SOCIAL CHANGE, GENDER AND VIOLENCE

Social Indicators Research Series

Volume 10

This new series aims to provide a public forum for single treatises and collections of papers on social indicators research that are too long to be published in our journal *Social Indicators Research*. Like the journal, the book series deals with statistical assessments of the quality of life from a broad perspective. It welcomes the research on a wide variety of substantive areas, including health, crime, housing, education, family life, leisure activities, transportation, mobility, economics, work, religion and environmental issues. These areas of research will focus on the impact of key issues such as health on the overall quality of life and vice versa. An international review board, consisting of Ruut Veenhoven, Joachim Vogel, Ed Diener, Torbjorn Moum and Wolfgang Glatzer, will ensure the high quality of the series as a whole.

The titles published in this series are listed at the end of this volume.

SOCIAL CHANGE, GENDER AND VIOLENCE

Post-communist and war affected societies

by

VESNA NIKOLIC-RISTANOVIC

Institute for Criminological and Sociological Research,
Belgrade, Serbia

SPRINGER-SCIENCE+BUSINESS MEDIA, B.V.

A C.I.P. Catalogue record for this book is available from the Library of Congress.

ISBN 978-90-481-6063-1 ISBN 978-94-015-9872-9 (eBook)
DOI 10.1007/978-94-015-9872-9

Printed on acid-free paper

To Ognjen, my future

TABLE OF CONTENTS

PREFACE

Vesna Nikolic-Ristanovic and I first met in 1994 at an international conference in Adelaide, Australia. Fortunately for us, we spoke on the same panel - the one dedicated to gender and violence. I was taken with her compelling research on the experiences of violence among women in East-Central Europe. Situated amidst war, economic collapse, political upheaval, globalization and the "new Europe," women in this region faced increasing levels of violence and victimization while struggling to hold their families and societies together. Most significantly, Dr. Nikolic-Ristanovic's research shows that large-scale global changes dramatically affect the most private aspects of the lives of men and women in East-Central Europe - their marital lives, their relationships with their children and parents, their friendships, their community ties.

Impressed by her presentation and our initial meeting, I began a correspondence with Nikolic-Ristanovic, from which I was to benefit considerably. We talked about the war in Serbia, her ethnographic research with women refugees, and the challenges she faced as a criminologist working in that context. After contributing a chapter to a book that Lois Lorentzen and I co-edited, *The Women and War Reader*, Nikolic-Ristanovic developed a research project that synthesized her scholarship on war, gender, violence and women's experiences in the public and private spheres. Her proposal was funded by the Harry Frank Guggenheim Foundation and resulted in this book. We can learn a great deal from it.

Social Change, Gender and Violence counteracts the tendency to view the collapse of the former Soviet Union and the Eastern bloc system in purely positive terms. "Transitionology," the near orthodoxy that has emerged and that is appropriately critiqued by Stephen Cohen in his book *Failed Crusade*, contends that Russia and the Eastern European states are undergoing a transition from communism to free-market capitalism and democracy. While that process will entail short-term difficulties, transitionologists argue that the ultimate outcome will be great for the peoples of that region and for international relations. Nikolic-Ristanovic is not the first to question that orthodoxy but her challenge is distinct. While recognizing the positive features of the collapse of Soviet and Yugoslav models of communism, she demonstrates that the economic collapse underway has devastating effects on the people of the region. Her project accounts not only for the economic changes, but for other large-scale changes affecting the societies of East-Central Europe: war; globalization; and radical political and cultural change.

Rather than limiting her study to macro level aggregate data, her research applies ethnographic methods to situate the lives of women and men, girls and boys, amidst these changes, melding both macro and micro levels of analysis. Her book shows that hardship falls disproportionately on women in the region. Women are most likely to be left in poverty. They often become heads of household, responsible for providing not only for their own children, but also for members of their extended families. Elderly women and young girls are particularly vulnerable to the effects of poverty. Women and girls constitute the majority of the refugees. Under these conditions of social stress, more women experience violent attacks from their husbands, male partners, and sons. Nationalist forces within the region have reinstated traditional gender roles in their mobilization of support for the state, further reducing women's social status and power. With the breakdown of the communist or socialist model, social protections previously guaranteed to women have eroded. Thus, while in some ways the "transition" is to be welcomed, in many other ways it spells disaster.

This research brings to bear the kind of analysis we need in order to understand societies in transition and societies at war. While a flood of books and articles, both scholarly and popular, have positioned one ethnic group against another in a battle for morality in East-Central Europe, Nikolic-Ristanovic's work reaches out to women and men from four countries: Bulgaria, Macedonia, Hungary, and Serbia - and to many more ethnic groups. When I spoke with her during her research, she expressed her anguish at hearing the stories of women from not only her home country of Serbia, but also Croatian women, Albanian women, Roma women, and others, who have suffered violence during this time of upheaval and change. Nikolic-Ristanovic showed what was common in these experiences, while avoiding a reductionist gender analysis that overlooks cultural differences. She calls on us to listen to women's stories, but does not reduce the problem of violence to male pathology. Instead, she has placed the lives of both women and men in context, showing how the difficulties produced by war and economic hardship destroy the relationships of people who love and care about each other. Nikolic-Ristanovic calls this phenomenon "the mirror" – the reflection of global change in our private and community lives.

Nikolic-Ristanovic's account reflects an author who is not only a committed social scientist, but also a woman who has experienced the upheaval firsthand. With this book, she shapes the interpretation of events that have dramatically affected her own life. Her dedication to the research under severe conditions stands as an emblem of compassionate scholarship – melding her heart and mind to explain and witness history unfolding in East-Central Europe.

Jennifer E. Turpin
University of San Francisco

ACKNOWLEDGEMENTS

This monograph is the result of a two-year research project funded by the Harry Frank Guggenheim Foundation. I am grateful to the Foundation; without it's support neither research nor this book would have been possible. My special thanks go to Karen Colvard, whose suggestions regarding research and deep professional and human understanding were so precious and encouraging, especially having in mind the fact that the realization of the research coincided with tragic events in my country in 1999. I also want to thank all my research assistants, Violeta Caceva (Macedonia), Magdalena Vanya and Anna Rapolti (Hungary), Tatyana Kmetova (Bulgaria) and Ivana Vidakovic (Serbia), for being so devoted to the collection of rather impressive research material in general, and to stressful, time consuming and complex interviewing and their transcribing, in particular. I want to thank all translators of my research material, as well as all those who were kind enough to accept being interviewed for this research either as experts, activists or members of the general population.

I especially appreciate the professional and human support I had from Ruth Jamieson from Keele University (England) from the very beginning until the end of this project, especially during my stay in England. I am grateful as well to all those who read and commented on the research proposal and drafts of this book and whose suggestions and ideas in different ways were important for my work: Jennifer Turpin from University of San Francisco, Susanne Karstedt, David Gadd, Annette Balinger, Anne Warall, Davina Cooper and Kyril Drezov from Keele University, Judith Armatta from Portland, Marina Blagojevic from Belgrade, Violeta Caceva from Skopje and Natassja Smiljanic from University of Central England (Birmingham). Also, I want to thank all Keele University Criminology Department staff and especially Tim Hope, the head of the Department, for creating an inspiring and supportive environment for my second year of work on this project. Last but not least, I want to thank my son Ognjen and the husband Radovan, for being just what they are - the support and inspiration which kept me going.

INTRODUCTION

Social changes, which occurred in post-communist countries in the late 1980's and early 1990's, brought new opportunities for positive developments and offered the possibility of choice. In most countries, the social transition brought an opening of borders, enabling an influx of positive as well as negative influences. However, even the general positive impact of social changes is typically followed by more negative consequences in the everyday life of the people. The most dramatic consequences of social transition manifested in a significant rise of unemployment and the loss of many social benefits. These developments are directly related to the replacement of planned, centralized economies by the market and the privatization of state property. Most people lost their previous social security benefits and, despite the fact that the general character of communism was "equality in poverty," the social transition was the source of numerous existential problems and serious stress. This was further intensified by the fact that, at the same time, the growing import of both material goods and the American way of thinking, i.e. consumerist spirit of the West urged people to achieve their "American dreams" at any cost.

However, the precise manifestations of social changes differ very much from country to country. The manner in which social change is manifested depends on the level of economic development achieved in the communist period, the model of communism accepted (Soviet or Yugoslav), and the degree of its influence in a specific country. Additionally, the existence and nature of other global social developments such as nationalistic movements and armed conflicts create specific features in the transition processes of some countries. However, social changes do not affect all people in the same way.

Many academics have already pointed out the impact of social changes on gender issues in post-communist countries. Watson, for example, argued that the transformation of the relationship between the public and private spheres lies at the heart of the process of change in Eastern Europe, and that the exclusion of women and the degrading of feminine identity are not contingent to, but rather a fundamentally constitutive feature of, the democratization of Eastern Europe. She also points out that this contrasts with existing accounts of social transition which have focused exclusively on the reconstruction of the public sphere, ignoring not only issues of gender, but also the functioning of "real society" in general (Watson, 1993:482). However, as many authors have argued, there are clear empirical indications that gender relations are also in transition – the rate of female participation in the new democratic parliaments is less than in state socialism, women are overrepresented among those who are unemployed, reproductive rights achieved during socialism were challenged, domesticity of women is widely projected as a social virtue, pornography became a new symbol of freedom, and the marketing of women's bodies is rising. The creation of a market economy in Eastern Europe "fundamentally entails the construction of a 'man's world' and the simultaneous propagation of masculinity in the public sphere, with domestication and the marketing of women. The degradation of feminine identity is an inevitable corollary of this process" (Watson, 1993:472).

In the former Yugoslavia, both social transition and the war as macro processes obviously influenced changes in gender relations on the micro level, which further contributed to different patterns of women's vulnerability to become victims of violence. Social changes in post-communist countries had a serious impact on women's vulnerability to different forms of violence, especially to domestic violence, trafficking in women, and sexual harassment in the work place. These influences were mediated by changes in the social and economic status as well as in the gender and ethnic identities of both women and men.

This book is the result of both my three years study of the connection between social changes and women's vulnerability to violence and much longer personal experience of living in a post-communist and war affected society. Thus, I have been not only an observer of, i.e. researcher, but also a participant in all these changes. This made my position as a researcher advantageous, while, at the same time, my situation as a human being was very complex and difficult. Being a participant was an advantage since, as I wrote elsewhere (Nikolic-Ristanovic, 1998:462), I was able to observe directly some aspects of my research topic, and unlike Western authors, to be quite familiar with various aspects of the life in both communist and post-communist society's milieu. Moreover, I myself felt like part of my own sample since I shared the fate of the people I was studying. This, as stressed by feminist ethnographers who emphasize closeness rather than distance in fieldwork relations, enhances understanding based on participant observation because of "total immersion in the world one is studying."(Reinharz, 1992:69). On the other hand, living in a society with an extremely high level of instability, uncertainty and stress, as well as with all kinds of rapid changes, was not very stimulating for concentrated intellectual work, let alone for doing research on specific phenomena at the specific time. In other words, in societies, which change so quickly, there is always risk that the research findings, which were accurate for one moment, become partly or sometimes completely inappropriate in a very short period.[1] This is why in this book I so often refer to the time of doing the survey or the moment of writing the book. Moreover, living in a stressful society and doing a survey on stressful events in the life of overstressed respondents often posed serious problems to both my interviewees and myself. This was especially true in Serbia, since interviews were done immediately after the Kosovo conflict and NATO bombing, when both interviewers and interviewees were highly stressed.[2]

The survey on which the book is based followed my study stay at the Central European University in Budapest at the beginning of 1998, where I spent two months as the Open Society Institute Higher Education Support Project research

---

1 Data about the development of social movements and legal reform are changing especially quickly. As observed by Dobash and Dobash (1992:13) "the task of characterizing a living movement while still in the process of development is inevitably more complex than charting one that has become a memory". However, in the society in transition similar problems appear when other social phenomena are researched

2 My research assistant in Serbia Ivana Vidakovic, although a psychologist by profession, had problems in both coping with painful interviews and transcribing them. She used to say that transcribing interviews was sometimes even more difficult than doing the interviews themselves. I myself found it very difficult interviewing even activists of women's groups in Serbia, who, thanks to the use of different self-help techniques, usually cope with stress much better than other people. Also, even analyzing the interviews was very stressful so that I often found myself crying while confronted with the overall suffering and hopelessness of my respondents (for similar experiences of other feminist researchers see Reinharz, 1992 34,35)

fellow. This is where I did preliminary research of violence against women in post-communist society. I learned how different social transition in different countries is, and how interconnected and complex are different aspects of social change. That preliminary knowledge, together with my personal experience, enabled me to design the concept of the survey which, during 1999 and 2000, I carried out in four countries: Hungary, Bulgaria, Macedonia and Serbia.

The main aim of the survey was to examine the ways in which social changes in post-communist and war affected societies influence the vulnerability of women to violence (domestic violence and sex trafficking). Having in mind that preliminary findings suggested the hypothesis that the impact of social changes on women's vulnerability to violence is mediated by changes in the everyday life of both women and men, the subject of research was determined as an examination of the impact of social changes to changes in everyday life of women and men as well as the impact of these latter to women's vulnerability to violence. Also, the impact of social changes, primarily the impact of the creation of civil society and the women's movement, on the attitudes of both citizens and the state toward the problem of violence against women is examined. In this regard, preliminary findings suggested the hypothesis that the development of civil society initiatives in post-communist countries led to the development of the women's movement and the movement for victim's rights and, in this way, contributed to improved social visibility of violence against women and created conditions for improvement of legal and other social responses to it. In addition, the research was expected to provide the answer to the question what is the greater influence: negative changes in everyday life of people produced by the development of a market economy and privatization, or the positive influences produced by the development of civil society[3].

Comparison of data for four countries (Serbia, Hungary, Macedonia and Bulgaria) allowed me to learn about similarities and differences in the impact of social changes on everyday life and violence against women. Also, it allowed me, having in mind different levels of realized changes and different social conditions as a whole in each of the examined countries, to test the above-mentioned hypothesis. The comparative research of these processes in countries which belonged to different models of communism, which were on different levels of economic development and which, because of these differences and some additional influences, such as war and inter-ethnic conflicts, achieved different levels of macrosocial change, allowed me a deeper examination of the nature of realized changes and, at least at an analytical level, differentiation between the impact of war and social transition on everyday life and violence against women.

The end of the Cold War and related events, i.e. social transformations and wars in former communist countries, produced significant changes on both the macro and

[3] The originally designed focus of research was slightly changes due to unexpected events in Serbia connected to the Kosovo conflict and NATO bombardment of Serbia. It means that the focus of the research is consequently broadened to include questions related to changes in people's everyday lives and women's vulnerability to violence which were produced by new macro level processes (conflicts, bombing but also new migrations and further worsening of the economic situation affecting in different ways all countries included in the survey). In addition, restricted access to information about Kosovo and the fact that it was actually cut off from Serbia, limited my research dealing with this part of Serbia in the measure in which it was possible

micro level. Both levels of change seemed to be so connected and interlaced that it was barely possible to understand one without exploring the other. Thus, the subject of research was an examination of the influence of macro processes to processes that happen on a micro level and vise versa. The exploration of macro-micro links included:

a) The links between macrostructural and microstructural changes (e.g. gender and economic structures);
b) The impact of microstructural (primarily interconnected gender and economic structural) changes on women's vulnerability to violence;
c) The links between microstructural and macrostructural changes (e.g.the development of civil society, the women's movement and legal reforms).

Consequently data were collected in a way that would allow learning about indicators of social changes on a macro level, on indicators of changes in people's everyday lives and about characteristics of violence against women, i.e. how it is related to changes in everyday life. I chose structural methodology (Hagan, 1988:256) as a main methodological approach for connecting empirical data with theory, i.e. for the analysis of the impact of macrostructural on microstructural changes and violence against women. I tried to look at violence against women using the conceptualization, which focus is on the causes and consequences of violence in the life course. The same conceptualization is used within structural criminology, which itself seems to be one of important theoretical explanations for my findings.[4] I explore changes in the life course of women and men during first ten years of transition from communism (1989-1999).[5]

The focus of my analysis is on the changes and transitions of the adult life of people in post-communist society, including both changes in comparison with life during communism and different changes that occurred over the last ten years. Looking at the biographical and subjective perceptual processes of individual women and men, based on the use of intergenerational and historical dimensions (prospective and retrospective research design), I analyze them in relation to broader structural changes in their countries. However, as stressed by Burgoyne (1987:51), during their adult life people are faced with many changes, which are not necessarily related to changes in the broader society (e.g. changes connected to moving or size of family). Thus, looking at these changes was necessary as well and enabled me to get correct picture about macro-micro links.

I explore in particular the dynamic relations between the individual women and men and other members of the family and household, and relations between the household and the changing economy within the wider society. The impact of socio-economic and war related changes on family structure, gender identities, relationships and violence against women is the focus of my analysis. I assume that a comprehensive understanding of the causes and consequences of violence requires

---

[4] The point of life course perspective, as stressed by Hagan, is "to emphasize that social events which are called delinquent or criminal are linked into life trajectories of broader significance, whether these trajectories are criminal or non-criminal in form" (Hagan, 1988: 260).

[5] I use the term 'life course' rather than the more familiar 'life cycle' since the latter implies fixed categories in the life of the individual and assumes a stable social system, while the former allows a more flexible biographical patterns within a continually changing social system (Cohen. 1987:1) Thus, the term 'life course' suits much better the unstable and changeable context of post-communist society.

that it be placed within the context in which it occurs and that it be examined from the perspective of both women and men (Dobash and Dobash, 1998:9). Or, as Mills (1970:12, quoted by Burgoyne, 1987:37) put it, "a social scientific analyses of contemporary issues and problems should enable individuals to understand how their biographical circumstances have been shaped by particular historical events and social changes. Also, this imagination should help its possessor to appreciate that 'by the fact of his living he contribute, however minutely, to the shaping of this society and to the course of its history, as he is made by society and by its historical push or shove".

As a result, I chose data collection methods that assure acquiring all information necessary to achieve the above mentioned aims. In this regard ethnography as multimethod research seemed to be the most appropriate for placing violence against women into a social context (Reinharz, 1992:53). I collected data in several ways - in Serbia and during my field trips to other countries included in the survey as well as through the important help of my research assistants.

Data on indicators of macro level changes were collected on the basis of available written materials on the characteristics of social changes in each country as well as through the statistical data and analyses. I collected data about the impact of social changes on people's everyday lives through interviews with ordinary people (women and men), through interviews with women's movement activists, academics and experts as well as from press clippings and other published and unpublished materials collected specifically for this research. Data on precise manifestations of violence against women were collected from the documentation of different organizations (women's groups, victim support groups, state institutions and similar), from press clippings as well as from other written materials. Also, I obtained information about the development of the women's movement and movement for victim's rights as well as data on the influence of their initiatives to improve the legal protection of women victims of violence through a specially designed questionnaire as well as through interviews with activists and academics. Also, I collected data on legal problems related to violence against women and legal reforms through interviews with professionals, academics and activists and through analyses of legal texts, research findings and other written materials. For gaining to information about some of the above-mentioned phenomena and processes I used direct observation and participation (e.g. women's movement and legal reforms).

Seventy-eight NGO's (21 in Hungary, 18 in Macedonia, 13 in Bulgaria and 39 in Serbia) were included in the survey. The majority of them were women's groups (18 in Hungary, 17 in Macedonia, 11 in Bulgaria and 34 in Serbia). All victim support and women's organizations which, according to previous information, were expected to deal with violence against women, were sent questionnaires and almost all of them, with only a few exceptions, returned completed questionnaires. For those who, for whatever reason, did not complete the questionnaire, data were collected through the use of other sources, such as brochures, information packages, interviews with NGO activists, articles etc.

The sample of professionals, academics and activists was determined on the basis of the preliminary information obtained by research assistants. It included the total of 45 women's group activists, judges, attorney lawyers, social workers, researchers, professors, psychiatrists and psychologists (10 in Macedonia, 14 in

Bulgaria, 11 in Hungary and 10 in Serbia). This kind of information collection was especially important because of the small number of research and published materials relevant to the topic of research. In addition, 98 persons (36 men and 62 women) were interviewed about the influence of social changes to their everyday life and women's vulnerability to violence. The sample was determined using age, marital status and employment as the main criteria. As a result, in each country 24 persons were interviewed (9 men and 15 women) with an additional two interviews with Kosovo refugees in Serbia. In total, there were three women refugees in the Serbian sample (two from Kosovo and one from Croatia). Those interviewed were between 30 and 60 years old - five women and three men belonging to each of following age categories: 30-40, 40-50 and 50-60 years. In determining the age structure of the sample I started from preliminary knowledge of the 40-60 year age category as the most threatened by social changes as well as from the fact that people of this age might be able to compare their present everyday life and family situation with the situation which existed 10 years before. Also, I chose the 30-40 year age category, because of the specific problems (unsolved housing problem, women who are married to new businessmen and similar) that this category is expected to face and which may be the factors that contribute to disturbed family relationships and women's vulnerability to violence. Those belonging to the youngest category of the sample were asked about their own everyday life experiences as well as to compare their own experience with the experience of their parents.

Because the main subject of the survey carried out through these interviews was an examination of the influence of social changes on the everyday life of people and women's vulnerability to domestic violence, the sample consisted only of people who were married, cohabited or were divorced, and were living with the partner for at least three years during the examined period (1989-1999).

The structure of the sample regarding employment was determined on the basis of the type of the husband's employment because preliminary research suggested the hypothesis that in the post-communist period men are more under work-related stress then women. This is mainly because of the traditional male role of breadwinner and one who is responsible to solve the economic problems of the family. These stresses, i.e. frustrations, were expected to generate men's violence as well. Starting from this hypothesis, the sample is determined to include women whose husbands are unemployed, employed in state institutions and those whose husbands are private businessmen as well as men who belong to each group. Both working-class and what should be middle class women and men are included in the sample.

The material was collected in the native languages of the respondents and was then translated by either my research assistants themselves or by translators from the countries where respondents originated[6]. Research assistants, who did interviews with women and men from the general population were previously introduced to feminist methodology and feminist interviewing techniques based on a semi-structured questionnaire (with special emphasis on active listening and empathy). In

[6] The exceptions were interviews with activist, experts and academics, which were done by me in either English (directly or through interpretation by my research assistants) or Serbian.

interpretation of findings I also relied very much on my interviewees and research assistants' comments. Bearing in mind the accepted methodological approach, I used qualitative analysis as a main method and quantitative analysis as supplementary for analyzing the large amount of ethnographic material obtained from the survey. Similarly as Connell (1995:89,90) noted, I also found that although the life-history method "always concerns the making of social life through time", which makes it "a first-class method for the study of social change", as well as one of "the richest methods in social science", it is also one of "the most time-consuming. Moreover, using it to study large-scale social changes requires a trade-off between depth and scope." Indeed, in spite of small samples of respondents in each country, the extensive amount of narrative material obtained from numerous sources was very difficult and slow for data processing and analysis so that Nud*ist computer program was important in making these problems affordable. However, on the other side, the obtained material was impressive and gave me significant access and insight into the complex reality of the lives of women and men in post-communist and war-affected societies. Hence, doing the analysis was also a real challenge and pleasure.

Research findings are, where appropriate, compared with findings for other post-communist countries as well as with findings on social change, gender and violence in Western countries. The fact that the impact of social change is analyzed using the example of the society under stress does not make the analysis less important for societies where the level of social stress is much lower. On the contrary, in societies under stress the changes are very quick and frequent and thus highly visible. This makes their identification and analysis easier, and the findings of this research comparable with and applicable to wider, i.e. more stable societies, where social changes occur, albeit less frequently and less quickly.

Findings are explored according to different social and criminology theories: masculinity (sex role and structured-action) theories, structural (power-control theory), and feminist criminology, as well as in relation to radical microsociology, resource mobilization theory and global sociology. Thus, apart from giving insight on the real dimensions of the impact of transition and war on people in post-communist societies, I also try to incorporate knowledge about post-communist, war and post-war society into a broader social theory on social change (crises, social transformation), gender and violence. Within that, I especially try to develop theory on masculinity and domestic violence, i.e. trafficking in women, as well as explanations of violence against women in contemporary society which consider structural factors, i.e. inequalities, on both national and international level (e.g. in the context of globalization). Thus, I try to look at violence against women as connected to oppression of both women and men (e.g. as a consequence of both patriarchy and economic marginaliation of both women and men). I argue that violence against women in post-communist and war-affected societies is significantly connected to the increase of social stratification, economic hardships, unemployment, instability, uncertainty and related social stresses, militarism, changes in (especially men's) gender identity (both reinforcement and marginalisation of masculinity) and structural inequalities brought by the new world order.

The book is organized in a way that allows me to proceed with analyses from the macro to the micro level and back.

Macro-micro analysis includes review of changes in four countries included in the survey and the analysis of the way in which they are translated on a micro level, i.e. in the everyday life of women and men. Then I explore how changes in everyday life influence gender identity (masculinity and femininity) and then how both changes influence women's vulnerability to domestic violence and trafficking in women.

Micro-Macro analysis looks at the development of the women's movement and feminism, and especially the battered women's movement and other women' and civil society initiatives, how they are connected with both macro and micro level changes and how effective they are in terms of achieved legal and policy changes.

In the conclusion I try to develop a theoretical explanation which looks at one more general level at the impact of social change or social crises on gender and gendered violence. Especially useful for an explanation of my findings as well as for the development of such theoretical explanation are the following ideas: Connell's ideas about hegemonic masculinity and emphasized femininity, Messerschmidt's and Hagan's ideas about interconnections between gender and economic (class) structures as well as other ideas which consider interconnections between structural and interpersonal violence (e.g. revised multivariate model of men's violence against women developed by O'Neil and Harway, model of web of violence developed by Turpin and Kurtz and Gilligan's theory of violence and shaming).

CHAPTER 1

SOCIAL TRANSITION AND WAR IN POST-COMMUNIST SOCIETY

1. INTRODUCTION

As some authors have already noted, living in transition is nothing new for former communist countries (Drezov, 2000:195; Bolcic, 1995:13). Countries which are presently faced with "post-socialist" transition[1] are a special group of countries of the modern era because their global societies have undergone two "transitions" during a period of some (five to seven) decades: first a transition from capitalism "to socialism" and now a transition "from socialism" to capitalism.

However, while in the "first transition" the global social system was to provide a new social role for workers as "direct producers", the "second transition" should establish an institutional framework for a new role of owners, entrepreneurs and managers. Also, in the "first transition" the "totality" of necessary social changes was reduced to the political and ideological changes, while in the "second transition" "the essence of the transition is placed in the domain of the economy, which boils down to privatization understood as privatization of state/socially owned firms (Bolcic, 1995:15) One of the important characteristics of the "second transition" is also the fact that it was very fast so that it did not allow people the time either to adjust their everyday lives to the requirements of global changes, or to understand the essence of these changes. And finally, the "second transition" is mostly designed according to the solutions in the political, economic and overall social "order"originally created in developed "Western" countries, which do not always fit to the conditions in the Eastern part of the world.

It seems that people did not have a clear idea of the cost-benefit ratio when they caste their vote for change of the political system. Or, even more probably, as I will show later, they neither had a lot of choices nor were able to predict the consequences which the change might have for their everyday lives. The collapse of

[1] Some authors also speak about transition to a new social order (Bolcic, 1995:14), while others use terms such as transformation from "communism" to "post-communism" (Blagojevic, 1998:19). Bearing in mind both Marxist philosophy and ideological discourse accepted in the former communist countries, the terms such as socialism, transition from socialism and post-socialist society may be more appropriate for naming former and present social systems in the countries included in the survey. However, in order to avoid confusion, throughout this work I will use largely accepted terms such as communism, transition from communism and post-communist society.

communism and disintegration of the former Soviet Union and Yugoslavia, followed by social and economic reforms within countries and the globalization and creation of a new social order outside of them, were echoed in dramatic changes in the everyday lives of millions of people. Burdened with a narrow perspective from the everyday struggle for bare survival, a large part of them are hardly able to understand and predict the global trends, which caused these changes. Nevertheless, macrosocial changes had a strong impact not only on the social and economic situation of individual people, but also on how they lived together.

In this chapter, using the sample of countries included in my survey, I will explore the main macrosocial changes, which occurred in post-communist society during the first ten years of transition. The principle aim of this chapter is to review the major similarities and differences among countries included in the survey (before and after the changes), to enable a better understanding of the changes in the everyday lives of people and violence against women, which will be analyzed in the chapters which follow.

2. HUNGARY, BULGARIA, MACEDONIA AND SERBIA: SOME CHARACTERISTICS OF THE COMMUNIST AND POST-COMMUNIST ERA

During the Cold War, Hungary and Bulgaria, on one hand, and Macedonia and Serbia on the other, belonged to two strikingly different communist entities. While Bulgaria and Hungary were the part of the Soviet bloc and Soviet model of communism, Macedonia and Serbia were republics of the Socialist Federal Republic of Yugoslavia, i.e. they belonged to the Yugoslav model of communism. However, the countries that belonged to the same bloc or model of communism sometimes differ more than those which share a different communist heritage but have strong cultural and historical ties. Also, the dynamics and directions of social transition in the post-communist period are strongly affected not only by the type of communism but also by both the political and economic position of the specific country within the former communist entity, i.e. by the status of its economy at the beginning of transition.[2] These four countries differ significantly in terms of the dynamic of both economic and political transition, i.e. regarding the level of economic reforms, real democracy and abandonment of communism achieved during transition. Also, they differ significantly regarding their relationships with both other East European and Western countries, especially in terms of Western interest and commitment in their stability, democratization and economic development. Also, one of the important differences between Serbia and all other countries is that ethnic conflicts and war had an important influence on the dynamics and directions of the Serbian transition.[3] Thus, social transformation in Serbia was slowed and, for a time, blocked, by wars

[2] However, in spite of differences in their economic situation in the pre-transitional period, it was common for all former communist countries that, before changes, they endured long lasting and deep economic crises which showed the impossibility of the continued existence of state-planned economies, i.e. of their partial economic reforms. (Lazic, 1995:61).

[3] As we will see later, although much less than Serbia, Macedonia and Bulgaria also experienced some consequences of ethnic conflicts in the former Yugoslavia.

and disintegration of the former Yugoslavia, UN sanctions and isolation of the country. [4]

As some authors have already noted, there is not one "transition to capitalism" but a plurality of economic strategies which are being applied, albeit within some shared parameters (Molyneux, 1996:232). Differences regarding history, national identities, religion, level of economic development before changes and type of communist system help to explain different patterns and manifestations of social transformation, as well as their different impact on the everyday lives of people. However, apart from great differences, all countries also share many similarities, especially in terms of economic problems and their concrete manifestations, i.e. consequences in the everyday life of their citizens.

2.1 *Socio-demographic, historical and political characteristics and changes*

The population in countries included in the survey range from 2 million in Macedonia to 9 million in Bulgaria, and about 10 million in both Hungary and Serbia[5]. In all countries the capital cities dominate the population map (Turnock and Carter, 1999:2; Turnock, 1999:73).

Macedonians and Serbs are Slavs, while Bulgarians are also predominately of Slav origin. Serbia, Macedonia and Bulgaria are countries where ethnic diversity is especially emphasized.

In Bulgaria, Bulgarians constitute over four-fifths of the total population, while Roma are the second largest ethnic group.[6] Also, Bulgaria has both Turkish Muslim and Macedonian minority related problems. There are also difficulties in Macedonia caused by a substantial Albanian minority, which seeks accommodation in cultural matters in the form of elevating the status of Albanian as a second national language and the creation of an Albanian-language university. The 1994 census in Macedonia recorded that 1.3 of 2 million of the population (65%) reported their nationality as Macedonian, while around 23 percent were Albanians, four percent Turks and there were significant Slav Muslim, Roma and Serb minorities. Hungarians originate from Magyars, who are mostly a part of the Finno-Ugrian race, who are thought to have entered Pannonia in 896. Apart from the Hungarians, Romanians, Slavs and Germans also live in Hungary (Turnock, 1999:75). Serbs constitute about two-thirds of the population in Serbia, while the rest are 15 different ethnic minority groups (Albanians, Hungarians, Roma, Croats, Muslims, Montenegrins, Romanians, Turks etc). The most numerous ethnic minorities are Albanians (17.1%), then Hungarians

4 These contradictory social processes are so complex that they make comparative analyses extremely difficult. It seems that Blagojevic is right when she calls these processes the transformation from "communism" to "post-communism" (Blagojevic, 1998:19).

5 Data for Serbia are based on 1991 census and should not be taken for granted, since the ethnic structure was changed due to war-related migrations – immigration of Serbian refugees from other parts of the former Yugoslavia as well as emigration of both people of Serbian and non-Serbian ethnic origin from Serbia.

6 However, since, as in other countries, Roma people tend to conceal themselves under another group identity, their number may be much bigger.

(3.5%), Muslims (2.5%), Roma (1.5%) and Montenegrins (1.4%). Albanians are a majority in Kosovo (southern part) and Hungarians in Vojvodina (northern part).

During the last 10 years, as a result of nationalistic politics of its Government and ethnic conflicts in the former Yugoslavia[7], Serbia experienced serious tensions between Serbs and ethnic minorities. Tensions were especially emphasized in relationships between Serbs, on one side, and Muslims, Croats and Albanians, on the other. The tensions between Serbs and Albanians led to the Kosovo conflict. Also, during 1999, when political relationships between Serbia and Montenegro became strained, new tensions appeared in relationships between the Serbian and Montenegrin populations in Serbia as well. In addition, Hungarian minorities' political parties' struggle for increased autonomy and Hungary's participation in the bombing of Serbia contributed to tensions between Serbs and Hungarians in Serbia as well.

Present-day Bulgaria occupies the eastern portion of the Balkan Peninsula, while Macedonia and Serbia are located on its Western part. The history of these three countries is characterized by the movements and conquests of many peoples. They occupy the territory that has always formed something of a bridge between Europe and Asia, providing a transit region and crossroads for people from east to west and north to south from time immemorial. Bulgaria, as well as Macedonia and south and central Serbia were under Ottoman domination for nearly five centuries. However, although Ottoman influence still remains visible and strong, Bulgaria's chief historical, cultural and, until recently, political ties have connected it with the former Soviet Union, whose most faithful satellite it was (Carter, 1999:71:108). Also, the inclusion of Macedonia into the Ottoman Empire was significant for both its culture and later development of ethnicity. Apart from the settlement of unusually large numbers of Turks, Macedonia experienced higher rates of conversion to Islam among the indigenous Slav population than most other Balkan regions under Ottoman rule (Popovic, 1986 quoted by Allcock, 1999:144). The centuries of Ottoman rule also witnessed the movement and settlement in the region of other diverse groups, such as Albanians, Vlachs, Jews and Roma. Despite diverging Cold war histories, Sovietized Bulgaria and Yugoslav Macedonia shared deep-rooted common traditions that went back to the Ottoman and pre-Ottoman periods of their history. Namely, as pointed out by Drezov, under the Ottomans the contemporary territories of both countries were part of a single linguistic and ethnographic area and, as a result of that, both countries remain intimately connected by common history, traditions and language. Their similarities became even more pronounced once they gained independence from Soviet and Yugoslav control (Drezov, 2001:413).

Unlike Bulgaria, Macedonia and Serbia, Hungary is not a part of the Balkans (southeastern Europe). Geographically, Hungary is a Northeast European country

[7] On the first pluralistic elections nationalistic parties won in all republics of the former Yugoslavia. "Building of national states became the main political aim which undermined the establishment of democracy and civil society, while establishment of a welfare state was also forgotten"(Vrcan, quoted by Milic, 1994, p.124). In the struggle for power between communism and anticommunism the winner was nationalism, while democracy lost again (Milic, 1994, p.124)

and, as put by Wandycz, although it was generally regarded as part of Eastern Europe, in terms of religion and culture, it belonged rather to the West (Wandycz, 1992:2). Together with Bohemia (Czechoslovakia) and Poland, Hungary differed drastically from the East, as embodied by Russia, or the Ottoman Empire that ruled over Hungary for only 150 years, i.e. until 1526, when Hungary came under Hubsburg rule (Austria). In the 19th century Hungary achieved autonomy and became an equal partner with Austria within the Austro-Hungarian Empire, which lasted until the beginning of World War II. During the Soviet era, Hungary found itself in a semi-colonial relationship of dependence on the USSR which was culturally, socio-economically, and politically more backward. (Wandysz, 1992:236). After the failure of the 1956 Hungarian revolution, 12 years of Kadar rule, characterized by reforms, had a significant impact on the everyday lives of people. The power and authority belonged to the Party but everyday life was gradually depoliticized and rendered more tolerable. Educational and cultural activities became much freer than before and in comparison to other Soviet bloc countries, contacts with the West started to be more regular and an emphasis was put on economic progress. Private initiative was permitted in agriculture, retailing, and services. This kind of communism was oriented toward the consumer ("goulash" communism) and as put by Wandycz, in fact was bribing people to acquiesce in the regime.

The country was the "best barrack" in the Soviet camp, which was recognized both in Hungary and in the West. However, in the late 1980s it was also becoming "an expensive barrack to live in" since prices were rising and many people had to have several jobs to make ends meet. The initial hatred for Kadar turned into a grudging acceptance by many people. But, as pointed out by Szalai and Orosz, the organic development of a second economy and hidden civil society, as organic development of bourgeois activity, ensured a smooth transition from the old order to the emerging one (Szalai and Orosz, 1992:144). Kadar's fall from power in 1988 marked the end of an era, but "no great personalities emerged on either the communist or opposition side"(Wandycz, 1992:255-66).

The contemporary Republic of Macedonia dates only from the reconstitution of Yugoslavia in 1945. Within the former Yugoslavia, Macedonia was consistently rated as the poorest of the Yugoslav republics (after Montenegro) and was largely economically dependent on Yugoslavia. In addition to economic underdevelopment, Macedonia also exhibited classic patterns of underdevelopment in educational provisions, unemployment and health (Ramet, 1995, quoted by Allcock, 1999:159). Similar to Bulgaria's close ties with the Soviet Union, Macedonia had the reputation of being unreservedly pro-Yugoslav, unlike the majority of other Yugoslav republics (Drezov, 2001:414). Thus, although no one in Macedonia ever imagined that Macedonia could survive as an independent state, the declaration of its independence was made in January 1992, following the insistence of the EU's Badinter Commission (Ramet, 1995, quoted by Allcock, 1999:159).

However, in spite of the strong dependence of Bulgaria on the Soviet Union and Macedonia on the Yugoslav federation, they were not affected in the same way by the liberalization/democratization processes started in the 1980's in their respective countries. Gorbachev's *perestroika*, for example, had an important impact on the beginning of Bulgaria's democratization. The Macedonian public, however, was barely touched by the liberalization experienced in Serbia and other parts of the former Yugoslavia in the 1980's (Drezov, 2001:416).

It is worth mentioning the interesting connection between both Bulgarian and Macedonian subordinated positions within respective communist entities and their later (during 1990s) subordination of national interests to Western strategic concerns. Thus it seems that during both the communist and post-communist time, Bulgaria and Macedonia had much less independence than Serbia and Hungary. During communism, as pointed out by Drezov (2001:422), the pro-Yugoslav attitudes in Macedonia often masked a dependence on Serbia. On the other side, during the post-communist era, dependence on Western countries provoked feelings among their population that they were neglected and discriminated against by the West, particularly in comparison to Visegrad countries, Hungary being one of them.

Another similarity between Macedonian and Bulgarian transitions is the slow democratization and long lasting dominance of the former nomenclature, i.e. communist party, disguised under a new name. In addition, preventive deployment of United Nations troops and the active involvement of the US since 1993, "played a key role in buttressing the Macedonian state and nation, allowing concerns for the stability to triumph over concerns for the quality of Macedonia's democracy" (Drezov, 2001:417). Thus, a non-communist Government came to power in Macedonia no earlier than 1998, while in Bulgaria also nomenclature interests dominated the political life of the country until 1997. In spite of that, democratization, in terms of development of pluralistic media, politics and elections, started in both countries already in 1989. However, at the time of the survey, political democratization seemed to be slightly more developed in Bulgaria, while marketization of the economy was more advanced in Macedonia. This latter difference is mainly connected to specificities of their previous economic systems - with Bulgaria facing greater challenges than Macedonia, because of its full nationalization of production and services as well as collectivization of agriculture, as a consequence of accepting the full communist model - which Macedonia, as a part of the former Yugoslavia, never experienced. Also, between 1989 and 1997, industry was neither restructured nor privatized in Bulgaria and it was managed far worse than during communist time, with asset stripping, privatization of profits and nationalization of losses (Drezov, 2000: 209).

One of important differences between Bulgaria and Macedonia and also between them and other countries is the level of their openness toward the Western world. Among four countries included in the survey, Bulgaria was obviously the one which was the least connected with "the West" and had the most widespread anti-Western propaganda during communism.[8] On the other side, Macedonia and Serbia as parts of the Yugoslav communist model were much more open toward the West and were much less exposed to anti-Western propaganda. However, there is the difference between Serbia and Macedonia's openness as well, with Serbia having much more

[8] In the 1970's and 1980's Bulgaria experienced some controlled development of contacts with Western countries, but it was so gradual and imperceptible that it was almost entirely neglected by Western observers (Drezov, 2000: 199).

developed communications with the West. As we already mentioned, the opening of Hungary started during the Kadar era but it was still much further behind Serbia in that regard. However, during post-communist period opening toward the West was most obvious in Hungary, while Bulgaria, Macedonia and Serbia stayed behind. These latter countries faced a tough visa regime[9], with Serbia being additionally isolated by the UN economic sanctions imposed on 30 May 1992, leading to NATO military intervention in 1999 and complete interruption of connections with the West after that until October 2000.

2.2 Economic development during transition

A pattern of economic integration in the region is emerging in different ways. The pace of economic reform in Southeast Europe has been relatively slow compared with the countries of Northeast Europe. Serbia, as well as some other states of the former Yugoslavia, was experiencing a war economy in which war-related expenditures, together with destruction and economic and social disorganization resulting from armed conflict, blocked reform and led to hyperinflation.

However, even the more developed Central-Eastern European countries, such as Poland, Hungary and Czech Republic, experienced an unexpectedly steep contraction in the first three years of transition. The cumulative loss of GDP in Hungary amounted to 18.3 percent between 1989 and 1993.[10]The current account deficit approached 4 billion dollars in 1994 and the net extreme debt reached 46 percent of GDP. The austerity program in 1995 and 1996 reduced the balance of payment deficit to 1.7 billion dollars and the net external debt to a third of GDP by the end of 1996. As Kocsis and Szanto point out, "Hungarians paid a heavy price for averting insolvency and for retaining the confidence of international finance: economic growth was virtually halted, and real incomes dropped by some 16 percent in two years, mainly as a result of inflation" (Kocsis and Szauto, 1997:145). Inflation had its peak in 1991 (35%) and after that time it was more or less kept under control, although it was still over 23 percent in 1996 (Kocsis and Szauto, 1997:145). Although considerably less than other countries included in the survey, the Hungarian economy also felt some negative consequences of the NATO war against Yugoslavia. The greatest impact on Hungary's economy resulted from NATO's blocking of the Danube which led to a decrease in revenues of the largest Hungarian shipping companies and producers who depended on river shipping (Dempsey, 2000:59).

However, although large, the drop in GDP in Hungary was the smallest in comparison to other countries included in the survey. The biggest drop occurred in Serbia (more than 60%), then in Macedonia (about 45%) and Bulgaria (almost 40%) (UNICEF, 1999:5).Ten years after the beginning of the transition only Hungary's GDP increased so that in 1998 it was slightly below the 1989 level. In other

[9] For example, Bulgaria was removed from the EU visa blacklist not earlier than at the end of 2000 (information received by Bulgarian_Studies @egoups.com on December 1, 2000)

[10] This fell in output was larger than that which occurred during the Great Depression of the 1930's (Rostowski, 1996, quoted by Bod, 1998:14).

countries, in 1998 GDP was still far from 1989 level. Thus, it seems that at the time of the survey the economic situation was much better in Hungary than in other countries, while the Serbian economy was in the worst state. Also, Hungary is leading in terms of the level of privatization, i.e. private sector share of GDP, while Macedonia is much behind it but still ahead in comparison to Bulgaria. Serbia comes far more behind all three countries - it is among those countries of Central and Eastern Europe which are at the very beginning of privatization, i.e. where the private sector share of GDP is on the lowest level (UNICEF, 1999:7). Hungary was also in the first "package" of Eastern countries to be considered for accession within the European Union in 2000. On the other side, Bulgaria, Macedonia as well as Serbia face no realistic chance of joining EU in the near term. However, the chances for Bulgaria to become a member of the EU are slightly better than those of Macedonia and Serbia since it is a part of those countries who may be considered in the second wave of EU enlargement. (Phinnemore, 1999:72-73).

The economic development of Hungary was in a large measure the result of the fact that Hungary was the country with a large, if not the largest part of foreign direct investment (FDI). According to Bod (1998), there have been years when the greater part of all FDI to the entire region, including Russia and Ukraine, has gone to the relatively small Hungarian economy. Foreign direct investment in Hungary is incomparable with foreign investment in Bulgaria, Macedonia, let alone Serbia.[11] For example, between 1991 and 1996, flow of the FDI into Bulgaria ranged from $42 million in 1992 to $100 million in 1996. Foreign investment started in Bulgaria only in 1992, while the same year investment in Hungary was already $1.459 million, reaching its highest point of $4.410 million in 1995 and then $1.986 millions in 1996. The highest foreign investment in Bulgaria, however, did not exceed $105 million (1994).[12] The sectorial composition of German, Austrian and US investment reflect the overall sectorial structure of the Hungarian economy. It is the US that leads in Hungary, as in most other countries of the region. However, most of the direct investments take place either in the capital or on the Vienna-Budapest corridor so that the long-awaited modernizing effect has so far been limited to the more developed areas of Hungary, making Government unable to create proper business conditions elsewhere in the country (Bod, 1998:38). Apart from the increase in import intensity, the reform led to transitional unemployment and temporary loss of state revenues. It has become standard practice in Hungary, as well as in other post-communist countries, to underreport the size of activity, number of employees and size of profits in order to avoid tax and extremely high social security contributions.

The Bulgarian economy has been hit by the collapse of the Soviet market, which formerly accepted 80 percent of Bulgarian manufactures, as well as by reduction in

[11] Foreign investment in Bulgaria was lowest among former Soviet satellites (Drezov, 2000:210), while Macedonia and Serbia mainly share lowest foreign investment in comparison to other countries of the former Yugoslavia.

[12] However, the trend was not rectilinear in Hungary as well. In 1994, foreign inflows represented less than half the level of previous year, and even less than in 1991, which was the year of sharp contraction. This year, new (Socialist) government practically stopped initiating any new privatisation transactions for several months and re-launched it again in March 1995.

Soviet oil deliveries, combined with a requirement to pay in hard currency starting at the beginning of 1991[13]. Thus, Bulgaria entered transition with an enormous foreign debt (US$10.7 billion in 1989) and the degree of past dependence on trade with the USSR constituted a major economic handicap during the first years of Bulgaria's transition (Dobrinski, 2000:583). Also, the Gulf crisis and economic sanctions imposed on Iraq intervened to prevent alternative deliveries from Iraq. Despite its potential, agriculture was weakened by a poor infrastructure and a workforce heavily tilted towards older people (the young people having left for the towns), including many relatively unskilled women workers. The emigration of 70 000 Turks from the Haskovo, Ruse and Varna regions contributed to worsening of the labor situation in 1989-90, when the state procurement system almost collapsed as farmers withheld supplies in anticipation of market reforms and high prices. Industrial depression was most evident in iron ore. Steel output collapsed by over 40 percent in 1991, while electronics and electrical engineering declined by a third. There was a sharp rise in unemployment to 15 percent. Rural western regions, including the wider Sofia area, seem to have been especially affected, while, at the same time urban parts such as Sofia city and cities of Montana, Plovdiv and Varna have gained (Nefedova and Trejvis, 1994, quoted by Turnock and Carter, 1999:16).

The Bulgarian economy was also hit by international sanctions imposed on FRY in 1992 and losses from that after only one year were about 6 million dollars. (Mateeva, 1998:116). The first ten years of the Bulgarian transition were marked by two severe economic crises, in 1991-1993 and later in 1996-1997. A weak and fragile recovery in 1994-95 followed a deep transitional recession in the initial phase and preceded a devastating financial turmoil, which ruined the country's banking system and left its public finances nearly bankrupt. During 1996-97, the cumulative drop in Bulgarian GDP amounted to more than 18% (Dobrinski, 2000:583, 581), and at the beginning of 1997 the country experienced an outbreak of hyperinflation reaching 1082.3%[14]. The severe economic crisis in 1996-97 triggered a political crisis and resignation of the ruling Socialist government. The new government constituted by a centrist-right coalition, initiated a drastic change in the course of economic policy, intended to push forward painful but necessary radical reforms, including restructuring of the enterprise sector and rapid privatization. After 1997, Bulgaria decisively moved away from communist domination of society, and "has come to a stable plateau" in its development in a whole (Drezov, 2000:215). The Kostov Government committed itself to a program for stabilization, reforms and economic growth in the country, based on a neo-liberal approach, which requires the State to largely withdraw from its dominant role in the economy. Financial stabilization and improvement marked the period after hyperinflation at the beginning of 1997 in most macroeconomic fundamentals (Dobrinski, 2000:597). However, as well pointed by Dobrinski, in terms of policy, delayed reform in

[13] Among the former CMEA-member countries, Bulgaria was the most closely attached to the Soviet economy, with its dependence on trade with the Soviet Union growing continuously even during 1970s and 1980s, when a number of east-European countries attempted to reorient some of their trade to/from some other trading partners (Dobrinski, 2000:582).

[14] *Monitor*, Centre for the Study of Democracy, No 5, 1999, p.6

Bulgaria is "hardly marketable to an electoral constituency", as enterprise restructuring and the macroeconomic adjustment problems involve highly painful and unpopular measures such as liquidation and closure of a very large number of unviable enterprises (Dobrinski, 2000:598). Also, during 1999 Bulgaria's economy was once again hit by the situation in Serbia. This time the Kosovo war and NATO bombing of Serbia led to additional economic loss provoking a further increase of both unemployment and poverty. [15] Bulgaria's contribution to the help of Kosovo refugees, although modest in comparison to Macedonian, was not welcomed by its own citizens who considered themselves in a not much better existential situation.[16].

Since Macedonia was the part of the former Yugoslav federation until 1992, it shared the former Yugoslavia's economic context during the first years of transition (1989-1992). At the beginning, both Macedonia and Serbia shared the positive effects of the economic reforms of Ante Markovic[17], which seemed promising in terms of both development of a market economy and improving the living standard of a large part of the population. However, the disintegration of Yugoslavia and the wars in Slovenia and Croatia in the early 1990's led to the collapse of reform since, as noted by Stokes, emotions in Yugoslavia had reached the point at which economic arguments ceased to have an impact (Stokes, 1997:132).

Macedonia, as one of the former Yugoslavia's poorest parts, was especially severely affected in economic terms. Thus, after becoming an independent state, Macedonia entered the transition from socialism in very specific and difficult conditions as well as without any experience (Dimitrievska, 1998:28). In addition to inner difficulties connected to transition to a market economy, the Macedonian economy has also been seriously disrupted by external factors, such as the indirect effects of the international sanctions imposed upon the Yugoslav federation (Serbia and Montenegro). These problems have been compounded by the blockade, which Greece attempted to impose unilaterally on Macedonia for as long as it insists upon the legitimacy of its claim to the name Macedonia.[18] The difficult economic situation is mirrored in both the sharp increase in unemployment and a large decrease in the GDP: the number of people who lost jobs as a consequence of privatization increased from 156 000 in 1990 to 249 928 in 1997 (Dimitrievska, 1998:28), while in 1996, GDP dropped 37.2 percent. in comparison to 1989 (Nanevski, 1998:50). However, the decrease in real wages was most striking in 1992, i.e. immediately after Macedonia became independent from Yugoslavia (Nanevski, 1998:51). Also,

[15] According to Bulgarian Government sources, the country was losing $1.5 million a day in exports after NATO rendered the Danube impassable. Bulgarian trade economy lost $70.7 million as a result of the war (Dempsey, 2000:65).

[16] *Ranno sıgnalızırane-polugodısen obzor* (Early signalising-half year report), December 1998-May 1999), Sofia: UNDP.

[17] Markovic was a market-oriented Communist who stressed deregulation, elimination of laws that hindered entry into the market, privatisation of small businesses, and creation of capital markets. The results of his reform were spectacular. Inflation dropped precipitously, foreign exchange reserves rose dramatically, and foreign debt declined. As a consequence, foreign investors were encouraged and flocked to Yugoslavia. (Stokes, 1997:130-31)

[18] Greek intransigence delayed international recognition of Macedonia and its pressure on Macedonia to accept recognition within the UN and EU under the cumbersome euphemism of the "Former Yugoslav Republic of Macedonia", only fuelled tension between the two neighbouring countries.

the first years of Macedonian independence were marked with high inflation, which in 1993 reached an annual average of 349.8.[19] Inflation was notably curbed in 1995 and stabilization of the Macedonian currency led to a positive effect on the global financial situation. However, in spite of that, the expected improvement in economic development was delayed due to the unfavorable situation caused by the above-mentioned blockades. In addition, in 1999, the Kosovo conflict and NATO bombing of Serbia contributed to the increase in tensions between Macedonians and Albanians in Macedonia. Consequently, an increased presence of military (NATO and UN forces) in the region as a whole and in Macedonia, in particular, had many consequences on both the economic and political life of the country. During the Kosovo war and NATO bombing, the Macedonian economy was seriously hit[20], since this already poor country was pressured to accept enormous numbers of both Kosovo refugees and NATO soldiers, without being given appropriate compensation by the West.[21] Also, the war forced Macedonian factories that do business with Yugoslavia to stop or curtail production, leading to an increase in unemployment or irregular wage payment.[22].

Unlike Macedonia, Serbia generally retained its position around the Yugoslav average in terms of its economic development within the former Yugoslavia. However, Serbia always had its own economic diversity mirrored in the gap between Kosovo as the poorest and Vojvodina among the richest parts of the former Yugoslavia. Similar to Macedonia and Bulgaria, the Serbian transition is also characterized by a neo-communist ruling elite. Unlike Hungary, these three countries were latecomers in the democratic transition, with Serbia being the latest, i.e. coming to the end of communist rule not earlier than 2000. Serbia's transition has been atypical in comparison to the majority of post-communist countries (Milic, 1995:137), and certainly is very different from global processes that happened in other countries included in the survey.

Privatization and transition to a market economy were very limited, since "shadowed " by the process of "ethnification" of society, where all social relations tend to be established in a manner which will provide for the "survival, growth of the nation (ethnicity), subordinating to the 'interests of the nation' all the other needs and interests of people (Bolcic, 1995:79). Thus, the first wave of social transformation, started in the early 1990's by Markovic's reforms, was later blocked and followed with several negative phenomena which had an anti-transition effect and made Serbian society look like a society undergoing a process of multilevel destruction rather than transition from communism (Milic, 1995:136). As well noted

19 Source: http://www.mchamber.org.mk/maceco.html , retrieved on November 10, 2000.

20 V.M. Bozinovska "Dve varijante za ekonomska katastrofa" (Two variants for economic catastrophy), *Vecer*, 22 April 1999, p. 11.

21 Immediately after the end of NATO bombing of FRY, at the Paris donation conference, Macedonia was given financial help which, however, was far from being enough to cover all economic loss Macedonia experienced in connection to the Kosovo war and NATO bombing - M.Radenkovic "Mirnodopska okupacija"(Peace time occupation), *NIN*, 9 September 1999, p.44-45.

22 Macedonian trade unions, for example, reported that 40,000 Macedonian workers were on "forced leave" and that 120,000 workers have not been paid in months (J.Cook "Macedonia 'On the Brink of Economic Crisis", *Financial Times*, July 20, 1999, p.3).

by some authors, Serbia's transition was characterized by the domination of destructive forces over the forces of construction (Milic, 1995: 137) so that the "construction of emerging society was late in comparison to deconstruction of the old one" (Lazic, 1994, quoted by Milic, 1995:137). Or, as Molnar put it, the "social situation in the new Yugoslavia and Serbia is most similar to the status of 'organized chaos', the case seen already in Nazi Germany" (Molnar, 1994, quoted by Milic, 1995:138).

In ten year period, Serbian society was hit by four big "shocks" with long lasting consequences: the breakdown of the socialist self-management system as the institutional basis of the former Yugoslav society; disintegration of the former Yugoslavia and creation of a new state (FRY-Serbia and Montenegro); civil wars in Bosnia, Croatia and ethnic tensions (Kosovo before conflict, Sandzak, Vojvodina) and ethnic conflicts in Serbia itself (Kosovo). Civil wars had especially severe consequences on Serbia's economy and social life in general. They were followed by large migration waves (immigration-refugees[23] and emigration of disappointed Serbian people, members of ethnic minorities who felt endangered in Serbia and young men who left in order to avoid military service), UN economic sanctions and complete isolation of the country,[24] as well as by NATO's 79-day military intervention in the Federal Republic of Yugoslavia.

As a result of civil wars (which were at their peak in 1993), economic sanctions imposed in 1992 and NATO bombing (1999), Serbia faced the deepest economic crises in 1993 and 1999, when GDP per capita came to the critical point of above 1000$ in 1993, and below 1000 $ in 1999. In 1993, the country was hit by hyperinflation, leading to price increases of 60 percent daily or 2 percent per hour. Inflation had disastrous effects in terms of both impoverishment of large segments of the population and severe social differentiation, i.e. concentration of assets and power in the hands of the ruling elite and those close to it (G17Plus, 2000: 49-50)[25]. The hyperinflation lasted for 24 months and, after an anti-inflation program was successfully enforced, the situation started to improve and GDP started to increase slightly. However, NATO bombing with its enormous destruction of plants and

[23] At the end of 1999, Serbia had almost 1 million refugees and internally displaced people, which made it the country with the highest number of refugees in Europe. Refugees came to Serbia in waves – the first big wave was in 1992, the second was in 1995 and the last one was in 1999, after the NATO bombing. In 1995, 250,000 people from a former Serbian province in Croatia (Krajina) were expelled and moved to Serbia in a very short period of about two weeks. In 1999, about 230,000 Serbs from Kosovo came to Serbia under similar conditions as the Krajina people (Mrvic-Petrovic, 2000:101). The large number of refugees was an additional burden for the Serbian economy, especially because humanitarian aid for Serbia was always much behind the aid given to other parts of the former Yugoslavia.

[24] UN sanctions were formally economic but their effects were global – political, cultural and moral, which consequences were long lasting even after their abolition (Lazic, 1995:75).

[25] Hyperinflation, together with bank fraud, based on the collection of foreign currency from people by false promises of high interest rates, was used deliberately by the ruling neo-communist party in order to obtain its citizens' last supplies of foreign currency. The same strategies were used by neo-communists in Macedonia (Nanevski, 1998:57-62), but the inflation was not so high and disastrous as it was in Serbia.

infrastructure caused significant economic damage[26] to the country's already weak economy and turned it even more backward than it was before. The first signs of the beginning of the national economy's healing were not felt before the beginning of radical economic reforms in 2001, which cost in terms of transition unemployment and poverty were not predictable at the moment of writing of this book.

[26] It is estimated that the total economic damage as a consequence of NATO bombing was $29.608.5 million and that the GDP fell 44.4 per cent in comparison to the previous year (Dinkic, 1999:9).

CHAPTER 2

LIKE A MIRROR IMAGE

Reflections of macro changes in the everyday lives of women and men

1. INTRODUCTION

As shown in the previous chapter, and similar to other post-communist countries, economic and political changes in all countries included in the survey led to changes in GDP, employment and real wages. Both economic development and the level of employment are closely connected to the level of privatization and the level of foreign investment, as well as to the direct or indirect impact of war, i.e. the intensity of that impact. The combination of severe recession and deeply flawed tax systems led to a large decline in government revenues as well. Although, because the communist state was so costly, the revenue decline was not a bad thing in itself, it had several quite negative consequences. First, it impaired the functioning of vital state institutions and made reform of institutional arrangements extremely difficult (UNICEF, 1999:9). It also led to the abolition of many social benefits, subsidies and services as well as to continual increases in taxes. And finally, one of the consequences of economic recession and punitive tax systems and costly and corrupted bureaucratic procedures was the growth of the informal sector and its associated labor markets. The growth of the informal sector (both 'shadow' and illegal economy) was a prominent feature of the transition economies of all countries included in the survey. However, it was especially apparent in connection to UN economic sanctions imposed on Serbia, which prevented trade and financial transactions with other countries, opening a large space for illegal activities, including organized crime. It especially generated fuel and weapons trade and foreign currency transactions, in Serbia as well in other countries included in the survey as Serbia's immediate neighbors (Bolcic, 1995:87). Transition from communism was also followed with an enormous increase in traditional crime, especially property crime and violence, with an additional impact of war on the increase of crime in Serbia.

All the above-mentioned macrosocial changes had a strong impact on people`s everyday lives. Macro trends are internalized as personal problems, so that individual women and men who confront problems in their everyday lives reflect social changes in a microcosmic snapshot (Huber, 1991:21). Although this impact is unique in a similar way as the historical context of post-communist societies is unique, it shares some features with changes in everyday life and gender relations in other societies which were also faced with some kind of social transformation or crisis (see Karstedt, 1993; Matsakis, 1996; Moeller, 1993).

In this chapter I will look at the ways macrosocial changes are mirrored in the everyday lives of women and men, i.e. in which ways the social and economic situations of individual women and men has been changed in post-communist societies. Identification of different patterns of changes to which individual women and men are exposed is crucial for understanding changes in gender identities and women's vulnerability to violence. However, although useful for getting an abstract idea about the nature of changes, statistics, i.e. quantitative data, are not sufficiently comprehensive to get a complete picture of different patterns of change faced by individual people. For example, it is crucial that we know about both the formal and informal employment structure within the family, i.e. whether a wife or husband, both of them or neither works and provides for the family. Also, in households with adult children, it is important that we learn about their employment status or problems in finding jobs as well as about concrete manifestations of changes in their financial situations and living standards.

Thus, in this chapter I will try to look more closely at translations of macro level changes in the everyday lives of people, relying in large measure on interviews with women and men in Hungary, Bulgaria, Macedonia and Serbia as well as on the other qualitative material, and only sporadically on quantitative data. Using life course perspective, I will turn to the last ten years of changes in men's and women's socio-economic situation, quality of life, living standard and housing as well as to their everyday life changes connected to the war. Afterwards, in the chapters which follow this one, I will examine how socio-economic and war-connected changes in the everyday lives of people affect gender identities, power relations and relationships within and outside the family as well as women's vulnerability to violence.

2. SOCIAL AND ECONOMIC CHANGES

2.1 (Un)employment and changes in distribution of economic power

After several decades of a planned economy and full (Soviet model) or high (Yugoslav model) employment policy, the emergence of significant unemployment in the post-communist period is a relatively new phenomenon in the countries of Eastern and Central Europe. The number of registered unemployed grew from about one million in 1989 (mostly in the southern states of communist Yugoslavia, such as Macedonia and Serbia) to eight or nine million by 1993-94 following the first wave of economic reforms. Three quarters of these people were registered in Central Europe and in the Balkans. The countries included in my survey, with the exception of Serbia, had the greatest decline in employment in the period between 1989-1997 in comparison to all other post-communist countries, with Macedonia and Hungary having the highest loss of jobs (33 and 30 percent respectively) and Bulgaria in the next highest group of countries with a 25 percent decline. As pointed out by Jakimovski, in the period between 1992 and 1995, Macedonia recorded a significant increase in people who lost the jobs and pensioners who were forced to retire before retirement age, as well as a decrease in new jobs. (Jakimovski, 1998:12). Thus, similar to the consequences of unemployment for people in the pre-retirement stage in Western countries, "the pre-retirement phase may well become a retirement reality for many as a result of the increasing redundancy rate." (Cohen, 1987:27).

In comparison to other countries, FR Yugoslavia and Serbia, as a part of it, had a moderate decline in registered employment (15%) (UNICEF, 1999:7-8). These differences are mainly connected to the differences in the level of privatization and state factory restructuring, which, as mentioned above, were the least developed in Serbia and the best developed in Hungary, among the countries included in the survey. Also, although in Hungary steady economic recovery has been under way for some time, the unemployment rate still stayed very high. However, while these well-known and tremendous shifts are frequently identified with the "social costs" of the transition process, less well known is the rise in self-employment, which more than doubled in most post-communist countries (Earle and Sakova, 2000: 588).

However, the gender gap in labor force participation does not appear to have widened considerably. Thus, both women's and men's participation in the labor force has decreased. Also, the financial pressure to maintain two incomes in a household remains tremendous, constraining women and men to continue to work or to search for work. Due to high pre-transitional employment rates, the share of women employed remains in the 40-50% range. For example, in 1997, among countries included in my survey, there was a slightly (by 4%) higher female unemployment rate only in Serbia. In Bulgaria, male and female unemployment rates were almost the same, while in Hungary and Macedonia male unemployment slightly exceeds the female. (UNICEF, 1999:28; UNDP, 1999:39).

Although there is little evidence that women are being largely removed from formal employment, it seems that the tensions created because of the need to care for children and the need to work for pay have grown, especially since that flexible options for reconciling these commitments, such as part time jobs, are still mostly unavailable (UNICEF, 1999:40). It also seems that in practice unemployment affects women in a greater proportion than official statistics show. As stressed by Toth, many women opted for early retirement in order to avoid unemployment.[27] Also, many women, who are currently on maternity leave or childcare benefit may find themselves unemployed after benefits run out (Toth,1997:70). Also, much of the reduction in women's economic activity has occurred among younger and older age groups. In general, available statistical data show that finding a job is particularly hard for young people as well as that youth unemployment rates are often higher than the average in well-established market economies (UNICEF, 1999:29). Thus it seems that age is more important than gender as a determining factor for labor force

[27] It is especially characteristic for women who lost a job after the age of 40, when they are usually not able to find a new one without retraining. However, as they become closer to retirement age, they are less ready for retraining (Gabriella Nemeskesy, interview, 1999).

reduction (Stenhilber, 2001:203). However, some evidence also suggests that employers, when reducing working hours or forcing workers on administrative leave, tend to focus on women while keeping more men full-time. In addition, for newly created employment, it has been observed that sectors and professions previously considered "female" are now becoming more mixed (Knothe, 1999, quoted by Steinhilber, 2001:203). Also, as stressed by many of my interviews, and as noticed in Western countries as well, the impact of unemployment is most keenly felt by those at the very early or very late stages of their careers (Cohen, 1987:26).

The available data show that in 1996/97 women earned less than men on average, with the gender gap ranging from 10 to 30%, rates comparable to, or smaller than, those in Western countries. However, only Bulgaria reports a large increase in the gender pay gap between 1990 and 1997. The data suggest that in some (mainly most developed) countries, including Hungary, since the introduction of reforms there has been a considerable narrowing in the gender pay gap, while ratios for FRY, i.e. Serbia, are relatively stable. It appears that significant occupational segregation by gender continues to exist in the region. During the transition, gender segregation is also becoming based on the ownership structure of enterprise, with women continuing to cluster in public sector jobs, and men being much more present in private sector employment (UNICEF, 1999:40). Having in mind that public jobs are paid significantly less, this has a serious negative impact on women's economic position during transition. However, although women "appear to be less inclined or able than men to move into self-employment and entrepreneurship - a vital part of the new private sector in many cases women already have strong a position in the private sector" (UNICEF, 1999:33-40), and the trend for those employed in the private sector is growing (UNDP, 1998:8). However, as pointed out by Steinhilber:

> "While men tend to dominate the newly privatized large-scale enterprises, women seem to have benefited relatively more from employee buy-outs and voucher privatization. Women have created fewer businesses than men, own smaller businesses, employ less people and do not engage in international activities to the same extent as men's companies" (Losowska, 1999, quoted by Steinhilber, 2001:208)

Another phenomenon which appears in transition countries is sham presidency of women, while the companies are run by their husbands (Kotzeva, 1999:8). According to research findings, two thirds of unpaid workers in Bulgaria are women who work unregistered in family businesses run by their husbands. Although they work very hard, they do not have any kind of insurance and are economically dependent on their husbands (Netkova, interview, 1999). Also, as mentioned by Jovanovic, women in Macedonia most often run small shops located within their own house or building where they have a flat, so that they can easily combine domestic chores and work (interview, 1999). In Bulgaria, most of the women-run companies deal with some kind of family business that is regarded as a way of supporting the family. These businesses are low-profit and slowly developing (Kotzeva, 1999:8). Also, it seems that, at least in Serbia but most probably in other countries as well, younger people (below 40) are more represented among those employed in private sector and private owners, while those over 40 dominate among state firms' employees (Milic, 1995:159).

Employment (informal and formal jobs) related problems and the economic difficulties as a whole seem not to be evenly spread among the representatives of the various ethnic and religious groups. They had particular effects on Roma people in all countries, and, in Bulgaria, on Bulgarian Muslims and Turks as well (UNDP, 1998:20). During the last ten years the growing social exclusion of these groups led to a new form of ethnic inequality and generated new kinds of social tensions and conflicts in Bulgaria. The threat of ethnic discrimination and abuse has become an everyday phenomenon for representatives of these minorities. As highlighted in the 1998 UNDP development report the two largest ethnic minorities (Turks and Roma) are among the most vulnerable and marginalised groups in Bulgaria. Children and women within these ethnic minorities are especially insecure, as they are subjects of both intra-and intergroup violence.

Also, there are differences between Albanians and non-Albanians both in Macedonia and Serbia (Kosovo). In Macedonia, for example, Albanians, both women and men, participate less in the labor force than Macedonians. While Albanian men often go to work abroad by themselves, leaving their families alone, or are involved in informal/illegal activities, Albanian women, following a strong patriarchal tradition, stay at home, or are unable to find employment due to the lack of education (Jovanovic, interview, 1999).[28] Similar behavior is seen among Kosovo Albanians (Report of Helsinki Human Rights Committee, 2000:9).

Although useful for understanding changes in the economic positions of women and men in post-communist countries, statistics on employment are far from giving a complete picture about it, let alone about the impact of employment changes on relationships within the family. In transitional countries being formally employed does not necessarily mean being paid for work, or that salaries are paid on time or that pay is sufficient to provide economic security at all (Prokovik, 1998:125). As a result, data on registered employment do not always give an accurate picture about the actual level of people's economic activity. For various reasons, registered unemployment is a poor indicator of the actual level of unemployment as well. Thus, some registered unemployed may in fact be economically active. Many people find either a primary or additional (second) job within the informal sector which, together with its associated labor markets, is growing in many transition economies. Not so rarely, the informal sector offers better paid jobs than the formal one and a section of the population earns significant additional income from such activities (UNDP, 1998a: 4). However, evidence on the hidden labor market and incomes derived from it is difficult to obtain.

In Hungary, for example, it is often estimated that one third of GDP is realized within the informal economy (Frey, 1998:7). One of rare study is a survey undertaken at the beginning of 1998 in Belgrade (Serbia). According to the survey findings, 30 percent of employees were engaged in unregistered labor market

[28] Earlier, Albanian girls used to leave primary school after finishing the fourth year. This was the way of the traditional family to keep them in the home. However, more recently, more and more girls, especially in urban areas, continue education and try to find employment (Coneva, interview, 1999).

activities in the form of second jobs and were motivated by economic necessity. About 40 percent of them were women, with the highest participation of women aged 30-40. (UNICEF, 1999: 8) Also, as pointed out by Steinhilber, "because of their lesser chances of getting a decently paid full-time job, more women than men take on homework and work without contract. On the other hand, it seems that more men than women are found in some forms of seasonal employment, for example in agriculture". (Steinhilber, 2001: 203)

The growth of the informal labor market means that more people (both women and men) are relatively unprotected and vulnerable to exploitation in their jobs (inappropriate wages, prolonged working hours, lack of any rights etc.), since their employers prefer not to report them as employees in order to avoid paying social and retirement benefits to the state (UNICEF, 1999:6; Efremov, 1998:138; Vaknin, 2000:1). The upheaval of transition, on the one hand, and the growth of the sex industry as an informal sector most interested in attracting women, has led to a rapid rise in the number of women who are, willingly or unwillingly, working as prostitutes and being at high risk of violence and exploitation.

Economic changes in post-communist countries resulted in significant social differentiation of the population as well. On one hand, there is the impoverishment of a large part of the population, while, on the other hand, a small number of people are getting rich. At the end of 1998, about 30 percent of the urban population in Macedonia could not afford to buy food.[29] Those who were already poor before the changes became poorer, while a large part of those who were middle class, became poor as well. The unemployed, pensioners, housewives and a large part of those employed in state institutions and enterprises are in the worst situation (Nanevski, 1998:52). Among those whose financial situation improved, private (successful) businessmen and managers on different levels prevail. Therefore, conflicting interests arose as well, such as those between poor and rich, employees and employer, young and older, the unemployed and the employed and the rural and urban populations.

The most intense interest conflict in Macedonia, according to Jakimovski, is between poor and rich people (Jakimovski, 1998:9-15). Income inequality among the population showed a tendency to increase in Bulgaria as well. For example, in 1996 the wealthiest 20 percent of the population received an income 5.8 times higher than the poorest 20 percent (UNDP, 1998a:7). In Bulgaria, in 1996 the annual inflation rate was at 311 percent with currency depreciation at 3,000 percent. The average monthly wage fell from the equivalent of about USD 110 in 1995 to USD 20 in the first months of 1997. The number of households with income below subsistence level reached 54 percent in 1996, households below the social minimum

[29] Interview with dr Jorde Jokimovski, quoted by S.Vukcevic "Solidna podloga za eksplozija" (Solid foundation for explosion), *Nova Makedonija*, July 5, 1999, p.11. Similarly, according to the survey carried out in Serbia in 2000 on a representative sample of 200 respondents, 30 percent of them said that they did not have enough money to buy food. More than two thirds of respondents answered that their income decreased, while 12 percent said that it increased over the last ten years (Z. Markovic, "Gladna sam, kradem sljive" (I am hungry, I steal plums), *Nin*, 27 July 2000, p.22-23).

made 41 percent in 1990 and 73 percent in 1996. The purchasing power of the population halved, creating changes in household consumption: the share of income spent on food increased from 36 percent in 1993 to 55.9 percent in 1997. The average monthly pension fell by 65 percent from 1990 to 1996 (Dakova and Indsheva, 1999:120).

The analysis of poverty in Serbia showed that all socio-economic categories of the population were affected by impoverishment. Among those most affected were families with children, single parent families and pensioners(Posarac, 1999:54; Puzigaca, 1999:111). However, this made the income imbalance between poor and rich even sharper than in other countries. In contrast to the major part of the population who became poor in a short period is a small group of those very rich, even by Western standards, who often earn money through criminal activities and are obsessed with uncontrolled consumerism and luxury (Milosavljevic, 1998:22). As in other post-communist countries and countries under economic sanctions, while the middle class disappeared, a new class of war profiteers has arisen especially as a consequence of economic sanctions and war (Women in Black, 1994a:100).

It is worth mentioning that a sharp social differentiation among refugees in Serbia was also seen. As Vucurovic pointed out in a workshop on the embargo organized in 1993 by Women in Black (Belgrade), the refugees come from two classes, the class of *nouveau riche* and the class of the poor. For example, the small number of refugees who belong to the first class are those who came earlier, even before the conflict broke out, with a large supply of foreign currency and/or were involved in war and embargo-connected organized crime (e.g. foreign currency trade) (Women in Black, 1994:101).

2.2 Formal employment and changes of employment status

My survey findings suggest that unemployment is one of the main but not the most serious problem which Macedonians, Bulgarians, Hungarians and Serbs have been facing during the first ten years of transition. While speaking about their own and existential problems of other people in their countries, the majority of my respondents, for example, put financial problems first and unemployment second. Macedonian and Serbian respondents also stressed housing problems.

However, since the beginning of transition, retaining stable employment and economic security became barely possible. Consequently, one of the most immediate changes which people experienced after macro economic reforms were introduced was connected to the loss of secure employment. The insecurity in that regard was best described by one of female respondents from Hungary:

> "The disappearance of existential security was a very hard thing... It is difficult to cope with existential insecurity. It is good that in many respects there is more freedom to make decisions, but at the same time there is crazy existential insecurity. For someone, who has felt secure all his/her life, it is difficult to get used to this...Since we used to expect that there would always be a job, there would always be some income, as well as pension...maybe not as good as compared to the West, but there was some secure atmosphere..."

However, not only formal employment is endangered. For those who, like Roma women and men, used to earn money through informal employment, employment insecurity meant the lack of informal employment, since demand for their services decreased with the general impoverishment of people. For example, in my Macedonian sample this was obvious in the case of a Roma woman, who used to work in other people's homes as a cleaning lady, while her husband used to earn money through singing at wedding ceremonies. However, in recent times, both of them had difficulty earning living since people could not afford to pay them.

Employment problems arose when one or both spouses lost or had to leave a job, had failed in private business or when they and their adult children could not find a new job. However, in spite of the fact that the majority of respondents and their partners were formally employed all or most of the time during the last ten years, the prevailing characteristic of their employment situation is that it was changeable, unstable and insecure. This means that less than half of respondents and their partners in each country, with the exception of Bulgaria, stayed at one work place all the time, but when changes of work place occurred, they were often radical and compulsory, i.e. as a consequence of either redundancy or lack of (or extremely low) income. Also, it does not mean that those who were employed all the time (whether at one or different work places) did not experience changes and insecurity as well. On the contrary, in all countries even those who maintained continuity of employment all the time during last ten years did experienced changes connected to transition and short, transitional, unemployment periods as well. For some of them it meant continuity in employment status but also and even more importantly, this meant significant changes in the organization of work, their duties and time spent at the work place. This is especially true for those who started their own private businesses, changed a state for a private job in looking for better wages or continued to work in the same, but privatized firms.

> " I was employed all the time during the last 15 years. I changed three firms, but never had breaks in employment status. I was working for eight years in a state institution. During 1992 and 1993 my salary was worth only 2 DM and this is why I went to work for a private firm. Fourteen months ago I changed jobs again and I am now working for another private firm"(female respondent from Serbia).

> "First, when I graduated I was working for the National Health Service in Tatabanya. Later, after the political changes took place, I was working for a charitable foundation and for two years I have been working as a private dentist" (female respondent from Hungary).

> "The professor I worked with helped me to find a place for practical training with his former student in the metal industry, in a factory. They liked me there so much that I stayed there after the training. From 1971 until the end of 1992. But the company ceased to exist. The employees were reduced to 10 percent of the former workforce. The company ceased to exist in such a way that it was transformed into private firm with six employees, and there were four people from my group that remained at the same place. In 1992, I started to work at the National Food-products Institute, actually in the same analytical kind of job. It was hard because I had to get used to many new things, it was a big change despite the fact that I was in the same analytical area" (female respondent from Hungary).

Also, as a consequence of ownership and related organizational changes, some respondents were moved to lower wage jobs.

> " I was employed all the time during the last ten years but I changed six jobs. I changed jobs as funds, self-management bodies, etc. got liquidated. Sometimes I got a better, sometimes a lower salary. I was just removed from one place to another. And I was silent...Everything is better than to be on the street. Just to 'collect' a couple of years for the pension" (54 years old female from Serbia).

But even those who stayed at the same work place often experienced a decrease in real wages and difficulty making ends meet with the money they used to get from their regular work. As I will show later, their efforts to improve their financial situations often led them to some kind of informal employment such as an additional job, rather than to changes of their formal employment. Thus the struggle for existential security and employment instability forced them to turn to the informal labor market. It seems that uncertainty in employment status continuity in a context of extreme instability, uncertainty and fluidity was the major characteristic of employment of both my respondents and their partners.

The frequency of employment changes seems to correlate with the frequency of events and changes on the macro level. Thus it is not unusual that employment changes were most frequent among Serbian respondents, who sometimes had to change jobs more than five times during the last ten years, often moving from state to private jobs and vice versa. Also, unlike respondents from other countries, often changes of jobs by Serbian respondents were related to economic sanctions and war rather than to transition, i.e. privatization, which was delayed and blocked by economic sanctions.

> "Since 1993 I have been most of the time on compulsory leave because my factory did not function normally due to economic sanctions. But this year (1999) my factory was destroyed by NATO bombing and my job ceased to exist formally as well. Over the last two years my husband was also on compulsory leave and got his salary mostly in goods." (female respondent from Serbia)

However, the prevailing characteristic of employment changes of Macedonian and Hungarian respondents and their partners is that they lost jobs solely in connection to the transition, and were, for a shorter or longer time, unemployed[30]. As already mentioned, unlike respondents from other countries, the employment situation of most Bulgarian respondents and their partners seems to be rather stable, with the majority of them being employed all the time. Moreover, Bulgarian respondents had more stable employment status even in comparison to their partners.

Findings about employment changes in Hungary, Bulgaria and Macedonia clearly reflect the level of privatization in these countries. Thus employment

[30] The kind of unemployment which prevails in Macedonia as well as in the most other economies in transition is not the kind of so called "healthy" unemployment which promotes labor mobility. Instead, it is permanent (structural), in the sense that same people are unemployed continuously for more than a year. For example, in 1997 more than the half of unemployed people in Serbia had been waiting a long time for employment. (Vukovic, 1999: 364). Moreover, "it is habit-forming: people lose their self-dignity, they become dependent on outside assistance, they are afraid to face reality" (Vaknin, 2000:1).

changes connected to privatization are most obvious among respondents from Hungary and Macedonia, where the privatization was most developed at the time of the survey. On the other hand, they were the least obvious in Bulgaria.

> "I am a biologist. I am unemployed right now, but I worked before. In 1992 I stayed at home with my first child and I stayed at home until May or June 1997. I went back in September and that is when I became unemployed. My job ceased to exist. The laboratory was liquidated, the boss was liquidated and so was the department, everything ceased to exist. I was doing research on medicine and they liquidated our department. I don't know more details because I was already crossed out when I stayed at home with the child that was also a way to reduce the overall number of people." (respondent from Hungary)

As already mentioned, the high level of employment instability in Serbia is connected to economic sanctions and war rather than to privatization. But, although obviously the level of employment instability is primarily an indicator of the level of vulnerability to the negative effects of economic changes, it also may reflect the level of people's readiness to respond actively to these same effects, which is also most visible in Serbia.

Employment stability does not differ significantly by the gender of respondents, although slight differences between male and female employment stability are found among respondents in all countries except Bulgaria. Thus, among Hungarian, Macedonian and Serbian respondents employment changes are slightly more frequent among female than among male respondents, i.e. partners of respondents. On the other side, both male and female Bulgarian respondents share the prevailing pattern of stability of employment status.

Another close link of macro changes and changes in employment status of individual people is found in timing and reasons for job loss. Thus the main reason for job loss of Bulgarian, Macedonian and Hungarian respondents is redundancy as a consequence of privatization and liquidation of insolvent state owned factories. For example, those Macedonians who lost jobs in state owned factories, mainly lost them in the period between 1989 and 1996, when, as pointed out by Dimitrievska, due to privatization, an army of "liquidated workers" was created in Macedonia, increasing from 156 000 in 1990 to 249 928 in 1997 (Dimitrievska, 1998:29). A similar situation is noticed in Bulgaria as well (Muleskova et al., 1999:50). Similarly, Hungarian respondents mainly said that they lost jobs during the first years of transition, i.e. between 1989 and 1995.

However, in Serbia, loss of jobs is more typically connected to economic crises caused by economic sanctions and war, i.e. to related economic malversations of political elite and war destruction.[31] Also, typical job losses related to ethnic tensions

[31] At least 300,000 people, 40% of whom are women, stayed without jobs as a consequence of destruction caused by NATO bombing. With the beginning of aggression, the number of employees in the private sector was limited to the necessary minimum, while more than the half of those employed in state firms were sent on "forced vacation" (Women - victims of aggression, Federal Government Report, 1999, p.13). One of the most striking examples of the unemployment crisis caused by NATO bombing occurred in the car factory "Zastava" in Serbian city Kragujevac: "The story about workers who stayed without job is the story about the majority people in Kragujevac... Everything here is

and war are those connected to ethnic discrimination, exile and general insecurity brought by war. Thus for the majority of refugees leaving home meant not only interruption but loss of employment status for a longer time. As pointed out by Milosavljevic, this fact shapes the overall social position of the majority of refugees (only 10 percent of them managed to get a temporary or permanent job). It has serious sociopsychological consequences since the majority (80%) of adult refugees used to have permanent and stable employment (Milosavljevic, 1997:12).

In all countries people also used to leave a job voluntarily in order to start their own businesses. If the business failed, they either could not find a new job and stayed unemployed, they started a new business or found another state or private job. Unemployment was sometimes a consequence of people becoming redundant by a private firm or as a consequence of its closing. This was usually connected to difficulties of new private entrepreneurs' adjustment to the new system and market economy. In Serbia, it was again connected rather to the economic hardships related to the war. It was most pronounced during severe the economic crisis caused by NATO bombing, especially during the bombing itself.

Since the general feeling of existential insecurity in every sense expanded during the bombing, people tended to avoid all unnecessary expenses. Thus, private entrepreneurs often either closed private firms, stopped work for some time or dismissed their employees and employed their relatives instead. People stopped going to work since it became dangerous or impossible because of destruction. Also, women left their jobs to care for children and their households. Similarly, some refugees became unemployed before fleeing their homes.[32]

In Macedonia, as well, apart from transition related reasons, job loss was also connected to political changes regarding inter-ethnic relations. For example, a male professor lost his job in one bilingual school because of his lack of knowledge of the Albanian language. The reasons for job loss seem not to be significantly dependent on the gender of respondents and their partners, i.e. it seems that they are similar for both men and women. However, on the other hand, some of my female respondents in Hungary lost jobs while on maternity leave.

While some people were not able to find a new job at all, others managed to find one sooner or later. Some people were without a job for only short time, during the privatization process, then got a job again in the same (after it became private) or another factory or institution. However, even a short period of unemployment and adaptation to changed organization of work connected to ownership transformation is often very stressful. For some people, insecurity lasted longer and they managed to find a new job only recently or kept getting and losing temporary jobs all the time after once becoming unemployed. A good example of that is a male interviewee from Hungary:

---

connected to "Zastava"...When it broke, the entire city broke. This is now the valley of hungriness." (V.Simic "Depresija u dolini gladi"(Depression in the valley of hungriness), *Blic*, 23 July 1999.

32 My earlier research showed that women, who used to be employed before the war, had stopped working when the war started, because they had either been dismissed from work, or had quit their job, because they had been made redundant or were unable to go to work due to disconnected communications. In order to make a living, in the absence of husbands, most of them had turned to farming, activities that used to be men's work etc. (Nikolic-Ristanovic at.al, 1996:17).

> "I have been working for my present company for three years. Before, I worked for a year at the real estate department of the 13th district local government. Prior to that, from 1993 until the end of 1995 I was unemployed, as the company that I was the director of was liquidated. At that time, I first started a private company that I ran for about two years, but then I got really sick when the company went bankrupt. I was unemployed again for more than a year."

Among respondents in all four countries three patterns of couple's employment status are identified:

1. Only one partner was employed all the time during the last ten years;
2. Both partners were employed all the time;
3. Both partners faced unemployment for some or all of the time during the last ten years.

Within the first pattern it is possible to distinguish two sub-patterns in relation to the fact whether the husband's or wife's employment prevailed over the last ten years. First pattern[33], i.e. where one partner was employed all the time, while the other was for some shorter or longer time unemployed, prevails among Macedonian respondents. However, for Hungarian and Serbian respondents, couples where both partners were employed all the time were the most characteristic. Among Bulgarian respondents all patterns are represented equally.

Respondents who had partners who were unemployed for a shorter or longer time were usually those whose financial situation was very bad. As expected, the most difficult situation is in households where both partners were facing unemployment for a longer time during the last ten years. However, both partner's continuous employment as a prevailing pattern among Serbian respondents should not be taken as proof that they were better off in comparison to respondents in other countries. On the contrary, this is only one of the most striking examples of the formal character of employment in post-communist and war-affected societies, i.e. proof of the relative character of employment as an indicator of socio-economic status of their citizens. Thus beyond the mask of formal employment of both partners, lack of economic activity and/or earning a living by one or both partners is

[33] Among Macedonian respondents only four respondents, including two males and two females, were employed all the time. This is in accordance with the analysis done by Macedonian Statistics Bureau, which found out that in 1999, the number of households with only one employed member, increased constantly. (S.M.Vankov "Nivoto na siromastija postojano raste" - Level of poverty is increasing constantly, *Nova Makedonija*, 20 October 1999, p.12). Also, an examination of labor force survey data, which was focused on the employment status of children's parents in Hungary in 1992-97, showed a large decrease (about 10 percent, or from 48 to 38 percent) in families where both parents had worked, and a slight decrease in those where only the mother had worked (from 6.6 to 5.6 percent). However, there was a marked increase in the proportion of children in households with only the father working (up to 6 percent), as well as a slight increase in children living in workless households (quoted from UNICEF, 1999:39). This has very serious consequences on the material well being of families, since families with one wage earner are considered to be in a very dramatic situation, i.e. among the most vulnerable groups of Hungarian society. As pointed out by Adamik, during communism, an artificial wage system had been adjusted to the model of families with two wage earners. Thus, during the first years of transition, it was especially difficult since there was no new wage system, inflation was more than 30 percent and prices were at "almost world-market level" (Adamik, 1993:208).

very often found.[34] It seems that, in essence, the prevailing pattern of employment status of Serbian couples is the same as among Macedonian respondents with even more stressful economic consequences.

The unemployment problem is, however, connected not only with the loss of a job but also with the shortage of new jobs. Thus, people who left a job because of illness or those who lost one before the changes had difficulties in finding a new one and experienced shorter or longer unemployment. Also all respondents who were unemployed for a shorter or longer time but managed to get a job recently are between 30 and 35 years old and the job they got is their first job. However, it is not rare that they accept jobs which do not fit their education so that even people with university degrees work as waiters, for example.

The shortage of new jobs affected adult children of respondents in all four countries. However, the situation in that regard seemed to be slightly better in Hungary in comparison to other countries included in the survey. Thus, unlike Macedonians, Bulgarians and Serbs, adult children of Hungarian respondents only occasionally had problems in finding a job. Unemployment mainly affected those with low education, while those with higher education and knowledge of foreign languages were mostly able to find a job without a problem. This is not unusual due to the high level of foreign investment and privatization in Hungary. However, all Macedonian and Serbian, as well as almost all (with only one exception) Bulgarian interviewees, who had adult children, who are no longer in school, said that their children have problems finding a job. They are either unemployed, i.e. economically dependent on their parents (or together with them on social welfare)[35] or work illegally (without insurance and any kind of protection) in private firms.

Young women often work as unregistered (illegal) workers in private cafés and small clothing shops. Also, even those who went abroad in order to find a job often work there illegally as well. On the other hand, like their parents, adult children sometimes have permanent jobs but do not have regular salaries, earn some money only from time to time doing ad hoc jobs, or the salaries are so low that they cannot cover basic existential needs. Among the worst is the situation of the family of a Macedonian Roma interviewee, according to whom, the children became drug addicts, with the daughter starting to earn money through prostitution as a consequence of job shortage and extreme poverty of the family.

2.3 *Informal employment*

In spite of the fact that many people managed to retain formal employment, the decrease in real wages and high inflation, connected to the decrease of GDP and other difficulties faced by post-communist economies, reduced the value of their

[34] They were often on compulsory leave, for shorter or longer period, since their factories were not working at all or they worked with decreased capacity, because of lack of raw material, etc. due to economic sanctions, because the factory or part of it was destroyed in war and similar. Also, sometimes they had to work normal working hours, without any or with only symbolic income.

[35] Extended periods of dependency of adult children as a consequence of unemployment are noticed in some Western research as well (see Cohen, 1987:27).

work and income so that they were forced to look for alternative ways to earn their living. This was even more true for those unemployed, whose fringe benefits either ceased or were insufficient to cover minimal existential needs. Thus both employed and unemployed people were forced to turn to the informal economy to earn their living. Moreover, everything that was mentioned before about instability, frequent changes and fluidity of formal employment applies even more to informal employment.

There are some differences among countries regarding people's readiness to accept informal work. The difference is mainly noticed in relation to informal jobs as additional to formal employment. For example, having an additional job was the prevailing characteristic of my (male and female) respondents in Hungary, Serbia and Bulgaria, but not in Macedonia. On the other hand, however, it seems that much more similarities among countries are found regarding informal jobs as substitutes to formal employment.

Macedonian respondents, who were employed in state firms, mostly were not able to earn a decent living through their regular jobs. In spite of that, they only rarely had an additional source of income, i.e. additional job. Also, those who had additional jobs have been working mainly within their professions. However, Bulgarians, Hungarians and Serbs, unlike Macedonians, only rarely saw state employment as the only source of income. Hence, state jobs were always combined with other sources of income. Moreover, in Bulgaria "part-time private employment, work on one's own plot or land, small-time trade, wheeling and dealing, working out of one's home", and "in most cases, the income derived from this kind of additional work, appears to be greater than income received at the state job" (Garnizov, 1995:19).

Women's additional work was often in the sphere of domestic work and, especially in Serbia, in relation to smuggling goods from neighboring countries or parts of Serbia close to a border. Also, apart from the above-mentioned work, people worked in different additional jobs within their own profession. According to some sources, in Bulgaria and Serbia the additional work is more widespread among men than among women (UNDP, 1998:8: UNICEF, 1997: 24). Sometimes, women worked both in state firms and in private firms owned by their husbands. Also, it was not unusual that, after retiring from a state job, pensioners continued to work in private firms.

As already mentioned, informal employment as a substitute for formal employment seems to be widespread in all countries included in the survey. For respondents from all four countries who were unemployed for a longer or shorter period during the last ten years, the common characteristic is that they had some kind of informal employment. Women, even those with higher education, often worked in the field of domestic work (e.g. caring for children or elderly, cooking, catering etc.) or cleaning (in homes, restaurants etc.). Macedonians and Serbs traveled to neighboring Bulgaria, Turkey or Hungary and smuggled goods to sell later in these countries.[36] Women more often than men accepted informal jobs which do not fit their education (Indshewa, Filipova and Marinova, interviews 1999). However, it was very difficult to earn money in this way, especially because demand for domestic help and related services decreased with the decrease in general standard of living (Coneva, interview, 1999).

Refugee women are in especially difficult situation. They are mainly employed in the private sector (where they work unregistered and without welfare), in shadow economy or as domestic workers. Because of their status they have even fewer chances than local women to get steady jobs. Faced with dramatic poverty, women are forced to accept the jobs, which are offered to them, although they are inadequate and poorly paid. The women who are hired by private employers or through student employment agencies face uncertainty and lack of job security. Moreover, they often have to accept extra jobs, are subjects of exploitation and face the possibility of being exposed to various forms of blackmail (Mrvic-Petrovic and Stevanovic, 2000:163).

Hiring personnel without a labor contract as a way to avoid taxes was one of the most frequent violations of the Labor Code in Bulgaria. Women, especially young ones, were more often than men offered short-term jobs, with minimum wages and without social insurance. Also, in comparison to men, they were more likely to take them and were more vulnerable to sexual harassment by employees as well. In contrast, women older than 35 have difficulty finding jobs, since employers prefer to employ young unmarried women without children, because they are not expected to take maternity/sick leave as often as married women with children (WaD Repport, 1999, p.2, Netkova, interview, 1999).

Unlike women, men choose to stay unemployed rather than accept low paid jobs, i.e. jobs which do not fit their education. As a consequence, when men become unemployed, they often stay long in that status, become angry, bored and are likely to become violent. On the other hand, men mostly tend to use their own professional education to earn money through informal employment or, if they have land, they do agriculture together with their wives or by themselves.

Serbia is some exception in that regard. Because of the extremely difficult economic situation, men as well as women often accepted all kinds of jobs, regardless of their education. Most often women and men were engaged together in smuggling and selling petrol, which was a source of income for many people as long as there was no possibility to buy petrol legally, due to economic sanctions. A statement of one of my respondents illustrates this well:

> "In the factory where I have been working over the last 10 years, I was often sent on compulsory leave. And even when I had to work, I did not get my salary. So I used to escape from the work place and go home to take petrol cans. Then I went to sell it on the street. My husband used to come home at 3 PM, have lunch and come to replace me. Then I went home to cook dinner, wash dishes, feed the kids and then again on the

[36] According to Jovanovic, in Macedonia smuggling was especially widespread among Albaninian and Roma men as well as among Roma women. Albanian men smuggled weapons as well. (Jovanovic, interview, 1999). Also, although Roma women always prevail among those who work as domestic workers, the number of Macedonian women domestic workers has been increasing during the transition as well (Coneva, interview, 1999).

> street. We were able to survive...Now when I see petrol I feel nauseated...Sometimes my husband also used to go to buy petrol in Romania and Bulgaria. Sometimes we used to buy it from other smugglers."

Sometimes, women do not know a lot about the kind of informal works their partners do. Their partners often say that they earn a very small amount of money or nothing. However, when both partners do not have regular salaries, they are forced to rely on social welfare and/or their parents' financial support even when one or both of them are engages in informal work. In 1999, as pointed out by Coneva, 65,000 households in Macedonia were living on social welfare, which was insufficient for them to cover their existential needs (interview, 1999). Refugees in Serbia and Macedonia were in a similar situation.

2.4 Work and leisure time changes

Apart from their obvious stressfulness due to the insecurity connected to them, employment changes had a significant impact on the organization and quality of life of people as a whole. This impact was most directly manifested in changes regarding length of both work and leisure time.

Looking at the connection between employment change and working hours changes, it is possible to identify two main categories of people: those whose working hours are now significally longer than earlier and those whose working hours mainly stayed the same, or even became shorter:

a) Those who used to work in state firms but later became private entrepreneurs, started to work for a private firm, in the informal sector or for an NGO, as well as those who have been doing both state and some additional job on a regular basis, and whose working hours are significantly longer now than earlier;
b) Those who have been employed in (usually the same) state firm all the time, with no or rare additional economic activities, and whose working time did not change considerably over the last 10 years or even became shorter.

In Bulgaria, the second group also included some of those who, since the start of transition, used to work in private firms all the time, but did not have an additional job and had the same working hours as they had previously in state firms.

Also, some Hungarian and Serbian respondents spent the same or less time in work because of the greater flexibility of their new job, change of job position, changed nature and organization of work, or decreased requests of their new workplace, whether in private or public ownership. Women with small children sometimes worked shorter hours even when they were self-employed since they needed more time to take care of children. In Serbia, a second group mentioned above consisted also of pensioners who work part-time, of refugees and other unemployed people who work on temporary jobs from time to time.

It is common for people in all four countries that both women and men who have a private business or work either in a private firm or in the informal sector (as an additional or main economic activity) do not have free time at all or do not have enough of it. A Macedonian male respondent said:

> "Now this is capitalism and one must work a lot. In fact one works without a break. Even when I sleep or go to visit my parents - all the time business is in my head."

The statement of a Hungarian female respondent is similar:

> "I spend eight hours at my work place and an additional (at least six hours) in our surgery. An average of 13 hours per day... Basically my husband and I work much harder and we earn much more and also pay much more, but this also ruins our family life. Spare time is not for the family anymore but for the private business. And everybody around me, my colleagues and friends, live in the same way as we do."

As mentioned above, additional economic activities were much more widespread among Bulgarian, Hungarian and Serbian than among Macedonian respondents. As a result, in these countries, those who recently started to work longer hours are almost equally present among those employed in state firms and NGO's, as well as among private entrepreneurs. It seems that for Bulgarians, Hungarians and Serbs changes in working hours and free time are connected with having or not having an additional job (or with the number of jobs they have) rather than with the type of their employment, as is true for Macedonians.

The lack of free time is characteristic of women who, regardless of the type of their employment, were put in the situation to assume the burden of both paid and domestic work (for example, because their partners lost a job or got sick).

On the other hand, those who worked only in state firms mainly had enough free time. As expected, those retired and unemployed (both formally and informally) usually say that they had too much free time. The way they spent this time was considerably different, depending in large measure on their gender. While men tend to be idle, watching TV and wondering around, without doing any housework or taking care of children, women take care of household and children, i.e. grandchildren. Even unemployed women sometimes say that they do not have free time, especially when they have more than two small children and/or old parents to care for. A Macedonian female respondent says about her husband:

> "When he was employed, he used to spend 8 hours in work. After he lost his job, he used to be all day out, coming back home at 2 or 3 AM."

A Hungarian female respondent, who runs a restaurant together with her husband, tells about her leisure time:

> "Well, if I'm at home at about 7 PM, I can't stop housework and looking after the kids, but maybe I should reschedule my life in order to have more active leisure time. Because now, when I sit down after a whole day's work, I just fall asleep in front of the TV. I'm sure that on the weekends the kids would like us to take them on outings more often, but I usually have to work at least one day at the weekend. That's the worst part of our job, that you can't say that you have finished for the day at 4 PM, you always have to be ready to work."

Also, in Serbia, female respondents sometimes did not distinguish between their domestic work and free time. They said that they had enough free time but, at the same time, they said they spent that time in doing domestic chores.

Looking at the changes connected to employment, it seems, as pointed out by Deacon, that it reflects diversity in people's level of self-activity, i.e. readiness to become active economic and social citizens (Deacon, 1992:11). It appears that, in

Macedonia as well as in Hungary, Bulgaria and Serbia one part of the population is ready and able to become active subjects in the new capitalism and the other part finds no solution to its problems in the new situation (Szalai, 1992, quoted by Deacon, 1992:12; Garnizov, 1995:11). Or, as stated by Wnuk-Lipinski (quoted by Szalai and Orosz, 1992:150)

> "More freedom means greater individual responsibility for one's own life and more individualized choice of one's life career. For some it may be an unbearable burden...To help the helpless seems to be, in this context, the most serious challenge to social policy in a post-communist society".

However, experiences of my respondents in Bulgaria and Serbia show that in societies where the economic situation is extremely difficult, being an economically active citizen is often not enough. In Serbia, for example, the number of those who, in spite of their readiness and capability, were not able to provide for their basic existence and achieve social security, was increasing constantly (Milosavljevic, 1998:20). For example, although those employed in private firms and private owners often had better living standard than those working for state owned firms (Milic, 1995:175), this difference was more pronounced during the first years of transition than later. Thus, it was not unusual that the feeling of helplessness was emphasized more among my respondents in Serbia and Bulgaria than in other countries, as well as that, in spite of their active coping with micro level changes, people felt frustrated since they could not make any change on the macro level. This latter was especially widespread in Serbia after NATO bombing so that the psychological state of the whole nation could be described as learned helplessness.[37]

2.5 Changes in financial situation

The decrease in employment and nominal and/or real wages and pensions, i.e. irregular or no wages (pensions), led to impoverishment of a large part of the population in post-communist countries. As already mentioned, financial insecurity was existential problem most often mentioned by respondents in all four countries included in my survey.

Respondents who did not face financial problems in any period during the first ten years of transition were rare exceptions. This is not unusual considering that in Bulgaria, for example, about 20 percent of people who are considered relatively rich consume more than the remaining 80 percent of the Bulgarians who are close to the edge of physical survival (Raichev et al., 2000:70). Or, as my respondent from Hungary said, "a couple of thousands of people got very rich, but not happier than the ones who became poor".

Both my survey findings and others suggest that the material wellbeing of the family depends on the economic status of all its members, as well as that there is a connection between the fact that only one family member is earning a living and the

[37] Dr M.Popovic, the interview in S.Ast "Lica bez osmeha" (Faces without smile), *Vreme*, 29 April, 2000, p.20.

economic difficulties the family is facing in post-communist society.[38] However, even employed people often do not earn money at all or only insufficient amounts or irregularly. For example, in Macedonia, almost one- third of employed people were on so-called "forced vacation" and did not receive any compensation. A similar situation was found in Serbia (Puzigaca, 1999:111).

The standard of living fell due to the abolition of subventions and rapid increase of prices and living expenses as a whole (Dimitrievska, 1998:29). Apart from economic changes connected to the transition from communism, in some countries, such as Serbia and Macedonia, financial difficulties and a decrease in the standard of living were connected to the war in the former Yugoslavia: the economic sanctions and isolation of Serbia, destruction of factories and infrastructure during NATO bombing (Serbia)[39] and the influx of refugees from Bosnia, Croatia (Serbia) and Kosovo (Serbia and Macedonia).

The majority of refugees in Serbia and Macedonia were accommodated in private homes of people who themselves have been living on the edge of poverty and did not receive any financial help. [40] Since the number of refugees in Serbia has been increasing constantly during the last ten years, the economic situation of the families who accommodated refugees was especially severe there.

Continual impoverishment was the prevailing trend in the financial situation of the families of my respondents from Serbia, Macedonia and Bulgaria, while among Hungarians improvement of their material situation became increasingly evident, especially over the last years. Also, there is a significant difference in the degree of economic hardships faced by respondents in different countries, especially at the time of the survey. As will be shown later with more details, at the time of the survey, the satisfaction of basic existential needs of Hungarian respondents tended to be less affected in comparison to respondents from other countries. On the other hand, the material problems faced by Serbian respondents seemed to be the most serious. Additionally, Serbian interviewees often stressed the war and overall uncertainty connected to it as one of the main problems that they and people close to them faced over last 10 years.[41] These data are obviously connected with the dynamics and level of development of transitional economies in the ten-year period in the respective countries.

As already mentioned, the economic situation seemed to be the most difficult among Serbian respondents. At the same time, as an extreme, the Serbian case is one of the most striking examples of the manifestations of macrostructural changes in the everyday lives of people. The coincidence of the chronology of changes on both the macro and micro level is easily observable. Hence the period between 1989 and

[38] See p. 27 for examples.

[39] Since NATO aggression against Yugoslavia, poverty increased even more. Already low salaries decreased and the payment of pensions and social benefits became difficult.

[40] S.Vukcevic "Solidna podloga za eksplozija" (Solid foundation for explosion), *Nova Makedonija*, July 5, 1999, p.11

[41] According to one survey, until 1993 every fourth household in Belgrade felt direct consequences of war. In 1994 even 16 percent of households in Belgrade accommodated refugees, while every fifth household supported refugees in some other way (Blagojevic, 1997: 30). After the exodus of Serbs from the Krajina (Croatia) and Kosovo, it became worse.

1993 (Markovic's period) was described as very good, 1993-1995 (economic sanctions, war and hyperinflation) as very difficult (but still people had foreign currency reserves from the previous period), 1995-1998 (sanctions were lifted) was better and 1999 (Kosovo conflict, NATO bombing and the most strict economic sanctions) as the worst or "catastrophe." For some people, however, 1993 was the most difficult since they had to cope with worthless earnings and empty stores as a consequence of hyperinflation.

Unlike respondents from other countries, none of the Serbian respondents, including those who started private businesses or have been working very hard on several jobs, answered that his/her economic situation improved since 1993[42]. Only rarely Serbian respondents said that their financial situation was good and stable over the past ten years (owing to their hard work) or that it was bad all the time (usually because of their personal situation which required substantial investment at the beginning of the nineties, e.g. building a house, having children at university etc.).

The prevailing characteristic of Serbian respondents was that they experienced extremely rapid change in their economic security over the year 1993 due to economic sanctions and hyperinflation in their country. [43] This was a shock from which they have not yet recovered:

> "From 1989 to 1992 it was still good. I had a good salary, about 1000 DM. My wife did not work at that time since we had a small child and we had been living in a rented flat. But my parents helped us since they had very good salaries, about 2000 DM each. Then everything became hopeless. I went to fight as a volunteer soldier in Slavonija (Croatia) but after a short time I realized it was not the same as I thought that it should be...When I came back the inflation started and I became redundant in the state firm where I used to work. My last salary had a value of 2 DM. I got a very good offer and went to work for a private entrepreneur. The first couple of years it was good but then the salary went down as the Deutsche Mark went up. The worst was when I left this job. I tried to start a private business but I was not very successful since I was faced with extortion. Last summer we hardly survived Then I found a new job. It is not a big salary but I have a permanent income. So, it was changeable, but the last two years it was very bad." (38 years old, lawyer, married, father of two minor children)

> "During the Ante Markovic time I could support my children and my financial situation was getting better quickly: I became the chief and had about 1000 DM salary. The rent I used to pay for the flat was 300 DM and the rest was more than enough for living.

[42] In fact, the only exceptions in that regard are paradoxically two respondents- refugees, who said that their material situation was improving constantly while they were in Krajina, i.e. Kosovo. The standard of living that they described having before coming to Serbia was in sharp contrast with the rest of respondents who lived in Serbia during the last 10 years. This is not strange because people from the Krajina often had land and other resources gained from an earlier time. Also, since Milosevic came to power, Kosovo Serbs did not have problems finding jobs and earning a living owing to the loss of jobs by Albanians, the flourishing black market and the nformal, including illegal, economy there (Helsinki Committee Report, 2000).

[43] The speed and intensity of the deteriorating economic situation and living conditions in Serbia was also evident in the fact that between 1989 and 1994, i.e. for only four years the GDP decreased 54.3 percent (Blagojevic, 1997:29). The sharpest inflationary increase and the most dramatic decrease of living standards ever recorded in world history deeply influenced the everyday life of Serbian people (Blagojevic, 1997:76).

> Afterwards my rent stayed the same while my salary went down. When my salary decreased to 150 DM I had to leave the job and look for another one...Everyone knows that we used to live better during hyperinflation, since we were able to cope somehow using checks and changing Deutsche Marks. But now the prices are going up, while Deutsche Mark is staying on the same level. I am sure that this time they will put such a pressure on us that we will not be able to survive"(33 years old with secondary school, divorced, father of two minor children).

The disastrous effects of the 1993 inflation on economic security and the overall life of the Serbian people, and especially women, is best described by a female respondent, a 42-year old university professor, married, mother of two, from Novi Sad (Serbia):

> "That time was horrible. I remember that my husband's sister came from Germany for Christmas. I got my salary and wanted to buy bread for us to have for Christmas. There were policemen in front of the shop, who were standing near the queue with automatic guns in their hands. I could buy 2 kilos of bread for my salary at that time. For my whole salary. But the queue was long and when my turn came there was no more bread. I came back home and started to cry since it was Christmas and I had to make bread myself".

The other also rapid change in the economic situation was experienced by those who came to Serbia as refugees from Bosnia, Krajina (Croatia) and Kosovo. The change is connected to loss of employment, i.e. earning and property, which caused the loss of economic security and put them in a status of dependency on poor social welfare and poor people in their host country. Statements like "We used to live normally but now we have neither spoon nor mug", "I left the house with all our belongings, everything, all life"[44] and "the whole of my life was packed in a bag"(Mrvic-Petrovic and Stevanovic, 2000:155) are most often descriptions of this change given by refugees themselves.

In Serbia, refugees had to cope not only with significant changes in their own economic situations but with the decreased economic capacity and living standards of their hosts in general (Nikolic-Ristanovic at al., 1996:44). As noticed by Mrvic-Petrovic, refugees quite clearly became an additional burden for the host families:

> "These families, although they initially demonstrated great sympathy for refugees, gradually became torn between the moral obligation to assist refugees and a material and/or emotional inability to do something about that" (Mrvic-Petrovic, 2000:180).

The extremely difficult economic situation in the Federal Republic of Yugoslavia in 1993 worsened the situation of refugees. Thus, as economic sanctions became increasingly austere and the economic crisis deepened, refugees felt it more than local people. As pointed out by Bosnian refugee Vera Stojkovic at Women in Black Workshop, "one by one, most of the privileges, such as free bus passes, are being withdrawn. Monthly packages with hygienic supplies have been curtailed, supposedly because of the reduced influx of humanitarian aid." (Women in Black, 1994:100).

For Macedonians, as for Serbian respondents, Markovic's period was mainly described as very good and the aggravation of the financial situation mainly started

[44] Z.Panic "Dobro je kad ne moze biti bolje"(It is good if it cannot be better), *Blic*, January 12, 2000, p.13

since 1993 as well. For them, as for respondents in other countries, aggravation of the financial situation was mainly the result of the influence of the following factors: job loss or irregular income of one or both partners; decrease of real wages due to inflation; retirement[45], i.e. low pensions, unemployment of adult children, who, together with their newly established families, continue to be dependent on their parents[46] and/or new expenses, such as school expenses, medications etc. They mainly describe the period between 1993 and 1997 (decrease in GDP, hyperinflation and the impact of economic sanctions in FRY) as financially the most difficult period, although at the time of the survey many were still living on the edge of survival.

Impoverishment is the prevailing characteristic of Bulgarian respondents as well. My Bulgarian respondents described the first years of transition as either stable or the worst years for them in terms of their financial situations. At that time, they faced the first severe economic crisis but still without a serious impact on their employment and social welfare. For some Bulgarian respondents, as for most of Macedonians, the period between 1993 and 1997 was the worst, which seems to be the most difficult period of the Bulgarian transition (Netkova, interview, 1999). This period was marked with another severe economic crisis followed with hyperinflation. In spite of their obvious efforts to make more money through (usually more than one) additional job and to move from state to private jobs, for the majority of Bulgarian respondents the trend of aggravation of their financial situation was still going on at the time of the survey.

For some people, however, their financial situation started to improve after some time. But even when respondents said that they did not have financial problems, they had to cope with financial problems at some time over the previous ten years. They only rarely said that they had a satisfactory living standard.

For Macedonian families, whose members managed to start private busyness and succeeded in it, where one or both partners who lost a job managed to get a new one, or where those whose earnings were not enough started to earn more through an additional job, their financial situations started to improve, most often after 1997.

Apart from successful private businessmen, Bulgarian respondents, who said that their financial situation was either stable or had been improving during the last ten years, were directors of state firms and NGO's, as well as scholars whose additional income came from Western foundation-grants, scholarships etc. However, Bulgarian respondents, who were employed in private firms or had private businesses, sometimes also described their financial situation as "getting worse and worse" or "absolute insufficiency." Even in the case of Bulgarian couples where both partners

[45] It is worth mentioning that retirement is not always connected to retirement age. Many people actually did not have a choice but to take an early retirement due to job loss and the lack of possibility for finding a new one.

[46] In post-communist countries it has been typical that children are dependent on parental financial support even when they start a home on their own (Toth, 1993: 216). In the situation of widespread impoverishment parents are often unable to offer appropriate support which leads to tensions and other problems in parent-children relationships.

were employed in private firms, the financial situation did not start to improve - indeed, it continued to worsen.

Sometimes, a stable financial situation also results from financial aid which people receive from their parents, or, in the case of Albanians from Macedonia, it often results from Albanian men's work abroad (Jovanovic, interview, 1999). Also, sometimes, aggravation or improvement of financial situation was affected by changes related to the family or the employment status of some members of the family (e.g. children were born, left home or got a job, someone retired or died etc.).

Unlike Macedonians, Bulgarians, and Serbs, Hungarian respondents only rarely had their basic existential needs affected at the time of the survey. Respondents often stress that they must work much more now to maintain the lifestyle they were used to earlier, or that they cannot afford to buy some goods at all or as much as earlier (e.g. fruits, books, clothes etc). The prevailing characteristic of the Hungarian sample is a feeling of constant economic insecurity connected to constant and uneven changes in the economic situation. Almost every respondent faced temporary, shorter or longer, financial crises, most often since 1994 and 1995, followed by recent improvement of financial situation. Financial crisis is often caused by one or both partners' loss of a job, a failed private business or investment in starting a private enterprise or a decrease in real wages, connected either to inflation or the increase in taxes. On the other hand, significant improvement usually started after getting a job, i.e. when private business started to make a profit. However, as basic needs seem to be affected less than in other countries, those who did significantly better in comparison to ten year before were also rare. As in Macedonia, those whose financial situations improved the most were respondents who were successful private businessmen, especially when both partners and/or children were running private enterprises (either together or separately).

2.6 Scared of life: changes in living standard and quality of life

For a large part of the Macedonian, Serbian and Bulgarian populations impoverishment was evident in a decrease in the standard of living and quality of life as a whole. On the average, before changes, people were able to buy better food, clothes, to go out to eat[47] and travel for holidays, or replace house equipment regularly. Now, they are hardly able to pay bills[48] and buy basic goods (Milosavljevic, 1998:20).

Most of people's income is usually spent on food but for some even buying enough food is not possible. According to some research findings, the average Bulgarian spends about 50 percent of his/her income on food and he/she is not able

[47] It is interesting that for the significant part of Bulgarian respondents eating out was still possible in spite of difficult financial situation. It may be explained by culture, by acceptable prices in a lot of restaurants as well as by the fact that it somehow became substitute for socializing at home. Namely, many of recently established private restaurants in Sofia, for example, are located in or near the houses of restaurant's owners and the food and atmosphere in them are rather like at home.

[48] In the autumn 1999, 550 000 households or about 1 million people in Bulgaria had their heating expenses covered through Government's social welfare scheme - G.Lanzov "1 mln dusi s pomoci za otoplenie (Million people with help regarding heating), *Nosen Trud*, 28-29 October 1999.

to buy foreign goods, which became available after the changes (Netkova, interview, 1999). In 1999, 100,000 Serbian citizens got their meals in public kitchens for poor people and 150,000 received other kinds of social support.[49]

House equipment as well as cars, if any, are often 10 or more years old. Some Bulgarian and Serbian respondents had to sell their cars to get money to live on. Also, because of the high prices and shortage of petrol as well as lacking money to maintain it, some Serbian respondents stopped driving a car even when they had one. Unlike their parents during the communist time, young people can barely afford to buy house equipment and, particularly, a car. Some research findings show that only 10 percent of Bulgarians can afford to buy new house equipment, i.e. electrical appliances. Eighty percent of them bought only a color TV during the last ten years (Netkova, interview, 1999).

Negative changes in everyday life resulted in a decreased feeling of certainty and life fulfillment and satisfaction as a whole (Coneva, interview, 1999). They also contributed to the development of a range of existential fears among the Bulgarian and Macedonian population, such as fear of unemployment, fear of hunger (Garnizov, 1995:17), fear of the future, or, as pointed out by Jovanovski, "fear of life rather than fear of death" (Jovanovski, 1998:95). According to public opinion surveys (1997, 1999) two-thirds of Bulgarians feel a strong alarm and constant fear of falling standard of living and impoverishment.[50] Current poverty in Bulgaria is characterized by its extremely broad scope and considerable depth. As a result, the key word in Bulgaria's transition is survival.[51] Apart from fear of hunger and fear of unemployment, the most frequent fears among the Serbian population were: fear of war, fear of illness and impossibility to be cured, as well as fear of expulsion, which was felt by citizens of all ethnic groups. In 1999, to the previous list of fears in Serbia, the fear of authority (Milosevic's regime) was added (Puzigaca, 1999: 118,119).

Macedonian respondents describe change in their family budget in the following ways:

> "We used to go on holidays, drive cars, buy flats, have nice food and clothes - now we don't have money to buy shoes."

> "My wife and I wear the clothes bought by our daughter who lives abroad. We do not accept money from her, just clothes as a gift. This is because we do not want her to know how awful our financial situation is."

[49] R.Dubajic in "Pomoc za izbeglice, raseljene i socijalno ugrozene" (The aid for refugees, displaced and others in need) , *Danas*, 22 October 1999

[50] Center for Marketing & Social Studies, 1997; International Center for Minority Studies & Intercultural Relations, 1999.

[51] Different forms of natural economy developed. According to BBSS Gallup data (based on a sample of 11,200 interviewed people) 9 percent of the people lived on self-produced food, and 45 percent relied mostly on homemade foods (Raichev et al., 2000: 70). Misery leads to degradation. In 1999, one out of ten Bulgarians neither bought toilet soap, nor was able to obtain it in another way. Every fifth Bulgarian, or 1.5 million people, was unable to obtain toothpaste. Every fourth woman was unable to buy or otherwise obtain underwear or deodorant. (National Representative Survey of "Mediana" Agency, January 2000, *Trud Daily*, 19.02.2000)

> "Until 1993 we used to buy furniture, but since then we are not able to pay even for our electricity bills. We used to get money for food from our parents. 1994 was catastrophe for us."

> " Until 1996 we managed somehow to cope with the situation and pay our bills and rent. After 1996 it became awful. During the winter, we often stayed without heating because we were not able to pay for electricity. We did not have money to buy food either. We used to pay our debts by working for the shop, which used to give us the food on credit."

Similar statements are given by Bulgarians and Serbs:

> "Most often, regardless of the kind of job one has, in state or private firm, he/she cannot earn a decent living. In most places, the wage is not enough to cover transportation expenses to reach the workplace. And when one should pay bills, there is no money for that."(Bulgarian)

> "Ten years ago we bought a flat. Now we do not have enough money to buy food." (Bulgarian)

> " Earlier I could afford to buy a car. Now, the biggest luxury for me is buying ham for my children." (Serb)

> "During Markovic's period we were able to buy a microwave. Everyone used to buy them so we did the same. But now, if anything breaks, it would be a catastrophe. This is what happened with our cooker: it broke and could not be repaired. We managed to buy a new one using some smuggler channels and had to pay 900 DM in cash for it. And it was a less expensive one. This is horrible price in our economic situation."(Serb)

On the other hand, those Macedonians and Bulgarians whose living standard improved, also improved their financial situation. They were usually able to buy new house equipment, including items, which the average citizen could not afford during communism, such as a computer, microwave, Xerox etc., but, as a rule, even they rarely had clothes dryers and dishwashers. However, the overall quality of life of those whose financial situation improved often became worse as well, since they became exhausted and did not have time to make proper use of the money they earned. It was especially evident in Macedonia. Although the financial situation of some Macedonians and Bulgarians allowed them, for example, to eat out or take a holiday, they now did that more rarely than earlier

> "We used to have less money but it was enough for living. Now we have much more - we can go on holiday, in restaurants, etc. but we do not have time for that. We do not have leisure time at all."(Macedonian female)

> "We used to go to restaurants more often with our friends and relatives. Now we are busy with work, official meetings and traveling" (Bulgarian female)

However, as already mentioned neither those Serbian respondents who had a private business nor those who used to have additional jobs or worked long hours in the informal sector saw their financial situation improve. Their main achievement was keeping their living standard on a decent level. They, especially women, used to sacrifice their own needs in order to provide for children. Even people who seemed better off in comparison to others were not able to buy a new car, flat or house equipment.

It seems that they suffered from a twofold negative influence of changes on the quality of their life: one as the consequence of economic hardships, which they could not avoid in spite of their hard work, and the other, as the consequence of overworking and lack of free time. Both had a severe stressful impact and contributed to their feeling of helplessness since all their efforts often seemed senseless.

Looking from the perspective of my respondents from Hungary, the standard of living of Hungarians was not affected as much as the standard of living of people from other countries included in the survey. The prevailing characteristic of Hungarian respondents was that at the time of the survey they did not have problems buying basic goods, such as food, and paying bills. However, the decrease in the living standard was obvious in Hungary as well. It was reflected in the fact that they could not afford buying goods, including food, of the same quality as earlier, that they were less able to invest in education and entertainment (including books) and that they could not afford buying some luxury items.

Another prevailing characteristic of Hungarian respondents was that they could afford to go out to eat. Unlike Macedonian and Bulgarian respondents, they rarely said they could not afford to eat in a restaurant at all. Hungarians mainly had all the house equipment that they needed and, if they had not bought new things recently, it was because they did not need them rather than that they could not afford them. I noticed that, unlike Macedonians and Bulgarians, most of my Hungarian respondents had bought new house appliances during the last ten years and these were appliances which were not affordable for them during communism, i.e. which were affordable only for those Bulgarians and Macedonians who could be considered the new rich (e.g. microwave, computer, HI FI, piano, etc.). Also, they mainly had one car (which was not always an old one). Some of them could afford to buy a new car but did not want to. Also, what Hungarians considered an old car was significantly different as compared to what an old car meant for Macedonians and Bulgarians.[52] Only rarely did Hungarian respondents not have a car or have had to sell one. However, unlike Bulgarian respondents who had to sell a car in order to survive, Hungarian respondents did it to get money to invest in other things, like house renovation or for buying a flat.

Looking at the possibilities for taking a holiday, as one of the indicators of a change in living standard and quality of life, I identified three groups of people: 1. those who used to go on holiday, but, over the last ten years, stopped doing it, went for shorter times or closer to home due to their financial situation; 2. those who, for different reasons, never went on holiday; 3. those who used to go on holiday, could still afford it, but no longer went or went for a shorter time due to lack of time.

Macedonian respondents were distributed almost equally among the above-mentioned groups, while most respondents from other countries who still went on

[52] For Hungarians, for example, a car bought at the beginning of the 1990-s was considered old, while Bulgarians and Macedonians considered old the new or used cars they bought more than 10 years ago.

holiday went for a shorter time or closer to home. Those who stopped going on holiday said the reason was lack of time or money, while those who decreased the time and/or distance said the change was due to a lack of financial resources. Also, some of respondents, especially those from Serbia, stayed in their own or a friend's cottage, or in available state hotels or school resorts for children.

The lack of time as the reason for not going on holiday was usually connected either with a private business or an additional job. It was common for those Macedonian respondents, for example, who had private employment that, in spite of the fact that their financial situation allowed them to go on holiday, they often did not go anywhere, spent holidays working, or, even if they went somewhere, they could not relax properly, since they kept thinking about business or work all the time while on holiday. Sometimes, men sent their wives and children to spend a holiday by themselves. Because they used to go for holidays together and be much more relaxed during communism, this had a serious impact on partner's relationships.

Rare cases (two) of more significant positive change was noticed only in Hungary among those who answered that they now could afford to go abroad, which was not possible for them earlier. This means that only rarely did my respondents have both money and time to go on holiday regularly and, especially, to leave their country. Both Hungarian respondents who answered that their possibilities for spending holidays improved significantly were private businessmen, whose partners were businessmen as well.

2.7 Housing

As with people from other post-communist countries, Macedonians, Bulgarians, Hungarians and Serbs usually live in their own[53], their parent's or rented flats or houses. For a large part of the population, the housing problem, which obviously existed during communism as well, worsened during the transition and as a consequence of war. Negative changes in housing were especially stressful for both refugees and families who accommodated them in Serbia and Macedonia.

The analysis of my respondents' answers about their housing situation shows three main patterns:

1. A bad housing situation (no flat or inappropriate one, had to move often, refugee etc.);
2. A stable and decent housing situation over the last ten years (has flat, but usually of inappropriate size);
3. A very good housing situation (very large houses, often meaning significant improvement over the last ten years).

These three patterns existed in all countries included in the survey, but they were distributed among respondents of different countries in different ways. A bad housing situation, with strong negative consequences for family relationships, for example, is the pattern which prevailed among Macedonian and Bulgarian

[53] Most often these are flats which they received, and later bought for symbolic money, from the state, and which were only rarely appropriate for the size of the family. However, some people also had private houses, which they built or bought.

respondents. Although less often, however, this pattern was also significant among Serbian and Hungarian respondents, where a stable and decent housing situation prevailed. Examples of the third pattern were rare.

Those who did not have a flat of their own and could not afford to buy or rent one were obviously in the worst position in all countries. Most often these were young people who were just starting their families and it was quite common for them to live with parents and/or other relatives for many years, with the couple's room being shared with their first child (Corrin, 1992:50). This usually makes life unsupportable since two, or even three families are living under one roof.[54] Sometimes, those who had been living in a rented flat for some time had to return to their parents home since they could not afford to pay rent and bills any more. An extreme example of this kind is described by a male respondent from Macedonia:

> "During Markovic's period, while we were able to pay rent, we lived in a decent flat. From 1996 until recently we lived in two rooms in the same flat with my mother. Three months ago, my brother, together with his family, came to live with us as well, and we had to move into one small room. Since then, we have conflicts between us all the time. It came to the point of violence so that even the police had to intervene."

Returning from a nuclear to a several generation family was also necessary for those who, in spite of the fact that they had their own flat or house, could not afford to live on their own. Sometimes, they sell or rent their own flat and return to live with their parents. Or their relatives sell or rent their own flat and come to live with them. Sometimes, as two respondents from Hungary did, they go to live in a house for homeless people instead. In Macedonia, as pointed out by Trajkovski, patriarchal loyalty and solidarity became more pronounced during the transition since people could not afford to live without the material support of a wider family or without saving money by living close to each other, i.e. together (Trajkovski, 1998:71).

In Serbia and Macedonia, the worsening housing situation was also influenced by ethnic conflicts, i.e. by the arrival of refugees and international military forces. The arrival of refugees, who were most often accommodated with friends and relatives, made the housing situation extremely difficult for both refugees and their hosts, whatever their earlier housing situation was. Also, as stressed by one of the Serbian respondents, the first wave of migration from the conflict area usually consisted of affluent people, who bought or rented flats in Serbia. This had an impact on the increase in rent prices and worsened the housing problems of people in Serbia.[55].

Those refugees who were accommodated in *ad hoc* created refugee centers were obviously in the worst housing situation in Serbia and Macedonia (Mrvic-Petrovic and Stevanovic, 2000:160; Mrvic-Petrovic, 2000:102). Some of the refugee centers

[54] The same is widespread within the Albanian population, but, as stressed by Jovanovic, it is related to tradition rather than to necessity (Jovanovic, interview, 1999). The same may also apply to Romany people in all countries and Turkish ethnic groups in Bulgaria, which (traditionally) large households are seen as a significant factor for poverty distribution among those groups (UNDP, 1998a:83).

[55] A similar situation was noticed in Macedonia but mainly in connection to the increase of prices related to the increased presence of international military forces in that country (Coneva, interview, 1999).

in Serbia looked like real "hallways to hell"[56], or like "ghettos for old and sick people"[57]. In a collective refugee center, the loss of privacy and family organization, i.e. family roles, is most striking[58]. After the expulsion of Serbs from Kosovo, following the end of the Kosovo conflict and NATO bombing, many, especially lonely old refugees became either homeless or moved from one relative to another. One of the best illustrations of the hopeless housing and overall situation of both refugees and their hosts in Serbia is found in the statement of Rada Vujovic, an old female refugee from Kosovo, quoted in the magazine *Vreme:*

> " So, when I see that I bother them much, I ask them for money to buy a train ticket and I go to another relative. Since I left Kosovo, I have made a full circle. I went to everyone - nobody expelled me but nobody also tried to retain me. The best was with the neighbor of my brother's son in Kragujevac. They accepted me since they are nice people. But after one week, I saw what their situation is: they did not have bread, they did not have money for themselves either, and they all slept in one room. They have only this one room. But everyone was fine toward me like I was their own. But I saw that I am the burden...I consider myself a traveling lottery - where I am going to die, this one should pay for my funeral. I would prefer to die somewhere on the road...So..Somewhere."[59]

A stable and decent housing situation was characteristic of those people who were lucky enough to have an appropriate flat that they obtained from the state or bought by themselves, by their parents or with their help, before or during the transition. This pattern prevailed among Hungarian and Serbian respondents, while it was less often seen among respondents from Bulgaria and Macedonia. This group consists, especially in Hungary, of people whose family structure did not change significantly during the last ten years, or the change was in terms that some of their members left to live on their own. In Serbia, in two cases, these were also those who occupied, legally or illegally, inappropriate common rooms in state buildings, had them rebuilt and made them more or less appropriate for decent living.

A more significant improvement, i.e. extremely good housing situation (unusually large houses) in comparison to the average one is characteristic of new private businessmen and businesswomen, directors of large state firms or those who managed to earn a significant amount of money through different additional jobs. In Macedonia, Bulgaria and Hungary, they often managed to replace earlier small flats or their parents rooms with houses of 200-300 square meters. Sometimes they also retained flats they bought from the state and used them in order to earn additional money through rent.

[56] Z.Tmusic "Predvorje pakla ispod zlatiborskog raja" (Hell vestibule below Zlatibor's heaven), *Blic*, January 8, 1999.

[57] B.Kaljevic "Lica bez osmeha" (Faces without smile), *Vreme*, April 29, 2000, p.21

[58] Psychologist Nada Polovina, in M.Milosavljevic "Mrzim svoju majku" (I hate my mother), *Nin*, April 27, 2000, p.30

[59] *Vreme*, January 15, 2000.

2.8 Gender and poverty

Although impoverishment affects both women and men, the factors which determine poverty have generally more impact on women than on men, due to the specific characteristics of gender and their relevant capacity and status. Poverty affects women in a more drastic way than men since they are expected to continue to cope successfully with an increasing burden of domestic work. A decrease in living standard is followed first and foremost by an increase of women's obligations within the family.

Women run households in a more primitive way and their capacity for using domestic help decreases. This was expressed in a specially drastic way in Serbia during the NATO bombing and in parts of the former Yugoslavia affected by ethnic conflicts. For example, as a consequence of shelling, bombing and other military actions, i.e. "strategies", people went a long time without electricity and water, which made running households and taking care of children extremely difficult (Nikolic-Ristanovic et al., 1996:18).

At the same time, men's contribution to childcare and household duties, as a rule, is modest and depends on their willingness to contribute or to be involved in it at all. This is confirmed by the answers obtained from respondents in all four countries included in the survey. Men mainly do not participate at all, or participate only marginally and in terms of a traditional division of labor. However, the cases where a less traditional share of household duties exists were occasionally found as well. They were mentioned more often by Bulgarians and Hungarians than by Macedonians and Serbs.

As Burgoyne (1987:54) stresses, the more closely the husband's masculinity and sense of self-worth is based upon identity as a worker and breadwinner, the more difficult it is for his wife to take over that role or to suggest that he should do more around the home. However, men's contribution seems to be more visible in terms of their increased contribution to tasks which are traditionally considered male but, in modern society, are mainly done by paid workers, such as repairs, building, decoration, different kinds of physical work etc. As with women's household work, men's contributions in these areas often saved the household budget a significant amount. However, it is very difficult to find the real ratio of male-female contribution in this respect since, apart from traditional female duties, women's extended household duties sometimes include those which are traditionally expected from men as well.

According to the Hungarian Statistics Bureau Survey, although domestic chores always have been mainly women's responsibility, since 1993 the average monthly time which women spent on them was more than 10 percent longer than the time men spent on paid work. This occurred in spite of the fact that the time which men spent on paid work decreased more than twice. Also, while women used 50 percent of the free time that they got after losing a previous job for doing their household duties, men use only one fifth of their newly free time for that. This situation poses unsolvable problems especially to those women who managed to retain their work place (Frey, 1998:8). Similar effects are noticed in Western countries. For example, as Cohen points out, a study of the impact of male unemployment among redundant steelworkers upon their family relationships offers little evidence of increased activity by those men within the household. Moreover, as with my findings, this study shows the existence of a corresponding reluctance on the part of wives to agree to what they perceive as an invasion of their personal domain (Cohen, 1987:28).

The increase in the time necessary for domestic duties may also be explained by the decrease in the number of households which are able to use external services, such as cleaning, babysitting, food preparation etc. For example, since 1986 the number of households in Hungary which used some kind of help was halved, while the number of households that could not afford or were not willing to use these services increased from one third to two-thirds. As pointed out by Frey, it is evident that, with the increase in poverty, there are fewer and fewer families who can afford to use services that have become too expensive for them. The availability of domestic services decreased as well, which additionally decreased people's ability to make use of them (Frey, 1998:8)

These effects are confirmed with my survey findings for all four countries, according to which, with rare exceptions of the occasional use of other services, the only help women have comes from their parents, relatives and kindergartens. While some used to have help (e.g. babysitting, cleaning, ironing, restaurants, etc.) on a regular basis or from time to time, others never had it, either because they could not afford it or because they did not need or did not want to use it. On the other hand, however, the answers about the time that women spend on household duties and child care show two opposite patterns connected to women's work outside the home, changes in family life and availability of domestic help. Women who spend less or no time in work outside the home and/or have small children, or take care of the elderly and/or grand-children, usually say that now they spend more time in household duties than earlier. In addition, in Serbia (obviously because of extremely difficult economic situation), some women said that they had to work more in the home as well as outside it in order to both earn a living and reduce expenses. Also, some women said that they spend more time in household chores in comparison with earlier since all things in their household are old and need more time for taking care of them. On the other hand, women who said that they now spend less time in household duties are usually those who now work longer hours as well as those who can afford some kind of help (most often those who have a private job or are private entrepreneurs). Also, women whose children are grown or who are divorced have fewer duties in their homes even when they work less outside the home than they used to.

However, one analysis of subjective feelings about the impact of impoverishment on men and women shows that both genders feel that they are those who are most affected. And interestingly, the feelings of both are closely related to their traditional roles. Men think that they are affected more because of their traditional role of bread winner, while women's assumption is based on their lack of conditions for the normal fulfillment of their role as housewives and mothers (e.g.cannot prepare a normal meal) and for taking care of how they look. (Dimitrievska, 1999:189).

Single women who are heads of households are in an especially difficult economic position. As in Western countries (Crompton and Mann, 1994:VI), divorce is one of the most serious risk factors for women's poverty. For example, in Bulgaria, in the period prior to 1990 divorce caused moral embarrassment rather than economic problems, while nowadays, the crisis overshadows the moral embarrassment and brings to divorced women another problem, which did not exist before - survival. Women, who in 90 percent of cases are granted parental rights after divorce, have to find ways to compensate for the lack of a second income (UNDP, 1998:17). Also, as pointed out by Speder, poor women in Hungary live either as single mothers or with one family member - most often with a son who leaves the family later than a daughter or returns to mother after divorce. Divorce is considered a greater poverty risk factor for women than for men in Hungary (Speder, 1997:130).

Women from Serbia, however, became heads of households as a consequence of war as well, and, unlike in transition countries which did not experience the war, in Serbia it happened regardless of their marital status. The outbreak of war usually means the military mobilization of men, so that women, whether they decide to stay or leave to take refuge elsewhere, are compelled to care for themselves, children and the elderly, without any support from their husbands (Mrvic-Petrovic and Stevanovic, 2000:152). Women, whose husbands were killed or became disabled in war, kept in prisoner-of-war camps or those who did not know where and how their husbands were, were in even more difficult situations since they were burdened not only by poverty and worries about their husbands, but also by serious traumas. This made their struggle for survival even more difficult.

One of the most powerful factors of poverty for both women and men is age. Young and old people are among the most severely hit by poverty. (UNDP, 1998a:83). As pointed out by Speder, among women, the old are most severely hit by poverty, while among men, the poorest are the very young (Speder, 1997:131). The economic situation of young people, especially young men, in Serbia was further aggravated in connection with their political background. Young people who were mostly against Milosevic were in the worst position, since they often did not have another choice besides emigration or the black market (Dankovic, in Women in Black, 1994:109)

Age reduces the capacity for labor and additional work, which renders pensions a major, and, in most cases, the only source of income. Due to the low level of pensions, people and households that depend on pensions, were poor (UNDP, 1998:15; Speder, 1997:130). Single old women in big cities were in an especially difficult position in Bulgaria, since their pensions could not be supplemented by income from personal farms, while the costs of electricity and heat considerably exceeded the capacity for support and normal life. They were definitely the poorest group in Bulgaria and Hungary, and, most probably, in other post communist societies. When they have their own flat, they are often forced to sell it, buy a smaller one and live on the difference in price. However, because they are old, they are vulnerable to fraud so that when it occurs they are left without either flat or money.[60]

The problems of the elderly are not only financial, but also social and psychological "since they are related to disappointment and loneliness, destruction of illusions and values" (UNDP, 1998:23). This becomes disastrous especially when old refugees, and, especially women refugees, are in question (Knezic, 2000:42)

3. EVERYDAY LIFE AND WAR RELATED CHANGES

Although all countries included in the survey felt the consequences of ethnic conflicts in the former Yugoslavia and NATO bombing of Serbia, as it could be expected, their impact on the everyday lives of people was the most striking in Serbia. Previous analyses showed some effects that war had on the social and economic status of people who were directly or indirectly affected by war. These consequences are often similar to those noticed in connection to earlier wars, such as the consequences of World War II on the life of German people. (Moeller, 1993:3; Karstedt, 1993).

However, apart from the obvious negative impact that war had in terms of decreasing possibilities for employment, earning a living, in aggravating the housing situation and the overall living standard and quality of life of people living in Serbia, especially refugees, it had other consequences to the everyday life as well. These consequences are often interlaced and multiple, and include especially:

a) forced interruption of normal life and overall stress caused by war;
b) migration (forced or to prevent of anticipated danger) and stresses connected with it;
c) men's absence from family life (because of participation in/avoidance of military service, etc.) and related changes of family structure and women's social and economic status;
d) disturbance of inter-ethnic relationships, changes of ethnic identities and ethnic discrimination.

The stresses, resulting from changes connected to the war, were always multiple, long lasting and cumulative. While refugees usually accumulate stresses resulting from war and their refugee status, people from Serbia had war stresses caused by NATO bombing on top of the stresses of social and economic changes resulting from partial transition, economic sanctions and ethnic conflicts in the former Yugoslavia.

War itself means sudden and forced interruption of normal life in such a way that any perspective was erased and this severe interruption itself is experienced as violence. In this way, the war was experienced both by refugees from parts of the former Yugoslavia affected by ethnic conflict and by the Serbian population affected by NATO bombing (Blagojevic, 2000:XIII; Vidakovic, 1999:56). For many people,

[60] Such one case was reported in Bulgarian newspaper *Nosen trud*: after being left without a flat and money, 83 years old Fidanka Nadeva, who could not live on her 42 levs pension, and who did not have a family of her own, asked from doctors to give her an injection and let her die (*Nosen Trud*, 12-13 November, 1999, p.24).

and especially for women, who make up the majority part of refugees, the stresses of war itself are followed by the stress of leaving home and becoming a refugee. The stress of leaving is especially pronounced when it is sudden and forced. The stress of sudden and compulsory migration was best described by a Serbian refugee woman from the Krajina, an interviewee for one of my previous studies:

> "We were sitting, crouching in our tractor, in disbelief, wondering if it was possible that we were leaving our homes and our land (...) I cried all the way through, not so much because of the house itself and the furniture we had left inside, but because of our lives that were being destroyed, because we were losing our identities, becoming estranged from all that had been so genuinely ours, like celebrating our *slava* (Saint's day). What we were leaving behind was an entire lifetime, unfolding memories, feelings, our childhoods, the house we were born in-all these things would never come back."(Nikolic-Ristanovic at al., 1996:XV)

Loss of previous social and economic status led refugees to economic and social powerlessness. Simultaneously with their geographic, social and psychological uprooting, refugees lost a very important part of their social security which resulted from their position in earlier informal, formal and institutional social networks. All these losses led to a deeply unfavorable socio-psychological and personal situation, where identities and subjectivity were lost, and one became dependent and in the position of object in the majority of social relationships which were established in exile. (Milosavljevic, 1997:12). Also, with the loss of employment, most social rights, except the right to health care, were lost as well. With the disintegration of Yugoslavia, many people lost their former citizenship but, because of war, did not manage to obtain a new one. Thus many refugees are not able to leave Serbia and try to find better conditions for life in other countries.

The life in refuge represents a trauma which is additional to the traumas of war and forced migration, so that we can speak about the accumulation of stresses, i.e. traumas. As well noticed by Vlajkovic, people in exile face two large groups of adaptation tasks: to overcome what they experienced before going into exile and to adapt themselves to everything that life in exile brings. Very often, it means: "overcoming and adjusting to the loss of a dear one, traumatic experiences, loss of home and property passed down through generations, loss of friends, loss of precious symbolic valuables like photographs of dear ones, changes of life habits, poverty, loss of professional identity, dependency on others, feelings of insecurity and helplessness, social marginalisation and social stigmatization and, at the same time, the necessity to preserve mental health, hope, life sense and the ability to make constructive decisions, essential for further life (Vlajkovic, 1997:23).

All that becomes even more pronounced and difficult to cope with when refugees find themselves in a country with a completely different culture and way of living (e.g. refugees from Bosnia in Western countries). Also, the problems of adaptation and refuge trauma become deeper with each new experience of compulsory leaving. Some refugees in Serbia were double, triple or four time refugees (e.g. those who had to flee from one part of Croatia to Krajina, from Krajina to Kosovo and then from Kosovo to Serbia proper).

Since the outbreak of war usually separates male and female members of a family, the number of temporary or permanently incomplete families begins to rise suddenly (Moeller, 1993:3). Although the number of complete refugee families, especially those from Krajina and Kosovo, is not insignificant, there is a preponderance of incomplete families among refugee families, where the absence of the husband or father is frequent.

The absence is temporary (temporary incomplete families), when the father or the husband is participating in war, is a refugee in some other country or is in hiding in order to avoid military service. On the other hand, permanent incomplete families are created as a result of the death of the husband or father. Both the permanent and temporary absence of the husband put an extremely difficult burden on women in terms of care for their own and their children's existence. Also, the psychological effects, although different in the intensity of trauma which they provoke, have some similarities as well.

Women, who lose their husbands in war suffer the trauma of loss and are confronted with taking on all family responsibilities, which are often extremely difficult to bear. On the other hand, women, especially refugee women, experience serious traumas provoked by separation from loved ones. This kind of separation was particularly hard for women from so-called mixed marriages. As pointed out by Mrvic-Petrovic, "their own ethnic affiliation could be a source of trouble in the new environment, no matter how much loyalty they showed towards their husbands' nationality. They 'betrayed' their nation without gaining a place among compatriots of their husbands." (Mrvic-Petrovic, 2000:137) Cut off from support in the new surroundings, these women relied too much on emotional exchange within their nuclear families. Thus, they suffered very much when they became separated or lost their husbands.

As noticed in other wars as well (Moeller, 1993:29), changes in family structure caused by separation, i.e. men's absence, often create problems in relationships when the family is reunited For couples of different ethnic origin it is even more complicated, since nationalism and abstract ethnic hatred spread by ruling elite, "very easily transforms itself into animosity towards the closest persons, such as a wife, children or cousins (Nikolic-Ristanovic, 2000:97).

However, it is worth mentioning that both socio-economic changes connected to war and changes brought by the disturbance of interethnic relationships, affected complete families as well, whether they used to live in Serbia or came there as refugees. Their impact was obvious in changes of power relationships within the family connected to changes of ethnic and/or gender and generation identity as a consequence of nationalism, economic hardships, and both men's temporary absence and participation in war. As we will show in the analysis which follows, these changes are responsible for a large part of violence against women, during and after the war.

CHAPTER 3

GENDER IN TRANSITION

1. INTRODUCTION

Social and economic changes, analyzed in the previous chapter, have had significant impact on gender relationships and women' s vulnerability to violence. However, as in Western societies, the relationships between changes in social and economic status and violence against women are rarely direct. Rather these relationships are mediated by stress, frustrations and/or changes in gender and other identities (ethnic, generation, class).

Gender structures contribute significantly to women's vulnerability to violence, including domestic violence, sexual harassment, prostitution and trafficking in women (Messerschmidt, 1993:8121-153). Thus changes of gender structures in post-communist societies are expected to have a strong influence on the vulnerability of women to these forms of violence.

In this chapter I will explore changes in gender structures in post-communist society against Connell's hegemonic masculinity/emphasized femininity and Messerschmidt structured-action theory. I will look at both changes in social constructions/representations of masculinities/femininities, i.e. normative gender identities, and changes of actual masculinities/femininities in post-communist society. The bases of these analyses will be Connell's (1987:183-88) notion of "hegemonic masculinity" and "emphasized femininity" as the culturally idealized forms of gender in a given historical setting. These forms, as further elaborated by Messerschmidt (1995:173) are "culturally honored, glorified and extolled at the symbolic level in the mass media". "In Western industrialized societies", as stressed by the same author, "hegemonic masculinity is characterized by work in the paid labor market, the subordination of women and girls, heterosexism and the driven and uncontrollable sexuality of men, and underscores practices toward authority, control and aggressiveness". Emphasized femininity is a form that complements hegemonic masculinity and is defined by Connell through compliance with men's desire for titillation and ego stroking and acceptance of marriage and childcare, and on mass level is "organized around the themes of sexual receptivity in relation to younger women and motherhood in relation to older women" (Connell, 1987:187).

My analysis of changes of gender role identities in post-communist society will be focused on changes of three specific social structures, which, according to Messerschmidt, underlie relations between women and men: gender division of labor, gender relations of power and sexuality (Messerschmidt, 1995:172). For exploring both normative and actual masculinities/femininities, I use my own and other survey findings. My survey findings on normative gender identities include those resulting from interviews as well as from content analysis of media representation of women. On the other side, the analysis of actual masculinities /femininities is based exclusively on the part of my survey which was based on interviews (with professionals, women's group activists, etc., as well as with women and men from the general population).

2. GENDER IDENTITIES IN PUBLIC REPRESENTATION/DISCOURSE ABOUT WOMEN AND MEN

As Messerschmidt (1997:10) puts it, "hegemonic masculinity" and "emphasized femininity" are neither transhistorical nor transcultural, but vary from society to society, and change within a particular society over time. In any specific time and place, then, hegemonic masculinity and emphasized femininity are culturally honored and extolled at the symbolic level (e.g. mass media) and are constructed in relation to subordinated masculinities and femininities (based on race, class, and sexual preferences, for example), to oppositional masculinities and femininities, and to each other. "Hegemonic masculinity and emphasized femininity", stresses Messerschmidt, "are the dominant forms of gender to which other types of masculinity and femininity are subordinated or opposed, not eliminated, and each provides the primary basis for relationships among men and women" (Messerschmidt, 1997:10).

Consequently, if we want to understand changes in actual gender identities and how they affect relationships and contribute to violence in post-communist societies, it is necessary first to look at changes in presentations of masculinities and femininities, i.e. to identify presentations which were normative during communism as well as those which became normative in post-communist societies. In fact, there is an ordering of versions of masculinity and femininity at the level of the whole society, which creates people's expectations about themselves and about other people. As a result, actual gender identities are always shaped in relation to people's compliance/ rejection attitudes toward the normative, which tend to be "more skeletal and simplified than the human relationships in face-to-face milieu" (Connell, 1987:183). The most important presentations in that regard are those connected to gender division of labor and sexuality, which I explore in the text which follows

2.1 Gender division of labor

During communism, the most publicized images of gender roles in regard to the gender division of labor may be described as housewife and breadwinner/shared bread winning (shared wage system) rather than housewife/breadwinner arrangement (family wage system). In other words, it means that women were expected to have two or three roles (paid work, housewife, mother), and men only one (paid work), which was also shared with the wife.

Images of masculinity seemed to have softened as a consequence of restrictions on the acting out of traditional masculine identity, while increasing the social significance of the feminine (Watson, 1992:145). Due to the absence of private property, politics and civil society, both women and men were neutralized as social actors. However, Watson (1992:142) is right when she notices that the neutering of men in the public domain was particularly emphasized, bearing in mind that they were expected to fit the position which was in obvious contrast with traditional expectations regarding their gender. In addition "the opportunities offered by civil society for the experience of 'success' were withheld from men under state socialism, while careers in the state-run public domain increasingly appeared to be devoid of value or sense."(Watson, 1992:142) Hence, men's role was rather passive, i.e. restricted in terms of both economic and political initiative in the outside world, or, as Blagojevic puts it, the male gender role became significantly "emptied", while male domination, unless it was based on physical strength and violence, got caricatured (Blagojevic, 1997:83). However, bearing in mind that, in spite of the formal equality of women and men and the fact that women obviously gained some advantages as well, patriarchy never disappeared, and conflicting images about both genders persisted throughout communist time. This was confirmed by my interviewees from all countries included in the survey, who agreed that it is difficult to notice any radical change in male identity since the macho culture was always very widespread in that part of the world.

State socialism, as Watson argues, provided a social context which acted to conserve patriarchy (Watson, 1992:144), which was already strongly embedded into the culture (Najcevska and Marinova, interviews, 1999). This also may mean, using Connell's terminology, that during communism traditional masculinity and femininity were subordinated to socialist masculinity/femininity. Having that in mind, it is not difficult to understand changes in public discourse, i.e. restoration of male dominance within it, which occurred after the establishment of a market economy and civil society.

Consequently, public images of women appeared as two conflicting images consisting of the image of New (Amazon) Woman (or superwoman, omnipotent woman) and the traditional image of woman as housewife and mother (Kotzeva, 1999a:85)

One the one hand, as Kotzeva (1999a:85) puts it, "the feminine vision of socialism is completely linked to the workplace and the public domain, owing to the mass-mobilization of women in state-run factories. The visual rhetoric of socialism is imbued with photographs of women, looking proudly from the seat of a tractor, a conveyer belt or other technical appliance, which is emblematic of the socialist progressive transformations and the human race's domination over nature...The visual space of the socialist society is inhabited by the new Amazons - they are labeled 'doers', 'fighters', 'functionaries', 'laborers', 'activists', and so on."

However, on the other hand, the traditional image about women as well as about men was never erased. Hence, women were equally expected to be good housekeepers and mothers. As pointed out by Bejkova, in Macedonia, for example, "woman was superior in comparison to man, but the public image was still such that the husband is the one who is the main breadwinner, while women's earnings are only supplementary and her main role is one of housewife and mother (interview, 1999). On the other side, expectations toward men's share of household duties and caring were always weak and unarticulated publicly. As Kotzeva says, women are the best representatives of collective life and the collective values of socialism - "they are named 'national heroines' as mothers, toilers and social activists" (Kotzeva, 1999a:86). As such they were expected to sacrifice their own interests to the "higher" interests of the state and nation. However, as Watson well noticed, women's subjective sense of self-esteem was enhanced during communism, at first place because of the pivotal role of the family, where the partners are economically independent, which simultaneously underlines the central importance of women's work, and thereby, adds to women's sense of self-worth. "It is the family, the domain of women," says Watson, "which becomes of crucial political and economic importance", which is in radical contrast to the status of the family in the civil society of liberal democracies (Watson, 1992:140). Thus, as we will see later, the problem that women faced during transition was connected exactly to the loss of self-esteem as a consequence of the loss of economic independence.

Many authors argue that after political changes public presentations of gender changed as well. Since traditional gender roles and power relations were accepted as "given" and "natural", whereas women's equality was identified as "forced" and "unnatural", re-traditionalisation and "renaturalization" of gender roles is something which started to be largely publicized as desirable. It seems that the focus started to be put on the fact (whether true or not) that "values like 'equality of women' and 'all around personal fulfillment of women' were not internalized and remained foreign to the 'socialist' lifework...The traditional family pattern - the breadwinner/housewife arrangement, which was to a certain degree eroded under communism though never seriously challenged - is reinforced". (Petrova, 1993:23, 27).

As Kotzeva (1999a: 88) stressed, referring specifically to the situation in Bulgaria, two discourses contributed to the trend toward re-creation of a traditional image of women in post-communist society: "return to the home" and/or "motherhood" discourse and "westernisation" and "normalization" discourse. "Return to the home" and "motherhood" discourse is expressed implicitly rather than explicitly and occurred alongside the rise of traditional (hegemonic) masculinity images. Both occurred as a consequence of market economy and liberal democracy, as well as under influence of nationalism and militarization of the society in some post-communist countries, such as Serbia.

"It is obvious that the development of a market economy and privatization encouraged the macho character of (post-communist society's) men", said Maria Adamik from Hungary (interview, 1999). "This kind of very clear ideology supported the idea that men have to be strong, that they have to have power and be dominant, that they have to cope with their enemies and have to defeat them - whether it is an advertisement for a car or money, the message is clear: you have to win". This support, what Watson already stressed, that the new gender relations are shaped by liberal democracy and market economy based on private property, which essentially entails the (re) structuring of opportunities and the creation of institutionalization of hierarchy based on market advantage. "Traditional ideas concerning difference, including gender difference, are playing a key role in shaping such exclusionary advantage in the new public sphere" (Watson, 1996:217). Thus, in (neo) liberal capitalism (which elements, together with the remaining elements of communism, post communist societies obviously have) "hegemonic masculinity" and "emphasized femininity" became associated with being a good provider and a full-time mother/housewife.

Social construction of masculinity is especially important since femininity (as all other masculinities) is subordinated to hegemonic masculinity. Thus masculine domination of the gender division of labor in both Western liberal democracies and post-communist societies is expressed, as Adamik noticed so well, as pressure on men to be "a good provider, to win, to succeed, to dominate" - since they are (should be!) breadwinners (Messerschmidt, 1993:67). Additionally, there is an impact of global capitalism or neoliberalism, which, as well noticed by Connell (2001:64), has an implicit gender politics:

> "The 'individual' of neoliberal theory has in general the attributes and interests of a male entrepreneur, the attack on the welfare state generally weakens the position of women, while the increasingly unregulated power of transnational corporations places strategic power in the hands of particular groups of men. It is not surprising, then, that the installation of capitalism in Eastern Europe and the former Soviet Union has been accompanied by reassertion of dominating masculinities and, in some situations, a sharp worsening in the social position of women".

"Return to the home" and "motherhood" discourse was especially evident in media coverage and campaigns regarding restriction of reproductive rights (Watson, 1996:221; Einhorn, 1993:40, Daskalova, 2001:247; Toth, 1993:214; Milic, 1993:112) and domestic violence (Nikolic-Ristanovic, 2001:291; Corrin, 1999:73) but also, and sometimes more explicitly, in public discussions about (un) employment and importance of the family.[61] Similarly as in Western society (Messerschmidt, 1993:66), the "familiar" accusation that the high divorce rate, juvenile delinquency and alcoholism can be directly attributed to women's absence from the family, is used in post-communist society as well. It seems that the role of woman as mother as well as self-sacrifice of woman for collective aims is central to the ideology of both communism and post-communism (Einhorn, 1993:40; Blagojevic, 1994:477). It is also central to the nationalism and war discourse in Serbia, as well as in other parts of the former Yugoslavia and elsewhere (Nikolic-Ristanovic, 1996:360; Corrin, 1999:74: Millett, 1977:165: Moeller, 1993:5). However, in connection to the rise of the women's movement, new or emancipatory images of women emerge alongside traditional ones as well (Daskalova, 2001:246; Nikolic-Ristanovic, 2001:285). But these images are still not strong enough and are mainly subordinated to prevailing social constructions of traditional masculinity and femininity.

It is important to notice that traditional images/discourse re-creation is closely connected to the economic difficulties and unemployment problems in the society as a

[61] H. Szilvia and P. Lajos "Szabadsag a rend keretei kozott" (Liberty among the framework of social order), *Nepszabadsag*, March 3, 1999, p.9

whole as well. Thus, although with changed structural conditions in Western capitalism in after the Second World War, new forms of masculinity and femininity emerged concurrently (Messerschmidt, 1993:70), backlash, which started soon after economic recession and neo-liberalism, put them aside again (Faludi, 1991). Hence, having in mind economic difficulties as well as idealistic images about the West created during communism as a reaction to anti-Western propaganda, it is not unusual that westernisation and normalization discourse served as an additional argument, i.e. justification, of new expectations toward women and men in post-communist society.[62]

As Kotzeva noticed, "where once Western Europe played a retrograde role and blocked the progressive steps of the countries beyond the 'Iron Curtain', now it has become a willing standard to be imitated" (Kotzeva, 1999:87). In addition, the very moment of post-communist changes coincides with re-traditionalization of the gender order connected to globalization, i.e. export of North American and European models worldwide (Connell, 2001:60). Consequently, westernization and normalization have been explicated through messages about implementation of European standards and models, with normalization being the key concept of the post-totalitarian language (Kotzeva, 1999:87).

However, as answers of some of my respondents from Bulgaria show, the impact of communist anti -Western and equality discourse is stile alive so that some people still accept it and reject new discourses altogether (return to the home and westernization). For example, a Bulgarian female respondent, 41 years old researcher, said that in present-day Bulgaria both women and men earn the living and they are equal. Also, she stressed that this is the "bourgeois model", which assumes that man is a breadwinner and decision-maker, while woman's activity is limited to the houschold and children. According to her, this kind of model was not accepted in Bulgaria during communism, nor is it now.

Future society was scen as basically "the opposite" of state socialism. However, since the experience of socialism was very different from its rhetoric of equality between women and men, "opposed to" attitudes of post-communist society meant also the refusal to embrace feminist principles which appear to be very similar to the values of Marxist gender politics (Morvai, 1994:64). As Connell stressed, the crises of gender order or its tendencies toward crises (e.g. emasculation of men during communism or development of a women's movement in the post-communist period - my emphasis) may also provoke attempts to restore a dominant masculinity (Connell, 1995: 84).

However, it does not mean that dominant masculinity in post-communist society became the prevailing cultural model. On the contrary, the answers of my respondents from all four countries showed that socialist gender ideology is still very much alive, alongside the rise of traditional gender images. The majority of my

[62] With the exception of Serbia, where the rejection of western values and nationalism/war discourse was used to intensify the traditional gender images. However, interestingly, after changes in Serbia in 2000 (at least immediately after them) , normalisation and westernisation developed the opposite meaning which, in regard to gender, may be described as emancipatory discourse (e.g. media's reaction to sexual harassment accusations of the leader of one of the parties from the ruling coalition in May, 2001)

female respondents, for example, answered that they would prefer to work even if their husbands are able to earn enough to support the family (for similar see also Toth, 1993:218; Lobodzinska, 1996:531; Molyneux, 1996:257; Csaba, 1998:42):

> "I will always prefer to work. I need to be with and among people, to communicate with them and to feel independent." (Bulgarian)

> "When a woman goes to work, she has a chance to change her surroundings, while being at home means staying only with the kids, plus the husband perhaps. And this is bad for him and for me as well". (Hungarian)

> "We were born into this society where we can have a sort of self-respect only if we also work. Mopping the floor or dusting the furniture is not the same as a "product" that I have created, these activities are without value in today's society...and there is also the financial side of it. So, if you work only at home, you can suffer from a lack of self respect for several reasons. I cannot imagine wishing to stop working. For someone who was brought up in an era when people had to work from the age of 14, and take responsibilities, it is just unacceptable to stay at home". (Hungarian)

> "It is not so easy to work when you have a family, but I would always choose to work. In order to break the monotony, in order not to be beside the sink and stove. I just started to do something, to sell things on the market. So I have some duty, something started to happen in my life. Otherwise, since I lost my job I used to stay at home by myself. I felt sad, there is nobody around all day. I sit alone and do not have any wish to work. I am just sitting and asking myself what are all these domestic chores for. I do not know whether this is a matter of habit, whether I should be unemployed for a longer time in order to get used to that...I am not used to being without work, I would always choose to work". (Serb)

However, apart from those who prefer to work, some women prefer to stay at home or, at least, to work part time or less (not to be forced to take additional jobs etc.) but, because of the difficult economic situation, are not able to realize that:

> "I would choose to keep working, but within normal limits. I mean not 16 hours daily, but only 6 or maximum 8 hours". (Hungarian)

> "If my husband could earn enough money, I would give up my additional job. I would go to work but also I would like to have some time to spend with my children."(Serb)

But, apart from continuing identification with socialist femininity, conflicting images that women themselves have about the gender division of labor are even more obvious. These conflicting images, inherited from the communist time, seem even more pronounced after changes. Following are some examples:

> "The man has to support the family, but he should not be the main decision-maker. The place of women is not at home, but their first obligations are to be wives and mothers." (female respondent from Bulgaria)

> "For instance, while I became an independent woman who works and earns a lot and my husband is feminine if it is necessary, does the dishes and takes care of the child, still it remained the woman's task, that it is still me who takes care whether the child has his clean clothes there, whether he's got his food, because otherwise it would not be there. And not because he (the husband) doesn't want to do that, but because he is different. A man is different. And then this remains the task of the woman, if she wants to hold a good family together, to take care of these things. I think the woman became too much

detached from this role, but I don't think that is good, and I consider it important that a woman takes this responsibility"(female respondent from Hungary)

Conflicting images become even more emphasized as transitional society develops. Toth, for example, compared data from her studies done in 1988 and 1994 in Hungary, and found an increase of those who consider that women should not work outside the home, that they should work in a two-part work cycle or part time. In her 1994 survey, she found that a significant proportion of the public is "genuinely nostalgic for the lifestyle in which women did not work or only worked part-time". However, on the other side, many of those who cannot find work or live at home on a childcare allowance feel they would benefit more from going out to work. According to Toth, this inconsistency is one of the most significant potential sources of conflict within Hungarian families (Toth, 1997:72).

Similar to findings of Daskalova's survey in Bulgaria showed, my findings also confirm that, on one side, women and men accept gender equality in general, while on the other side men are expected to be the main or sole breadwinners and women's roles as mothers and housewives are given priority. This is especially evident in answers about the expectations regarding taking initiative in coping with problems that the family faced when changes occurred. The answers which prevailed are those which stated that the husband was expected to take initiative (38 or 36.8%). Also, the answers that both of them are expected to take initiative were widespread as well (27 or 26.2%). However, those who said that the wife is expected to take initiative were the least frequent and their answers are often followed with an explanation in terms that the husband was not expected to do that himself because he was ill, did not take care of the family at all, was in the military, or similar (14 or 13.6%).

In Serbia, the creation of an image of tough, dominant and combative masculinity was connected to the ethnic conflicts and war as well. As Connell (1995:77) pointed out, hegemonic masculinity is strongly connected to the military. Although mythologies of war, past battles and man's role as a soldier have been largely circulating throughout Serbian history (which itself consists of a number of wars), the creation of militaristic masculinity in recent history, as I wrote elsewhere (Nikolic-Ristanovic, 1998:466), became especially pronounced at the beginning of 1990's and as a part of nationalism and war propaganda. The use of military rituals and the religious consecration of war as inevitable for defending "our brothers" in other parts of the former Yugoslavia, both contributed to the militaristic images of masculinity, i.e., to borrow MacWilliams's terminology (1998:132), to build "armed patriarchy". Thus it seems that the mechanisms of militarized gender order creation in the former Yugoslavia were quite similar to those found out elsewhere (Hatty, 2000:128). As was well noticed by Korac, "it took time and a lot of manipulations and war propaganda to create 'national enemies' and paranoia within ethnic-national communities, and consequently a 'real man', a 'patriot' who would fight back in 'defense' from 'the eternal enemy' of 'our' ethnic-national communities" (Korac, 1994:510).

The deployment of military rituals included use of uniforms, weapons, flags, music - in the media as well as within the broader culture and in everyday life (e.g.

in magazines, daily newspapers, on radio and TV, in streets, cafes, restaurants etc.). Cultural models of masculinity which were, as in other wars (Hatty, 2000:139), offered during and after the war, included those of soldier, breadwinner and family man. On the other side, complementary femininity models included women's sacrifice as mothers and wives (strongly promoted by Serbian Orthodox Church) as well as women as sexual objects and entertainers of soldier - widely propagated within popular culture. Hence militarized (hegemonic) masculinity and emphasized femininity served as the most powerful cultural models offered to Serbian men and women during most of the 1990's.

A good illustration may be the 1995 Christmas message from the Patriarch of the Serb Orthodox Church, which called on women to stop "killing their unborn children, to bear more children despite economic hardship and to learn from mothers who lost their only sons in the war and who now regret not bearing more sons who could bring them consolation (Nikolic-Ristanovic, 1996b:360). As pointed out by Jamieson (1998: 495-6), we can speak about re-ordering of gender in the context of war, or about the prevailing norm about the gendered division of labor in war which calls on men "to do the fighting (and dying)", and on women to "do the waiting" and self-sacrificing. Similarly, Dowler (1997:78) argues that the war in Northern Ireland constructs gender roles in oppositional terms - men are perceived as violent and action-oriented and women as compassionate and supportive of the male warriors.

2.2 Sexuality

Socialist femininity, expressed in what Kotzeva calls "new Amazons", served not only to publicize women's place within a gender division of labor, but also to counteract the aesthetic language of bourgeois representations of women as figures of fashion, consumerism and "sex parasitism". Since the socialist East was suspicious of the excessive pleasures and sexual freedom of the 'decadent' West, it strictly controlled women's sexuality and eroticism so that chaste women were presented as the symbols of a new spirit of communist-style Puritanism and abandonment of passions and desires (Kotzeva, 1999:85). At the same time, male sexuality was suppressed as well. The strictness of the control and suppression of sexuality correlates with the closeness of the ties the precise country had with the former Soviet Union, i.e. was in inverse proportion with the openness of the country toward the West.

Changes in gender images about sexuality are best mirrored in the explosion of beauty/fashion magazines and pornography. As Daskalova (2001:249) says, "the message conveyed is that beauty is the most valuable female 'asset' and that every woman should try to make herself sexually attractive to men and to become a source of men's pleasure".

Due to strict rules during communism, in the majority of post-communist countries pornography did not exist at all. [63] However, changes brought the rise of

[63] The former Yugoslavia, (which both Serbia and Macedonia were part of), was in some way the exception, since rare soft porn magazines started to come out already in the early 1970's. This was a

both soft and hardcore pornography. The expansion of pornography, which followed social changes, was one of the earliest and most obvious expressions of democratization of society, frequently seen as a synonym for new freedoms and opening toward the West. In Serbia, it was rather connected to both slow and contradictory democratization and the ethnic conflicts in the former Yugoslavia. The latter contributed to an increase in demand for all forms of the sex industry, while, contrary to other countries, the influence of the West became less effective (mainly as a consequence of economic sanctions imposed by the UN).

Suppression of sexuality during communism, more or less, delayed the sexual revolution in all countries so that social changes were seen as an opportunity to compensate for all that was missed for so long, as well as for achieving individual instead of collective identity. In Connell's words, this "has to do with a new structure of cathexis centering on what might be called hegemonic heterosexuality...The reorganization of emotions that allows this externalization of cathexis is perhaps the truth behind Foucault' claim of an increasing incitement rather than repression of sexuality" (Connell, 1987:157). At the same time, global mass media additionally reinforced this trend through circulation of stereotyped gender images, "deliberately made attractive for marketing purposes" (Connell, 2001:61). As Taylor and Jamieson showed very well, economic processes connected to globalization, such as rapid liberalization of trade and economy across the world, led to an increase in the role that sexuality plays throughout the public culture (Taylor and Jamieson, 1999:264).

In post-communist society media re-constructed the traditional opposition between men's sexual needs and women as passive sexual objects and men's property, which is further used to justify violence and blame the victim. As Stishova points out "among the images rendered taboo by Soviet power, nudity was one of the most prominent. The legalization of sex in post-Soviet cinema became part of the battle for *glasnost* and freedom of speech, and what is more, part of the battle for emancipation of the individual, repressed by total prohibition, and for the emancipation of culture, emasculated by hypocrisy."(Stishova, 1996:190-191).

"After the changes in Hungary it was suddenly possible to see pornographic literature everywhere, together with the daily newspapers. At the beginning, pornography was accepted as a part of new freedoms, of democracy, but later people started to be disgusted", says Lenke Feher (interview, 1999). Thus it is not unusual that any opposition to pornography has been, especially at the beginning of transition, experienced as opposition to democracy (Stishova, 1996:191). However, as many authors argue, pornography is a kind of violence against women and can provoke other kinds of violence. As Valverde points out "whether or not violent, porn actually causes violence, women do feel violated by its imaginary."(Valverde, 1985:121). In addition, pornography can be seen as a very good example/illustration of how the mass media picture women and relations between men and women, i.e. it

---

consequence of less strictly applied legal regulations as well as of the fact that the former Yugoslavia was more open toward the West.

can be defined as erotisation of women's subordination (Jeffrey, quoted by Attwood, 1996:259).

In post-communist society pornography is usually not limited to specialized porn magazines. It is obvious in the culture as a whole, from daily newspapers, advertisements, films to TV (Attwood, 1996:259). After ten years of transition, among the countries included in my survey the most striking example in that sense was Bulgaria. On the other hand, the presence of pornography in daily newspapers and magazines, which are acceptable to a large public, is recently limited only in Hungary[64].

It seems that presentation of sexuality shifted from images of women and men as asexual or partly sexual beings (in communism) to images of hegemonic masculinity and emphasized femininity associated with traditional opposition between men's (uncontrollable) sexual needs and women as passive sexual objects. Similarly as discourse about the gender division of labor, this discourse is also largely influenced by imitation of Western images about sexuality. As Messerschmidt points out, in Western industrialized societies "hegemonic masculinity is currently established through an alleged uncontrollable and insatiable sexual appetite for women, which results in a 'naturally' coercive 'male' sexuality. Thus, this kind of normative heterosexuality is based on power relations and, consequently, it defines masculinity "through difference from, and desire for, women. Therefore, "normative heterosexuality is not only a major structural feature for understanding gender, but for understanding masculinities and crimes committed by men as well" (Messerschmidt, 1993:75, 76).

3. ACTUAL MASCULINITIES/FEMININITIES

Although most women and men tend to fit offered gender images, they usually do not fit cultural models of masculinity and femininity. As Connell puts it, the image of masculinity that the ideologists of patriarchy sell is not intended to fit since cultural models are heroes only in contrast to the mass of men who are not (Connell, 1987:110). One example, with a number of consequences for actual gender identities, is the "family" wage model, which was never a reality for much of the working class, but nevertheless became formative not only for modern definitions of masculinity and femininity but also for the character and direction of working class politics. Also, as Connell stressed, the number of men rigorously practicing the hegemonic pattern in its entirety may be quite small, but the majority of men gain from its hegemony, since they benefit from patriarchal dividend, "the advantage men in general gain from overall subordination of women" (Connell, 1987:156 and 1995:79). As a result, there is not one, unique, but rather more and different masculinities or femininities, which are all, produced in the same cultural and institutional setting (Connell, 1995:36). However, it is very important that the tension between the normative and the actual experiences is sorted out, in order to

[64] For more details about that see Nikolic-Ristanovic, 2001, p.284-295

develop a more accurate picture of the nature and impact of gender relations (Walklate, 2001:61) and to understand violence as a part of them.

Gender is unavoidably involved with other social structures so that it interacts with race, class, nationality, position in the world order (Connell, 1995:75), as well as with age or generation. As Messershmidt points out, these social structures vary by social situation and circumstances. In their daily activities individuals attempt to be identified socially as, for example, female or male, or middle class or working class etc., and to conduct their activities in relation to their circumstances. According to structured -action theory, which seems to be applicable to the explanation of gender, social change and violence in post-communist society as well, people do gender, race, class and other social structures differently, depending on the social situation and the social circumstances they encounter (Messerschmidt, 1997:4). As a result, there are multiple masculinities and femininities. Also, as pointed out by post-structuralist critics of psychology, gender identities of individual women and men are fractured and shifting, because multiple discourses intersect in any individual life (Hollway, quoted by Connell, 1995:72). Thus, it seems that gender identities are created under the influence of both specific social situations where one finds her/himself and ideals of gender identities propagated by society. In addition, this influence is mediated by the psychic structure of any individual woman and man (Jefferson, 1997:543). Or, as Messerschmidt says, "social actors self-regulate their behavior and make specific choices in specific contexts". (Messerschmidt, 1995:174).

Because people do gender, race, class etc. in specific social situations, they reproduce and sometimes change social structures. Hence, there are numerous ways of constructing masculinity and femininity, but also class, race, nationality, position in world order and generation. Accordingly, they must be viewed as "structured action - what people do under specific social structural constraints". The concepts "hegemonic/emphasized", "subordinated" and "oppositional" masculinities and femininities permit investigation of the different way men and women experience their everyday world from their particular positions in society and how they relate to other men and women (Messerschmidt, 1997:6,12).

Looking at social changes in post-communist societies through structured-action theory lenses, one can assume that the former relatively unified gender identities started to be more and more fragmented as a consequence of ongoing social stratification (Adamik and Valkova, interviews, 1999).[65] Gender identities of individual women and men interact with their new economic position, with their belonging to a specific ethnic group, i.e. nation, their age and participation in the military, as well as with prevailing cultural models.

As I already showed, one of the main consequences of social changes is the sharpening of social differentiation between a small part of very rich and a large part of poor people, with an almost disappearing middle class. This had important consequences to the creation of different masculinities and femininities as well to the

[65] A similar effect was already noticed in other societies where the context changed markedly, leading to class stratification development (Connell, 1987:125).

emergence of different models of family class relations (see Hagan, 1988:171). On the one side, there was the rise of traditional (hegemonic) masculinity, while, on the other, multiple marginalized masculinities arose as well. Complementary to them are emphasized and marginalized femininity. Also, occasionally I found oppositional or emancipatory masculinity and femininity.[66]

Thus, we can speak about the masculinities and femininities of rich as well as poor and middle class, from a dominant ethnic group and from an ethnic minority, and those who belong to superior nations as well as those from nations which have inferior (economic and political) status within the world order. Additionally, we can also speak about transnational business masculinity.[67] Within the above-mentioned masculinities, however, there are also multiple masculinities, such as economically active as well as economically inactive, young as well as old, heterosexual as well as homosexual, etc. In addition, under influence of nationalism and war, different masculinities and femininities arise depending on individual man's belonging to specific ethnic group or nation as well as on their acceptance or rejection of militaristic discourse, duties etc. What is important is that there is hierarchy between masculinities themselves (hegemonic and marginalised), on the one side, and between masculinities and femininities, on the other (Connell, 1995:77). Or, as Walklate (2001:65) puts it, the version of masculinity which possess hegemonic power (e.g. white men) not only serves to provide individual men with a sense of themselves "as more or less of a man", but it also serves to downgrade other versions of masculinity (e.g. ethnic minority men) as well as downgrading femininity.

Although the impact of transition, nationalism and war on the way women and men do their gender is strongly connected and interlaced, for analytical reasons (to the extent it is possible) I will look at the impact of the transition and war separately. It is important to notice that the impact of war and transition on both gender identities and relations is very similar, which is not unusual having in mind that their common constituents in terms of their impact on the everyday life of women and men, as already shown, are similar as well.

[66] As Messerschmidt puts it, "because femininities are constructed in the context of gender relations of power, femininities are polarised around accommodation or resistance to masculine dominance. Forms of femininity sustain themselves in contrast to one another and to situationally specific types of masculinity under which they are subordinated." Thus femininity can be understood only as a relational construct. (Messerschmidt, 1995:173).

[67] According to Connell, transnational business masculinity is a hegemonic form of masculinity in the current world gender order, which is "associated with those who control its dominant institutions: the business executives who operate in global markets, and the political executives who interact (and in many contexts, merge) with them" (Connell, 2001:65)

3.1 Actual masculinities/femininities and transition

3.1.1 Hegemonic masculinity and emphasized femininity

There is an evident rise of traditional masculinity among those men who became rich, i.e. in different ways successful in the new society, and who tend to fit the cultural image of breadwinner, combatant, potent, tough, and, in Serbia, militarized maleness. Among these men successful private businessmen, managers, new state elite, and men from the military prevail, as well as criminals, especially those involved in war crimes and newly emerging organized crime.

Re-establishment of private ownership, as noticed by Blagojevic (1997:80), brought back, at least to some men, the part of their traditional role of breadwinner. These men tend to fit the new cultural ideal of hegemonic masculinity in different ways - from the way they look (toughness, weapons, luxurious cars and mobile phones as widely recognized new status and macho symbols) to the way they act in gender relations (e.g. breadwinner/housewife and omnipotent man/helpless doll pattern).

However, the men who fit traditional masculinity are rare and they are often, especially by my respondents in Serbia, identified as mafia men, criminals, foreigners or new political elite. As one woman from Serbia says, "practically there are not real men. If we see one, he either earned money illegally and now pretends to be 'real' or he came from abroad. Otherwise, there is no chance here for a man to be 'real'."[68]

Complementary emphasized femininity, in terms of woman's place within the traditional gender division of labor, is available only to a small number of women as well: it correlates with hegemonic masculinity so that women who identify themselves with emphasized femininity are mainly those whose partners belong to the small segment of rich men.

In terms of sexuality, however, emphasized femininity is much more widespread, especially among young women who tend to achieve the new cultural image of woman as a doll, i.e. sexual object. Men's and women's attempts to achieve the traditional cultural model of sexuality are most obvious in the rise of prostitution and other forms of the sex industry in post-communist society[69]. The place which men have within the economic structure usually determines the role they have within the sex industry as well (e.g. as street pimps, brothel owners, traffickers or clients). However, whatever their economic position, women who identify themselves as sex objects are always subordinated to a man. What is different are relations between different forms of

[68] It is worth mentioning that among some ethnic minorities, such as Albanians, Bulgarian Muslims and Turks, hegemonic masculinity has always been present as part of the tradition and only recently started to change among young generations of some men and women. Among Albanians, for example, even during communism it was quite usual that men worked abroad. In such a way they earned a lot of money and were able to support their large families, while their wives were rigorously limited to the household and child bearing (Coneva, interview, 1999; UNDP, 1998:21).

[69] These attempts, however, do not coincide always since many women are not in the sex industry because they identify themselves as sex objects but rather because they are identified in that way by others (e.g. young girls who are forced into prostitution by their partners, parents or traffickers).

emphasized femininities (e.g. street prostitutes, call girls etc.). Thus, although there are different subordinated masculinities, they are always hegemonic in relation to women.

3.1.2 Marginalised masculinities/femininities

The consequences of social differentiation on power relations between men and women, but also among men and women themselves are evident. Since only small number of men and women somehow fit the ideal of hegemonic masculinity and emphasized femininity, the large majority actually possess masculinities and femininities which are subordinated or opposed to hegemonic normative (Messerschmidt, 1997:10). Thus, a range of different gender identities arose in connection with the specific socio-economic position of individual women and men, depending first on their employment, i.e. job stability and earnings. Ethnicity may play an important role as well.

Whether they accept it or not, the majority of men and women in post-communist society, as in Western society during periods of economic crises, instability and inflation (Messerschmidt, 1993:68), are not able to fit the traditional gender division of labor, i.e. family wage arrangement. However, in post-communist society this problem is exacerbated by the fact that, as we showed in the previous chapter, people are often not able to fit the socialist identity, i.e. shared wage pattern, either. Thus, looking from a perspective of a gender division of labor and gender power relations, we can identify different gender identities, depending on the partners' employment and material status, changes regarding status they had during communism and their relation to cultural gender models.

The gap between the actual social situation and cultural model associated with a specific gender is especially important for the creation of specific, marginalized[70] gender identities. The bigger the gap, the bigger the frustrations and feelings of powerlessness. As a male respondent from Hungary said:

"There is such a tendency in society that a man should be the breadwinner and have the dominant position. But this is only a tendency because the vast majority of men cannot maintain their families on their own. However, the expectations of men reflect this attitude more and more and that breeds absolute contradictions again."

Also, marginalization of masculinity increases as far as the instability and uncertainty of socio-economic status increase. It affects more those who once had a stable social status, such as middle class men, than those who always struggled with income and job stability. Thus, a man's frustration and powerlessness are especially emphasized when the change in his social situation is so sudden and unanticipated that it does not allow him any time to adjust to it (e.g. a middle class man who lost his job because of transition redundancy or a former soldier from Croatia or Kosovo, who became a refugee in Serbia). Consequently, among respondents from the

[70] In order to assure consistency in analyses, I use a term marginalization here in the same way as Connell: to refer to the relations between the masculinities in the dominant and subordinated classes or ethnic groups. In that sense, marginalization is always relative to the authorisation of the hegemonic masculinity of the dominant group (Connell, 1995:81). Another term, which may be used as well, is troubled masculinity, introduced by Hearn (Hearn, 1998:39).

sample, marginalized masculinity was most stressed by Serbian and least by Hungarian respondents. Also, marginalized masculinity of Roma men became even more pronounced as the economic situation degenerated.

Keeping in mind the above-mentioned elements, we can identify two groups of patterns, each having two variations, of what is popularly called crises of masculinity, depending on whether a man economically contributes to the family or not:

Table 1.Crises of masculinity patterns

Man who contributes	Within shared wage system
	Within traditional family wage system
Man who does not contribute	Lack of family wage (when both partners are dependent on social welfare, relatives or others)
	Reverse family wage system (social incompatibility)

Although marginalized masculinity is less likely to be found among men from couples where both partners were economically active all the time (within a shared wage system), if it occurs, it is usually connected to a man's unsuccessful attempts to fit the hegemonic (e.g. fails in private business or politics) or socialist masculinity in terms of the main or similar provision for the family (e.g. he used to earn more or similar but now has a lower wage in comparison to his wife's).

Thus, the crisis of masculinity within the socialist wage system is connected to men's failure to fit either traditional or socialist male identity, depending on the cultural model he associates himself with. In this case, woman's identity mainly stays unaffected, since, whatever the ratio between her and her husband's wage, she still shares earning with him and thus conforms to socialist femininity.

However, the problem may arise when the woman start to identify with the new cultural model of traditional femininity and hence begins to put pressure on her partner to adjust to complementary male identity. Thus a woman's feeling of her own inadequacy arises as a consequence of her dissatisfaction with her husband's lack of identification with the new cultural model of masculinity. This has a further effect on a man's frustration and may reinforce his identification with hegemonic masculinity, even when he otherwise identifies with a socialist one.

Apart from families of wealthy men who are able to be the sole or main provider, traditional gender division of labor exists also in those families where the man is the main provider, in spite of the fact that he is not able to support the family in an appropriate way. This is a kind of marginalized masculinity which Connell calls protest masculinity - one which "picks up themes of hegemonic masculinity in the society at large but reworks them in a context of poverty" (Connell, 1995:114). This pattern is mainly found among couples where the wife is not able to earn a living at all (whether she lost a job, left it or was not able to find a new one, or is not providing for the family for other reasons) or she earns only a symbolic amount of money, while the man is still in a position to earn a living although inadequate.

In this case, the man' s frustration comes from the fact that he is not in a position to fit the traditional male identity, but may also be connected to, or rather reinforced by his wife's inability to share the burden of providing as it is expected within the socialist division of labor. It actually depends on the cultural a model man identifies with. For a man who tends to identify with hegemonic masculinity, the crisis results from the fact that he cannot fit this ideal and it is further reinforced by his wife's pressures on him to reach this ideal. The following statement of a Serbian woman is a good illustration:

> "As a mother, you must get money to feed the kids. And from whom are you going to ask money if not from your husband and their father. My parents are not able to help us anymore. My father died recently and my mother does not have any earning as well. Then I ask everything from my husband. And sometime he has, but sometimes he does not have anything to give me. He would be happy if he was able to provide for the children, I am sure. But when I ask for money from him, he gets nervous and starts to shout at me. It is not because he does not want to give money for the family but because he is not able to do that. As children get older we need more money, while at the same time we have less. Earlier, I did not have to ask for money from him since I was earning a living myself and was not dependent on him."

On the other side, men, who still tend to fit only the socialist male identity, experience a wife's lack of economic contribution as the main cause of their own failure, exacerbated by the wife's own expectations toward him. This is especially pronounced among middle aged men, who have been used to a shared wage system most of their lives and feel somehow in a vacuum between the male role they were socialized for, and both their new social situation and new cultural expectations. As a result, they are often either not ready or not able, keeping in mind the precise social situation in which they find themselves, to take initiative and to conform to expectations they, their wives and/or their surroundings have of them. A Serbian respondent, for example, says about her husband:

> "I am a very active person, but when earning a living is in question I prefer to leave that to the husband. This is especially emphasized in my case by the fact that my father used to be the real breadwinner, the head of the family. When my father stopped being able to help us financially, I expected my husband to take over his role. Unfortunately, reality was different. Not only that my husband did not take over the role of breadwinner but he also seemed to feel bad about being expected to do that. I experienced his behavior as very frustrating and hurtful. This caused tension in our relationship and was especially intense during the last years when it was very difficult to make decisions anyway. I even thought that I made a bad choice, I though about divorcing him as well. His response to my expectations is always that I have the wrong family model, which is frustrating for him, and that equality is much better, much healthier for both of us."

Thus feminine identity compliments marginalized masculinity in a way that a woman either identifies with emphasized femininity, as in the case of the above-quoted Serbian respondent, or her femininity is also marginalized since she finds it difficult to accept the role of housewife and mother as her only or main role. In this latter, we can speak about the crisis of femininity which is closely connected to change in the socio-economic position of women who were employed and economically independent most of their lives. Hence, these frustrations leading to low self-esteem are found most often among women who were forced to retreat from the labor market in middle age or in their pre-retirement period.

Marginalization of masculinity is especially evident when both partners are without jobs, i.e. without some kind of stable economic activity. Feelings of failed masculinity and dependence on others are especially expressed in refugee families, where change in their social situation is sudden, as well as where a man's inadequacy as a provider is sometime additionally affected by their post-traumatic stress disorder as a consequence of war. Marginalized femininity is often complimentary to that, but it is worth noticing that loss of economic role is always followed by more frustrations among men than women (Bejkova, interview, 1999).

This is not unusual since, as a rule, women respond to crisis situations in a more active way than men (e.g. since concerned to support their children, they are much less selective when looking for a job than men; they are always active at least in the household). Also, loss of a job for them does not mean the end of all useful activities, socially recognized status and position, as is the case with men (Csaba, 1998:41).

In addition, owing to conflicting images of femininity they were exposed to during communism, women have fewer problems limiting themselves to the private sphere than men, regardless of the cultural ideal of femininity they tend to fit.

> "Nowadays women adapt more easily to life difficulties because they are more practical, they are mothers and take care of survival - they stay within the limits of their traditional role. But men do not fit anymore the model which was imposed on them - that they should be the head of the family...and when this 'head' is based on some illusionary ego, everything is torn apart. As he is castrated, lost. Powerlessness is what ruins him. He comes home unhappy with himself, and a wife then starts to complain: ' we do not have this and that...' And then he goes to the pub and gets drunk." (male respondent from Serbia)

However, for women who are put in an extremely difficult economic situation assuming the traditional feminine role, as I have shown in the previous chapter, is a source of frustration as well because their financial situations do not allow them to perform their household duties and childcare properly. This was especially evident in Serbia, in connection with both the economic crisis and war.

In spite of the fact that couples who are dependent on others are usually in the worst economic situation, it seems, based on my survey findings, that the strongest feeling of male identity crisis is felt not by this group of men, but by those who are economically dependent on their wives. A gender division of labor, which is the reverse of the traditional one, is a serious challenge to male self-esteem. It may have both positive and negative consequences to women's gender identity as well.[71]

A feeling of inadequacy or, as Gelles calls it, status incompatibility[72], has multiple effects on a man. First, since they do not contribute to the family budget at all or their contribution is disproportionately small in comparison to their wives', they feel frustrated since they cannot achieve at least the ideal socialist male identity. The gap between the new cultural ideal of masculinity and the situation in which the men find themselves appears to be the largest, since both the traditional gender division of labor and gender power relations are seriously affected.

The gender division of labor is then such that the woman is the one who is associated with the public sphere more than the man. Although, as I already showed, this only rarely means that the man takes a significant part in household chores and childcare, the very fact that he is the one who stays at home while the wife goes out to work is something he experiences as extremely frustrating, since it contradicts both traditional and socialist expectations of men. In contrast to women, who, when they are unemployed, consider it normal to undertake all household chores and childcare, men do so only rarely. As Waddington et al. point out, the immediate impact of male unemployment on a wife is that her husband is permanently around the house and not apparently contributing much (Waddington et al., 1998:234). Although unemployed men spend more time at home, they do not become more domestic in their orientation since they continue to do "less than their fair share of housework (Morris, 1990; Jowell et al., 1992, quoted by Hearn, 1998:50).

The inadequacy, which is felt by a man in this situation, is reinforced by the intensity of the influence of traditional cultural images, i.e. the breadwinner/ housewife pattern in post-communist society. As in Western society, where this pattern prevails as inherent to the capitalist system (Mies, 1997), changes in work, employment and unemployment can have profound effects on men, both young and old. Loss of a job is likely to involve "loss of status, which may be accompanied by frustration, financial problems, domestic difficulties, and sometimes a greater assertion of a form of 'masculinity' through crime and violence" (Hearn, 1998:50; Waddington et al., 1998:233). Men's unemployment may have disproportionately negative effects on women partners and may reinforce rather than change men (Hearn, 1998:50).

The fact that the wife is the sole or main breadwinner increases the man's feeling of powerlessness, which often leads to an increase in his attempts to compensate for the loss of external power by any means, one of which not so rarely is violence (Schechter, 1982:236). However, it does not mean that there are no examples of those who lose gender-related power both outside and inside the family, but these cases still seem to be sporadic.

[71] It is interesting that this kind of marginalised masculinity is especially ephasised by Macedonian respondents (both men and women), who explained it by "the coming matriarchy, emancipation or increased aggressiveness of women".

[72] According to Gelles, status incompatibility is when the husband, who society expects to be the head of the family, has less education and a poorer job than his wife (Gelles, 1997)

In the situation where a woman is the sole or main breadwinner, she usually finds it very difficult to cope. However, woman's frustrations are not connected so much to the fact that she takes on the whole responsibility for supporting the family, but rather to the fact that she undertakes all family responsibilities, i.e. roles (breadwinner, housewife, caretaker). As a result, her identity shifts from socialist double role or double burden to all roles or all burden identity. It is to some extent comparable with fluctuating femininity, as a combination of conventional gender practices (such as cooking and childcare) and atypical gender practices (such as the role of breadwinner, and sometimes violent behavior as well), each practice justified by appropriate circumstances. Or, in other words, some events demand "hard" femininity, while others justify emphasized femininity (Messerschmidt, 1995:184).

Women who are forced to be sole breadwinners experience their everyday lives from a specific social position and as a consequence they construct femininity in a uniquely appropriate way. As we will see later, this was especially pronounced during the war. And, although some women find this position empowering, many actually go through severe crises since they find it difficult to respond to all roles with the same success. As a rule, their role as a mother suffers the most and, especially in the presence of an intensified cultural model of women as mothers, this is the role in relation to which they feel most guilty and frustrated. Their frustration is further reinforced when their partners do not make efforts to share family responsibilities with them.

A self-employed hairdresser, refugee in Serbia, for example, says:

> "Earlier he was less often at home and he used to earn money as well. Now I must work all day in order to earn a living and then, when I come back, I need to do the household chores. Although he is all the day at home, he does not want to do anything."

Also, another Serbian respondent, who is employed in a private firm and has a husband who works only from time to time, says:

> "Our division of labor is traditional, but when I am really overburdened, he helps as well. He is at home and does not work at all. We have arguments about that all the time. I think that he has a lot of spare time and I should undertake a lot of household chores, but his male ego does not allow him to do that. I wanted to hire a cleaning lady but he did not agree...He said he has a wife, he does not live on his own so that he should work in the home or hire someone to do it."

A crisis of masculinity may be also aggravated by age, i.e. by the inability of young men to identify both with traditional masculinity and as an adult, economically independent member of the family. Prolonged dependency of young men on their parents often leads to their failure to meet both gender and generation related expectations and power relations. This is often a source of serious frustrations and aggravations in family relationships, which are especially pronounced when a young man is dependent on his mother alone. On the other side, extended dependence of young women on their parents usually leads to intensification of traditional patterns primarily in relationships between father and daughter (e.g. the father continues to treat the daughter as if she is underage -

controlling her, interfering in her relationships etc.)[73] As well noticed by Allatt and Yeandle (1985:21, quoted by Coffield, 1987:97), "the shift in the balance of power in the labor market also denotes a shift to a more traditional society. Change in the labor market enhances the familial power of some parents fortunate enough to have access to the job market."

3.2 Actual masculinities/femininities, nationalism and war

As already noted, one of the most obvious impacts of war on gender is the re-traditionalization of the gender order through the rise of hegemonic masculinity and emphasized femininity in terms of a gendered division of labor, gender power relationships and sexuality. However, it would be too simplistic to argue that all men and all women tend to fit (hegemonic) militarized masculinity and emphasized femininity, as well as that all accept or reject these norms in the same way and with the same consequences. Also, what I want to argue here is that the way militarized masculinity is performed depends very much on the kind of war in which a particular man is involved, on his social situation, moral and psychological features as well as on his ethnic origin or belonging to a specific nation.

Nationalistic rhetoric and war propaganda in Serbia only sporadically used the language of an open call for aggression and attack on other nations. War discourse was deliberately used in a way which manipulated people's feelings about their "brothers"[74] in need in other parts of the former Yugoslavia, and urged them to enlist to help protect their territories and families. Especially effective in that sense were pictures of massacred bodies, crying children, burned houses and other images of excessive violence against Serbs in Bosnia, Croatia and Kosovo. Reinforced with a widespread military culture, these pictures often provoked men's anger and urged them to vengeance.

However, those who were most easily convinced to use weapons and join the war were criminals as well as police and army men who were forced to participate in it as a part of their duty as well. A part of them obviously saw it as an opportunity to act out hegemonic masculinity, or hypermasculinity in a way that would not ever be tolerated in peacetime. They performed this kind of masculinity both by killing people and doing other war crimes as well as in different kinds of expressions of toughness and aggression when returning (temporary or permanently) home. As I wrote elsewhere, this is exactly that criminal-warrior type of masculinity, which was widely propagated in Serbia, especially in the early 1990's (Nikolic-Ristanovic:1998:475).

On the other side, those who went to war convinced that they were doing "a good man's job" (as volunteers or conscripts), hoping that they would come back as national heroes, usually ended as deeply disappointed, frustrated men. Having grown up with pictures of heroic battles of their fathers during World War II, and being convinced that they were going to protect their own homes or the homes of

[73] For similar findings in UK see Coffield, 1987:93.

[74] This was additionally emphasised by the fact that many of them really had close or distant relatives, acquaintances or friends there as well as by reviving atrocities committed to their families in the past.

their compatriots, they soon became disappointed having found themselves in a situation where they had to commit crimes against innocent people if they wanted to survive or avoid being treated as feminine.

Aggression in war is not only a way for men to protect their lives, "but their masculinities as well" (Levy, 1992, quoted by Karner, 1998:229). Thus, as well noticed by Karner, "lashing out at their own fear and victimization by the enemy, they became the aggressors by killing to excess or participating in gratuitous violence." (Karner, 1998:228) And, even worse, many of them were actually entrapped in the anger and urge for vengeance after seeing their own comrades killed. As Karner (1998:226) noticed for Vietnam veterans, "when anger was introduced into the game of combat, the competition became even more abhorrent than the 'normal' or acceptable level of warfare, and violence became gratuitous."

Similar to Vietnam veterans, Serbian men came back home with their "instinct for an immediate violent response intact", i.e. still very dependent on violence. In addition, they felt disappointed in themselves as men as well as deceived and victimized by those in positions of leadership in the military and government. As I wrote elsewhere, many of those who were "normal" men before the war and who were manipulated by national politics were later angry or had a sense of guilt and were accused of being participants in a politically wrong and "dirty" war (Nikolic-Ristanovic, 1998:476). Potential victims of their rage and violence were those who revived their sense of hopelessness, uselessness and guilt for killing in warfare, especially if they were of the same ethnic origin as that of their wartime enemies (Jelkic, 1996:85).

What Karner noticed with Vietnam veterans applies for Serbian men as well: ex-soldiers "quest for manhood initially led them to the military, which in turn left them with a continuing need to find acceptance as men, which led them to participate in what she calls 'toxic masculinity'" (Karner, 1998:230-231). However, they usually end with a lack of self-esteem and marginalized masculinity, since they usually have a problem regaining their earlier status within the family. The lack of stable employment and a strong economic position led them to feel inadequate or betrayed, especially when they are put in a position to be dependent on their partners, as well as when the war led to emancipation and/or empowerment of the partner. Their feeling of powerlessness is especially strong when they were, as Croatian and Kosovo Serbs, put in a situation to surrender and leave their homes as refugees, becoming dependent not only on their wives but on inadequate state welfare and the mercy of unknown people.

However, not all men respond to war propaganda and even to military recruitment (even when it is accompanied by the threat of punishment) in the same way. It was noticed that working class men and men from rural areas tend to respond more readily which obviously confirms Connell's assumption about military and paramilitary forces, police and working-class milieu that emphasizes physical toughness and men's association with machinery, as tied together by an ideology linking masculinity, authority and technological violence (Connell, 1987:109). Men from urban areas and the middle class men were the majority of those who in different ways avoided conscription or found ways to stay as short a time as possible in the war. As was noticed by Hearn (1987:17), the threat and possibility of conscription and other military involvement cause deep oppression of men. Also, this kind of oppositional masculinity is widely considered feminine behavior so that it is not unusual for these men as well to show feelings of inadequacy in relationships with women close to them.[75]

The impact of war in the former Yugoslavia on masculinity is also connected to the increase of emphasized ethnic identity and disturbance of relationships between different ethnic groups as a consequence of the ideology of nationalism. It led to the creation of different masculinities in relation to belonging to a dominant or marginalized ethnic group. So, in Serbia, hegemonic masculinity was mainly associated with the Serbian man, while men from all other ethnic groups were associated with marginalized masculinity. As we will see later, this had especially important consequences to gender power relations in ethnically mixed marriages, leading to conflict and violence in connection with both hegemonic and marginalized ethnic masculinity.

One of the theoretically most neglected forms of masculinity created under the influence of war is the form of marginalized masculinity which is created in modern wars, led by superior military forces, such as NATO, against small and undeveloped countries, such as Serbia or Iraq. The conflict between, on one side, expectations from men embedded in the ideology of patriotism/ militarism, which in Serbia was especially emphasized before and during NATO bombing, and the feeling of fear and powerlessness of ordinary men expected to defend themselves and their families, on the other side, had serious consequences not only on their self-esteem but on gender relationships as well. Their inability to oppose superior power gendered their national identity "feminine" and therefore powerless. This is very well confirmed in the words of my respondent who spent three months in Kosovo:

> "I never felt passive and helpless except when I was in a trench in Kosovo, during NATO bombing. I felt passive, helpless and angry. Moreover, there was no one whom I could turn my anger against."

The feeling of actual powerlessness was increased even more under the influence of Government and military propaganda after the bombing, which kept telling men that they were victors in the war against better-equipped enemy, while at the same time disastrous consequences in their lives told them the opposite.

The impact of war on femininity is actually quite similar to the impact of other forms of social crises or social transformations, such as transition, as was well shown by Karstedt (1993), and as I showed before in this book. Thus, similarly to the transition from communism, war leads to re-traditionalisation of women's role as mothers and housewives.

As in other wars (Karstedt, 1993:145; Moeller, 1993:3), in the wars in the former Yugoslavia (both ethnic conflicts and NATO bombing of Serbia), women performed their traditional duties in much more difficult conditions and with more effort than usual (e.g. long periods of time without electricity and water, serious shortages of

[75] For example, the experiences of Women in Black from Belgrade, who supported men who wanted to desert from the military, showed that women are often victims of abuse by the same men they helped to avoid military service (Zajovic, 1995:174)

food and other essential goods, in difficult economic conditions and impossibility to use new technology, etc.). But, paradoxically, the re-traditionalisation of the gender division of labor brought by war, i.e. tightening of external patriarchy, also renewed a stronger position of women in the home as a consequence of the fact that economic crisis made the gender-specific functions of family maintenance especially important (Karstedt, 1993:147; Nikolic-Ristanovic et al., 1996:VII). For example, during economic sanctions and NATO bombing of Serbia as well as during the siege of Sarajevo, the families were more dependent on women's skills to run the household than on their economic resources. This was a consequence of the fact that, because of shortages, people were not able to buy elementary things, including food, even when they had enough money.

As Blagojevic (1994:476) puts it, patriarchy at the global level is matched by a sacrificial micro matriarchy at the micro level. Thus, the structure of authority gives power to women at the level of primary groups, where they achieve domination through self-sacrifice. It is important to notice the continuity of this pattern in communist and post-communist society as well as its obvious intensification in a completely disorganized society affected by war.

Another paradox of feminine identity during the war is the fact that many women assume all burdens or a multiple role identity. As I showed before and as others showed writing about other wars (Matsakis, 1996:123), this is a consequence of the fact that during and after the war, for various reasons, many families function as single parent or woman headed households. It seems that we can assume the existence of an unusual combination of empowering and domestication of women, which, as we will see later, may affect the way in which they respond to marital problems and spouse abuse following war.

However, performing all roles is especially difficult in abnormal war conditions and post-war economic crises. The situation is further aggravated if, at the same time, a woman is living with a man with PTSD, war caused disability and/or with other war related problems, and who is rarely ready to do any domestic work[76]. The situation is especially difficult for refugee women, whether they are in exile alone with children, or together with the husbands who do not have paid jobs and are frustrated as men. In this situation both women and men suffer all the consequences of the reverse role model of the family I spoke about earlier in this chapter.

[76] For similar experiences of Vietnam veteran wives see Mitsakis, 1996:130, and for women in the Germany after World War II, Moeller, 1993:9.

CHAPTER 4

DOMESTIC VIOLENCE

1. INTRODUCTION

Research recently conducted shows that domestic violence is widespread and a serious problem in post-communist societies, and that this problem may increase and become even more severe (UNICEF, 1999:80-83; Nowakowska, 1999). All research findings seem to provide evidence for the assumption that everyday life changes brought on by the transition from a planned to a market economy, further aggravated in some countries by ethnic conflicts and war, contributed significantly to women's vulnerability to violence at home. Impoverishment, decreased access to paid jobs as well as employment instability and complete insecurity became significant risk factors for women's vulnerability to domestic violence and contributed to the decrease of possibilities for women to leave violent men. If we add to that slow legal and policy changes, widespread corruption and prejudices related to domestic violence, as well as a strong patriarchal tradition in the countries under examination, the situation where women who are victims of domestic violence find themselves often seems hopeless.

In this chapter I will look at the available data about prevalence and characteristics of domestic violence in countries included in my survey, as well as at the impact of changes in everyday life and gender identities on women's vulnerability to violence and their possibilities to escape that violence. For analytical reasons, once again I will look separately at the impact of ethnic conflicts and wars in the former Yugoslavia - this time on domestic violence. I will analyze my findings in the light of several theories, bearing in mind my assumptions that it is a very very complex phenomenon, with many roots and causes, present in every society, and in societies under stress, in particular.

2. PREVALENCE AND CHARACTERISTICS OF DOMESTIC VIOLENCE IN HUNGARY, MACEDONIA, BULGARIA AND SERBIA

2.1 Hungary

Research carried out in Hungary in 1998 is one of the rare prevalence studies done in Eastern Europe. The study was based on a representative sample of 1010 women over 18 years of age from different regions of Hungary. Thirteen percent of the women said that their husbands had beaten them (usually more than once) and 22 percent said that their male partner had threatened them with violence. Nine percent of the respondents stated that domestic violence happened to a friend of theirs. As Toth points out, they may also be the victims themselves but found it easier to talk in the third person. Ten percent said that they had been raped by a partner. The same research also suggests that alcohol plays a major role in cases of domestic violence.

Respondents also often mentioned jealousy, difficult economic conditions and unemployment as excuses for violence. In addition, research findings show that unemployed and economically dependent women make up 22 percent of victims of spouse abuse. The research also gives evidence about the range of spouse abuse in the past, i.e. during the socialist time; findings suggest that every fifth woman has witnessed her father beating her mother. (Toth, 1999:30)

According to Morvai's estimates, in Hungary, about fifty women die every year as a result of domestic violence, while approximately every tenth woman is beaten by her husband/partner. Also, Morvai's research finding showed that more than half of all female homicide victims were killed by their partners, as well as that in 77 percent of cases of women killed by their partners the court found that the victim had been previously battered by the perpetrator (Morvai, 1998:109, 111) According to police estimates, the number of women killed by their male partners in Hungary is between 150-180 yearly. (Wirth, forthcoming)

However, in spite of the fact that domestic violence was a reality for many women during socialism and that it is getting worse during the transition, prejudices about domestic violence are still strong. Accordingly, every seventh woman from Toth's research said that even if a husband beats his wife brutally, it is a private matter. Also, every fourth Hungarian woman believes sexual violence within marriage does not exist, i.e. the wife should always be available to her husband. The study also investigated whether respondents know about the recent criminalization of marital rape. Although surprisingly for the researchers, more than half of the respondents had heard about it, forty-five percent had never heard of this important regulation. (Toth, 1999:32)

Hungarian women only rarely ask for help from authorities. The majority of women (65%) explain this phenomenon as a manifestation of a woman's feeling of shame. The second reason often mentioned by women is fear. Many women pointed out that abused women became even more defenseless after they reported a husband's brutal violence. Consequently, they think that it is hopeless to turn to the authorities without more efficient protection for the victims.

2.2 *Bulgaria and Macedonia*

Research on domestic violence as a human rights abuse, conducted by the Minnesota Advocates for Human Rights in both Bulgaria and Macedonia, shows that domestic violence is a serious and widespread problem (Minnesota Advocates for Human Rights, 1996, 1998) In addition, these studies suggest that there are currently no appropriate legal solutions for the protection of victims of domestic violence, that the police react inappropriately, and that courts do not take seriously their obligation to punish the perpetrator of violence. There are no statistics on domestic violence and the national governments do not provide any social services to victims of domestic violence. The research suggests that the main predictors of domestic violence in Bulgaria and Macedonia are the traditional subordination of women and their economic dependence on men.

Research on domestic violence in the Varna region (Bulgaria) confirms that domestic violence seriously affects women in Bulgaria. The research is based on the analysis of medical documentation for 1546 medical examinations of victims of domestic violence conducted during 1996, 1997 and 1998. The analysis shows that the majority of victims of domestic violence were women (81.6%) with women from age 20-40 being the most vulnerable (50.9%). The majority of perpetrators are husbands (65.2%). However, apart from husbands, children (13%) and other members of the family (18.5%) also appear as perpetrators. Research findings also show that there is a rise in cases where elderly parents are victims of their own children, suggesting that, in these cases, violence is mainly connected to the economic dependence of adult children. (Radoinova, unpublished). Also, another survey, carried out in the Bulgarian town of Burgas, showed that 45 percent of female respondents were abused at home, while 65 percent witnessed it (Kostova, unpublished).

Data from the sociological survey conducted in March 2000, by the Agency for Social and Marketing Research NOEMA, on a sample of 1123 women and men, shows that domestic violence is a serious and widespread phenomenon in Bulgaria (Zlatanova, 2001:42). Victims of physical violence are mainly women, 22.2 percent of whom answered that they were beaten by their partner often (4.4%) or from time to time (15.8%). The results show that sexual violence among spouses is the second most widely spread form of domestic violence. Again, women are the actual victims. Approximately 11 percent of the women over 18 define themselves as victims of sexual violence. 52 percent of respondents answered that they know people who are continually molested.

Two surveys of violence against women and children conducted by Eurobarometer in 1999 within the 'Daphne'[77] project reveal that the majority of Western Europeans and Bulgarians are of the opinion that this form of violence is widespread in their countries. Unlike Bulgarians, however, they have become aware of the problem from the mass media. The data from the survey in Bulgaria shows the opposite – problems of domestic violence are mainly discussed at home or with friends and have not yet become a public issue.

Violence is registered among all age, educational and professional groups. The percentage of educated people living in big cities, with income above average for the country, who have admitted that they were victims of domestic violence, is slightly lower than that of people with lower education, with income lower than average for the country, and living in smaller towns and villages. This fact indicates that the phenomenon is rooted in the traditional ideas of the role of men and women in Bulgarian society. Patriarchal relations, the sense of dependence on the family and relatives still dominate among Bulgarians. According to 86 percent of the respondents, violence among spouses and in the family exists within Bulgarian society. A quarter of them think domestic violence is rare, a third share the opinion

[77] Jertvi na nasilie (Victims of violence), *Evropeiski dialog*, No 4, November-December 1999.

that it is neither rare nor widespread, and every eighth person says it is widespread. An inconsiderable part of them think violence among spouses/partners does not exist. Every third adult man in the country answers that 'violence among spouses is not widespread', whereas every third woman says violence among spouses is a 'widespread phenomenon'.

Research based on interviews with 491 (male and female) students from Skopje (Macedonia) shows that 35 percent of all respondents and thirty-three percent of female respondents witnessed domestic violence in some period of their lives. Twenty percent of male respondents and 16 percent of female respondents answered that domestic violence was present in their own home. Although this research suggests that domestic violence is widespread in Macedonia, it unfortunately does not distinguish between different kinds of domestic violence according to the relationship between victim and perpetrator. However, as in the Hungarian and Bulgarian studies, this research also suggests that financial difficulties and unemployment are important contributing factors for domestic violence. (ESE, 1997) These findings are supported by another study conducted in Macedonia, which shows that marital and family conflicts (violence included) correlates with financial problems of the family. The same study also shows that, apart from spouse abuse, domestic violence often includes parent-children violence as well (Coneva and Darkovski, 1995:14,16).

The first survey on prevalence of domestic violence in Macedonia, conducted during 2000 on a sample of 850 women older than 18, further confirms the results of earlier studies. Hence, 61.5 percent of respondents answered that they were victims of mental violence, 23.9 percent were victims of physical violence and 5 percent were victims of sexual abuse within the family. Most often the abuser was a partner - (81.7% – in 70.8% present partner and in 10.9% former one), while 18 percent of respondents were abused by other family members (in laws, parents, siblings and distant relatives).

The survey showed that violence against other members of the family is connected to the existence of multi-generation families as a consequence of both tradition and economic hardships related to the transition. Even 35.1 percent of respondents said that they were beaten more than 10 times and in 70.3 percent of the cases violence occurred during the last five years. Physical violence was reported most often by Roma women, who are also among those in the worst socio-economic situation. (Caceva and Coneva, 2000:23-25, 67).

Also, 65 percent of respondents, who answered that they were not abused in the family, said that domestic violence is widespread within the Macedonian population. 37.5 percent knew women who were abused in the family. Eighty percent of them also said that economic crises connected to the transition contributed to the increase of domestic violence in Macedonia. Nearly two-thirds (62.7%) said that domestic violence was related to economic factors, i.e. poverty, unemployment and housing problems, while 14.7 percent thought that it was related to several generation families living together (Caceva and Coneva, 2000:51-53).

2.3 Serbia

The only prevalence study on domestic violence carried out in Serbia is the research on spouse abuse conducted in 1993[78]. The research was based on the sample of 192 women chosen at random from the general population in Belgrade. (Nikolic-Ristanovic, 1998:473) More than half of the women (112 or 58.3%) from the sample reported that they were victims of some kind of spouse abuse. Ninety-four or forty-nine percent of the women reported psychological violence while thirty-six or 18.7 percent of the women reported that they were victims of wife battery. Also, 18.7 percent of the women reported that they were being raped by their husbands.

Wife battery was usually followed by other kinds of violence. Women who were battered by their husbands were simultaneously victims of psychological abuse (38.9%), sexual violence (25%), or victims of both of these abuses (52.8%). Most often, women reported that the reasons for their husband's violent behavior against them were quarrels regarding money (14.3%) or parents (10.4%). Other reasons often reported by women were quarrels regarding children and the husband's alcoholism and jealousy. Even women who acknowledged that they were beaten often were not willing to label it violence and avoided answering more concrete questions. Similar to the findings of Toth's research in Hungary, these results may prove the high degree of tolerance of violence as a consequence of the generally strong patriarchal structure of the Yugoslav family, e.g. learning that it is normal for a woman to suffer violence, especially psychological violence, from her husband.

The women's status survey, which was conducted by UNICEF in Federal Republic of Yugoslavia in 1997, on a representative sample of the female population aged 20-55, found that 56 percent of respondents sometimes experience coercion in their relationships, while 16.3 percent of them experienced it often (UNICEF, 1997).

Research based on an analyses of cases reported to the Belgrade SOS Hotline for Battered Women and Children and the Counseling Service Against Domestic Violence, shows that in Serbia, apart from social transition, changes connected to ethnic conflicts and NATO bombing also had an impact on women's vulnerability to domestic violence. For example, the SOS Hotline survey suggests that, although molesters are most often actual husbands and partners (65%) or former husbands and partners (13.3%), since the beginning of war in 1991, the number of violent sons has been increasing (from 6.4% in 1991 to 8.7% in 1995), reaching its highest point in 1993.[79] 11.4 percent of the women reported death threats twice as often in 1993 than in previous years. The use of weapons in domestic violence also increased with the beginning of the war. After the start of the war, about forty percent of the women who called the SOS Hotline reported that their partners were threatening them with pistols, bombs and similar weapons. (Mrsevic, 1999:428)

One recent analysis of cases reported to the Counseling Service Against Domestic Violence in Belgrade, covering a two-year period (June 1996-June 1998), showed that

[78] At the time of writing of this book the prevalence survey on domestic violence in Serbia based on the sample of 700 women was going on.

[79] This was the year when the war in Bosnia culminated, as well as the year when in Serbia inflation reached an enormous rate and the level of crime reached its highest point.

652 women victims of domestic violence called or came to ask for help (once or several times). Fifty-two percent of the women who asked for help reported both psychological and physical violence, while 30.2 percent were solely victims of physical violence. In this latter instance, only the most serious consequences of violence were reported, such as a broken nose, ribs, teeth etc. 10.1 percent suffered only psychological violence. Most often, the abusers were husbands (70.2%), sons (7%) and fathers (4.2%). In 3.06 percent of all cases, violence was related to refugee status, while violence committed by ex-soldiers was reported only in four (0.6%) cases. Obviously, the war-related violence was reported less often, which is not unusual since the data relate to the period after the wars in Croatia and Bosnia (Nikolic-Ristanovic, Milivojevic, 2000:22).

The analysis of cases reported to the *Counseling Service Against Domestic Violence* during the NATO bombing demonstrates that more women asked for help during the bombing than in previous periods: 54 compared to 46. Also, the combination of emotional and physical abuse was reported more often than in previous periods: 34 in comparison to 27 cases respectively. Women who asked for help during the bombing reported only violence by men who were not engaged in the army, i.e. who remained at home. Women mainly reported long-term violence, which either continued with the same intensity or became worse during the bombing. In a few instances, women mentioned that domestic violence started at the time of the bombing. The abuse of alcohol as a contributing factor in domestic violence increased during the bombing to 10.7 percent. Women often stated that their husbands' and sons' increased consumption of alcohol was caused by the fear of bombing and "long hours," since they stopped working when the bombing started. (Milivojević:1999:46)

3. EVERYDAY LIFE CHANGES, GENDER AND DOMESTIC VIOLENCE

Previous research already has drawn attention to the impact of everyday life changes caused by social transition and war on women's vulnerability to domestic violence. However, these research findings give only superficial insight and do not illustrate details about the different patterns of the impact changes in everyday life have on women's vulnerability to domestic violence. Moreover, the studies do not show how everyday life changes affect gender identities, although this is essential for understanding the multiple and complex connections between social changes and violence against women in the home. Namely, gender norms and changes in gender identities are considered an important causal factor of domestic violence in all societies (Schur, 1987:159), but their impact is especially emphasized in societies in crisis, i.e. transition, since, as I will show later, this impact is intensified by social stress and its negative impact on communication skills. Also, the available studies do not give much insight into the impact of the interconnection between structural changes and changes in different microsocial structures and identities (generational, gender, ethnic) on women's vulnerability to domestic violence. Similarly as Hagan did argued regarding delinquency and crime in general, I argue that in order to understand "fundamental interconnections" between gender, class and violence against women "it is necessary to take into account the work-related positions of heads and spouses in households."(Hagan, 1988:258).

It is obvious that a more detailed analysis is necessary if we want to understand how changes in everyday life influence women's victimization in the home. To shed more light on this complex issue, I used both qualitative (main) and quantitative (supplementary) analyses of various sources of information about domestic violence, including domestic murders, in Hungary, Serbia, Macedonia and Bulgaria.

As shown previously in this book and as I will show in this chapter, my research findings suggest that social changes, such as social transition and war, are mirrored in all spheres of life and that they significantly affect personal relationships thereby, creating situations in which domestic violence is likely to occur. Changes which occur on the macro level provoke micro level changes which negatively affect both the women's vulnerability to violence and the possibility of leaving the molester and to get protection.

Although marital relationships are primarily affected, disturbances of relationships between children and parents and among in-law relatives are also frequent and may lead to violence. This latter instance is especially characteristic of Serbia and Macedonia, where the economic situation seems to be the most severe and, consequently, the trend that several generations live together (Trajkovski, 1998:71) the most frequent in comparison to other examined countries. In Serbia and, during the NATO bombing, in Macedonia as well, the situation was even more complicated in families who accepted refugees. In this case, the worsening economic and housing conditions, i.e. serious disturbance of family life caused by influx of refugees, sometimes led to violence. Consequently, women were vulnerable to violence from their partners, adult sons and sometimes daughters (including sons-in-law and daughters-in-law) as well as from their fathers, fathers-in-law and other in-law relatives living with them.

3. 1. Vulnerability to domestic violence: the impact of transition from communism

Economic changes resulting from the transition to a market economy strongly influence the way people live together. The negative consequences on relationships within the family were clearly demonstrated in interviews with people in the four countries under examination, where 53.6 percent of respondents said that their family relationships had gotten worse during the last ten years. Family relationships seem to get worse especially in Serbia and Macedonia (76.9 and 58.3 percent respectively in comparison to 39.1 percent in both Hungary and Bulgaria). In addition, only 24.7 percent described this worsening as tensions, while the rest said that their relationships were seriously disturbed, often including psychological violence. Moreover, 78.3 percent of the respondents also know families where relationships recently got worse.

In my survey I found that the breakdown of relationships often included psychological and physical violence (mainly on the side of the male partners with few cases of violent sons, parents and in-laws)[80].

Forty-four or 45.4 percent of respondents said that they suffer from psychological abuse with almost half of them also abused physically. In the majority of these cases (29 or 65.9%) the abuser is the victim's partner, while children, parents and in -laws appear as abusers in 15.9, 13.6 and 4.5 percent of cases, respectively.

Twenty-four or 24.7 percent of the respondents stated that physical violence was present in their home. In the majority of cases (22) the abuser was a partner - typically a male one. In four cases abusers were children (in two cases both children and male partner were abusive), while in two cases the abuser was an 'in-law'. Thirty-seven and one-tenth percent of respondents also said that they knew families where physical violence occurs. There was also a high percentage of cases where the person interviewed did not know whether there was violence in families s/he knew (29%). Although respondents mainly spoke about violence against women, in several cases, both women and men mentioned that women were also violent against their husbands.

Relationships worsened mainly when the husband, wife, or both of them lost their job, when the husband had difficulty finding a job, or when the husband or wife started a private business, and/or when their financial and/or housing situation worsened. On the other hand, getting rich quickly was also a contributing factor for the deterioration of relationships, especially when the husband is *nouveau riche*. Similarly, the deterioration of relationships between adult children and parents, as well as with relatives in-law was connected to financial difficulties, unemployment or the lack of job prospects, poor housing situations, the cohabitation of several generations, as well as drug addiction, and a relative's return from fighting in the war.

Data from all sources suggest that poverty and sudden and quick changes in social and economic status, together with a high level of instability and the difficulty of making decisions in such circumstances, caused a high level of social stress[81] and

[80] It is interesting to note that the answers about (psychological and physical) violence seem to be a better indicator of readiness of respondents to speak about this sensible topic and private matters in general, rather than the exact indicator of the existence of violence itself. It is obvious from my interviews that respondents from Hungary and Serbia, who most often answered that there was violence in their family, were also much more ready to give detailed accounts of changes that happened in their lives. This is in accordance with cultural and historical differences between the countries, which I mentioned at the beginning of this book, and which had a serious impact on differences in mentality of people, especially women, in these countries - with Bulgarian and Macedonian women being much more under the influence of rigid patriarchal socialization and much less ready to speak about family matters. On the other side, similar to other surveys which included men, I also noticed the men's tendency to minimize or deny their violence. Thus, in order to get a more correct picture, I made sure that in each country in at least one case both partners were interviewed.

[81] Western research also found connections between poverty of unemployed families and high level of stress they experience (Burgoyne, 1987:54). Also, they stressed the connection between instability of statuses and uncertainty, on one side, and stress and frustrations, on the other (Roberts, 1984, as cited by Coffield, 1987:890).

contributed to destabilization and disorganization of family relationships and to family violence (Jovanovski, 1998:91; Coneva, 1998:134; Milosavljevic, 1999; Polovina, 1999; Zegarac and Brkic, 1998:23; Zlatanova, 2001:33). They also led to difficulties in the fulfillment of gender and generational roles, and did not allow the space necessary to accommodate to the new situation.

In addition to economic changes, political changes also had a negative impact on relationships within family, which in most countries was especially emphasized at the beginning of the transition when political polarization of the society was most emphasized. Acute polarization of the society caused a new type of family conflict, grounded upon the political confrontation between family members - partners, parents versus children, brothers versus sisters etc. (Vicheva, 1999:14). In Serbia, this kind of negative impact, together with a disturbance in inter-ethnic relationships and armed conflict, has been present almost all the time since the beginning of the transition. The result, as usual in similar situations, is often stress especially in men, and depression, anxiousness, and low self-esteem in women, which, as I show later in this book, contribute to violence against women as well. (Andersen, 1988:77).

3.2. Spouse abuse

From my interviews and other sources, it is possible to identify two main forms of influence of everyday life changes connected to transition which have impacted women's vulnerability to spouse abuse:

a) Violence connected to enrichment of men who are successful in private business, shadow economy, etc. or are involved in organized crime;
b) Violence connected to impoverishment, unemployment and related gender identities changes.

These forms of influence are often interlaced with changes in ethnic or political identities, and the overall impact is mediated by social stress, problems in communication[82] and/or changes in gender identities. As expected, having in mind findings about changes in the economic situation and gender identities explored in previous chapters, the second form of influence seems to prevail both among my respondents and in other domestic violence cases I analyzed.

As in Western countries, the characteristics of the man with whom a woman is involved are actually a "better predictor" of a woman' s odds of being victimized by violence than are the characteristics of the woman herself." (Browne, 1987:35). In addition, as noticed by Mooney (and disregarded by radical feminists), social differences between men create varying forms of masculinity and different types and degrees of violence against women (Mooney, 2000:107).

As I have already stressed, economic changes brought on by the transition period had two main effects on men's social status and masculinity. On the one hand, the

[82] Vesna Stanojevic, from Counseling Service against domestic violence, Belgrade (Serbia), noticed, in her work with women victims of domestic violence, that the lack of communication skills is an important contributing factor in cases where violence occur. "People never learn to respect different opinions, i.e. how to communicate and solve problems peacefully within the family", says Stanojevic (Stanojevic, interview, 1999)

better social and economic position of some men led to the intensification of male identity and a renewed traditionalism of gender roles within the family. On the other hand and most possibly more frequent, the decrease in the social and economic status of a large portion of men as well as the increase in status incompatibility,[83] social stress, and social isolation are also strongly related to the risk of wife abuse. For this latter group of men, it is characteristic that crises of masculinity or marginalization of masculinity – i.e. the widening gap between social constructs of hegemonic masculinity and their possibility to fit them – may contribute to their violent behavior in the family.

Poverty and unemployment seem to affect women in the way that they are now more often dependent on men than earlier. This model seems to prevail among couples where violence occurs, suggesting a connection between domestication of women and a renewed traditionalism of gender roles on one hand, and domestic violence, on the other hand. This is in accordance with the assumption that traditional gender roles divide women and men from each other (Andersen, 1988:78), at the same time creating both the favorable context for violence to occur as well as decreasing the economic and social potential for women to leave the molester. (Nikolic-Ristanovic and Milivojevic, 2000; Caceva and Coneva, 2000:65) These assumptions also fit with research findings suggesting the significance of women's economic dependence as the factor of wife abuse which is directly related to the institution of marriage in its traditional form. (Schur, 1987)

However, re-traditionalisation of gender division of labor and gender roles has different consequences on masculinity and femininity, depending on the place women and men occupy within social structure and on changes related to that. Namely, re-traditionalization, as I showed in the previous chapter, can, but does not always, mean that masculinity is (successfully) associated with hegemonic masculinity. Hence we can distinguish between two forms of masculinity in relation to the traditional gender division of labor, i.e. women's economic dependence on man, where domestic violence is likely to occur:

1. When the man is the main (or only) breadwinner and is successful in securing the financial wellbeing of the family (hegemonic masculinity/emphasized femininity pattern);
2. When the man is the main (or only) breadwinner but he is not able to secure financial wellbeing (marginalised masculinity/emphasized femininity pattern).

The first form of masculinities is the part of what Hagan calls "unbalanced class relations" or "authority-subject relationship", which comes "closest to matching the conditions of the ideal type patriarchal family". The other one is closer to an egalitarian family with neither spouse having workplace authority with the consequence that the family is located in "obey class" (Hagan, 1988:172-3).

On the other side, crisis of (socialist) femininity, which is connected to the loss of paid jobs by women (especially those educated who used to have economic independence during communism and often feel degraded in the role of housewife) is

[83] According to Gelles, status incompatibility is when the husband, whom society expects to be the head of the family, has less education or is less paid than his wife. (Gelles, 1997)

an additional risk factor for spouse abuse (Vicheva, 1999:14). This new social position leads to women's frustrations, as well as to a decrease in their self-esteem and ability to resist violence. These factors combine to make women even more vulnerable to violence.[84] But paradoxically, women's better social status may have the same effect when an increase in women's economic status creates status incompatibility and leads to "a most unusual family class relation" - where the man is either unemployed or employed in a position "without authority", while the wife is employed in a position "with authority." (Hagan, 1988:172)

3.2.1 Hegemonic masculinity/emphasized femininity pattern and spouse abuse

The connection between structural changes, the renewed hegemonic masculinity/emphasized femininity pattern, and violence against women is confirmed by data examining why women became dependent, the violent men's social and economic position, and the methods used by men to keep wives in violent relationships.

The most common reasons for women's dependence on violent men are: they cannot find a job; they lost a job due to economic changes, either due to their ethnic origin or after becoming a refugee; they do not work or left a job because a partner prevented them from working, convinced or forced them to spend more time in the home, or become formally employed in his private enterprise; or they work or are retired but earn a disproportionately small amount of money in comparison to the husband. By contrast, the violent husbands of these women are often economically independent and earn enough and sometimes considerable money. They are most often involved in both legal and illegal work (shadow economy), have private businesses or are in influential positions in state bodies. The extreme examples of the connection of domestic violence to a renewed traditionalism of gender roles and the institution of marriage is found in cases of refugee women who married men living in Serbia.

One of most extreme examples of violence connected to newly won hegemonic masculinity is found in marriages of the *nouveau riches*, i.e. those men who got rich shortly after the social transition changes. When they get rich and start to feel powerful they start to isolate women. As pointed out by Nadia Kozuharova from *Animus Association* (Bulgaria) and Dusko Minkovski from *Skopje Center for Social Work* (Macedonia) (interviews, 1999), these women are in the position of wealthy housewives, who must stay at home under the control of their partners.[85] Together with psychological and physical abuse, these men usually use economic violence such as:

[84] Regina Indshewa, WaD, Bulgaria, the interview, 1999, and Vesna Stanojevic, Counseling Service against Domestic Violence, Belgrade, interview, 1999.

[85] The specific expression of hegemonic masculinity is found among Albanians in Macedonia, where men use to work abroad and leave their wives in complete social isolation, with their relatives whom they had to obey. When the man came back, his family usually complained about the wife's behavior, which often precipitated his violence (Janeva, interview, 1999). Also, in their recent survey, Caceva and Coneva found that Albanian women prevail among victims of mental abuse in the family in Macedonia and that it is connected to a strong patriarchal model and isolation of the Albanian family. As an illustration, they give the example of Albanian men who forbid their wives to work outside the home, even when their economic situation is difficult. They explain that with Albanian men's fear of their wives' economic independence which they perceive as threat to their traditional position (power) within the family (Coneva and Caceva, 2000:67).

not giving money to their economically dependent wives, not allowing them to work, blackmailing them in different ways, and especially with children, expelling them from the house and/or using physical violence to prevent them in their attempts to become independent. Moreover, in order to confirm their new masculinity, these men often find lovers and sometimes even bring them home and ask their wives to serve both of them or use other humiliating practices. If the women used to work, even when they had good jobs and salaries, these men tended to force them to leave their jobs and in these cases the re-traditionalisation of woman's role itself was part of men's violence, i.e. his controlling behavior and the physical violence was the part of men's "strategy" to maintain the new family order he himself established. A good example is found in the case from the practice of Nadia Center for Victims of Domestic Violence in Bulgaria, where another risk factor is added as well - the impact of the strong patriarchal Turkish tradition:

> R. (39), Bulgarian, had been married in a Turkish family for 19 years. The first years of her marriage she had no conflicts with her husband. At that time she was struck by the fact that everybody obeyed only the father and mother-in-law and did what they said without question. She and her husband had good jobs and made good money. With the help of her parents they managed to build their own house and moved out. And then the problems started. The husband decided she did not have to work and made her leave her job. They already had a daughter and, although there was someone to look after her, the husband insisted that his wife look after the child. He later confessed that the real reason was that he did not want her to 'meet' other men at work because he was jealous. Gradually, the 'order' in their house became very much like the one in her husband's family. She always had to be 'on the alert' – the meal had to be cooked, the house cleaned, brandy and beer in the fridge and the table had to be laid five minutes after he had come home and she herself had to wait on him 'obediently'. She had to 'report' to him who she had talked to during the day, whether she went out and who she had met. He forbade her to go out and meet friends and he did not let them visit her. She could visit her parents once a month. Usually, after these visits he would beat her because she had been away from home. He started drinking heavily and when he got home at night she and the children (they already had a son as well) were already asleep. If they did not meet him at the door, he would beat them, sexually insult her and would not let her go out for 4-5 days (until the scars from the beating disappeared). She became very depressed, they her took to a doctor to be treated for 'neurosis' in another town. In 1994 she attempted suicide.

Sometimes, after forcing his wife to leave her job, the man also forces or "convinces" her to work (sometimes only formally) in his new businesses. Usually, this serves two aims: to enable the man to avoid paying taxes and to control and exploit his own wife. Sometimes, violence is limited to the psychological and economic level but it is not so rare that physical violence is also added (Koycheva and Toth, interviews, 1999).

The *nouveau riches* also include those men who got rich over a short period of time through different illegal activities, including war crimes, organized crime and corruption (e.g. as corrupted policemen[86]). Men involved in organized crime became increasingly powerful during the transition period. Thus, in their relationships with

[86] According to 1996 ICVS carried out in Belgrade, the police is among the most corrupted professions in Serbia (Nikolic-Ristanovic, 1998a). Also, police officers were largely involved in ethnic conflicts.

women, violence is often connected to the extreme reinforcement of hegemonic masculinity/emphasized femininity and includes total subordination, control, and social isolation of the woman. Women who live with these men are in a very delicate situation since they know a lot and live in fear of being killed. They consider their partners omnipotent and do not have support from neighbors who often think that they deserve to be victimized since they stay with mafia men. In addition, men who are involved in organized crime live in constant stress caused by fear of mafia male-to-male violence and tend to vent their stress in the home.[87] Coercion to prostitution and abuse of women for pornography as a form of wife abuse is mentioned in all countries but most often in Hungary. This is not unusual because the prostitution and pornography industries are the most widespread in Hungary among countries included in the survey.

In the families of those men who recently became (more or less) successful sole breadwinners, one common reason for family disputes and violence is the increase in time men now spend out of the home because of work. Family disputes and violence result from overwork and stress as well as from general insecurity in the workplace and potential earnings. Wives' complaints about the men's absence and lack of time for domestic chores and the children may additionally increase the stress and offend newly won male pride. As well noticed by Messerschmidt (1993:145), "wife beating arises not solely from gendered subordination but also from women actively contesting that subordination." The tension is especially heightened when the man's success in public and absence from the private sphere is confronted with the wife's loss of a job and return home, i.e. limitation of her life to the private sphere (crisis of socialist femininity). Hence, they are faced with the worst possible mix: a man who is successful but overworked and, a highly educated woman who used to have a regular job is now forced to stay at home as a housewife dependent on her husband. A good illustration is provided by a highly educated woman interviewed in Hungary:

> "Practically our conflicts stem from the fact that my husband doesn't want to deal with the family, either with me or the problems related to the renewal. It means he doesn't want to participate in the labor division and actually he's tired...It is interesting that the financial issues usually don't develop to the point of a knife, but rather the division of labor - it means domestic chores, as well as the division of time spent with the children. That causes very ugly conflicts... The financial situation definitely makes one helpless. Because when a woman stays at home and she doesn't have an income, even if she receives maternal allowances or whatever they call it nowadays, she is still helpless because she cannot say that the income is hers. Now normally, if they really love each other, this doesn't even occur, and what the husband earns is common. But the truth is that the majority of people think that – and this is the normal, average view – what the husband earns is his and he is the master of his house, and many times he stresses that physically as well... It leads to situations that are quite rough and violent conflicts from which I cannot decide yet whether my husband is sick and that's why he's like that or he has just simply gotten a taste of that power, and as the breadwinner of the family he dares to form the right to use such rough, physical violence."[88]

[87] Interviews with Nadia Kozuharova (Animus, Bulgaria) and Gyorgyi Toth (NANE, Hungary).

[88] Similarly, a study of unemployed women in Poland in 1990 found that most women said that unemployment had affected their domestic relationships, usually in a negative way. For example, one respondent said: "The lack of money caused quarrels between my husband and myself. My husband says he won't work for my upkeep, and delights in saying that if it were not for him, I would die of hunger."(Watson, 1996:226)

As pointed out by Huber (1991:19), a complex interplay of gender ideology, feeling, and behavior determines the division of labor. When the supply of male commitment to share childcare is far lower than female demand for it, a high level of marital tension is most likely to occur. The whole situation, where both man and woman are frustrated because of feeling of uneasy with the burden of new gender roles and uncertain of their financial situation, affects their communication as well. As Juliet Mitchell observed, oppression within the family created in women "a tendency to small-mindedness, petty jealousy, irrational emotionality and random violence, dependency, competitiveness, selfishness and possessiveness, passivity, a lack of vision and conservatism". These qualities, she emphasized, were not false stereotypes created by male chauvinism but "real effects, the inescapable results of the woman's powerless condition within the family"(Mitchell, quoted by Bouchier, 1983:70). This is especially emphasized in the cases, like the one quoted above, where earlier independent women find themselves in dependent economic positions. This is how above-mentioned woman from Hungary commented on her problems in communication with her husband:

> "Many times it is caused by my isolation too, really, because I am also very irritated sometimes, because it causes tension in me too that I cannot get out from the apartment. And then I am also irritated. And I am not saying that I don't yell, I also yell. It is not true that the woman gets a beating because her husband is so to say mad, perhaps there is something like that too because there is, I heard and read about such cases. There are such cases. But most of the time it is caused by alcohol, the effects of alcohol. But there is no alcohol at our place. But the truth is when I'm tired, it is almost as if I am drunk. One's tongue doesn't work the same way when one is very tired, when one is dizzy... and one becomes aggressive the same way."

3.2.2. Marginalised masculinity/emphasized femininity pattern, status incompatibility and spouse abuse

As I already mentioned, not all men who have dependent wives are able to earn enough. In these cases, violence is connected to the husband's inner conflict between the desire to retain the role of family provider and his frustrations at not being able to meet his own and society's expectations (marginalised masculinity).

Sometimes, as in the case of a Macedonian respondent, these husbands complain because their wives do not work, leading to a further lowering of women's feelings of self-esteem, which was already endangered by the fact that they were forced to shift from socialist to traditional (marginalised) femininity. When a severe financial situation, for whom she is blamed by both her husband and herself, living in multi-generational family and alcohol are added, it is not strange that already bad relationships become dramatically worse and start to include severe physical violence as well (he broke her thumb). A similar pattern is found in the case of a Bulgarian woman, described by Minkova (interview, 1999):

> "The woman chose to retire because she is disabled somehow. She was working for 30 years and now she decided to retire in her fifties and to stay at home. Normal age for retirement in Bulgaria is 55. This caused a lot of problems since her husband was not jealous or controlling her but he had another way for violating her and this caused the

> problem since she does not bring in money any more. He abused her psychologically and also through specific kinds of threats like breaking furniture and small things like cups, plates etc. This is how he demonstrated his power."

However, even more often men do not allow their wives to work and improve the family's economic situation since they feel this may hurt their image of masculinity.

As I already showed in previous chapters, during the transition period, everyone's economic position is more fluid than stable. Changes in men's behavior toward their wives often coincide with changes related to the financial situation of the family. In addition, during the transition period, privatization was experienced as a big challenge to and test for male identity. Consequently, violence was intensified with worsening of the financial situation and when men failed in private business. The example given by my female respondent from Macedonia show that very well:

> Both husband and wife were without jobs during severe economic crises in the period 1993-1995. The conflicts they had before became more severe when they lost jobs and became even worse when the wife got a job and was the sole breadwinner (1995-1998). While he was supported by his wife, the man tried to start a private business but failed. However, in order to pay his debts, he had to sell their apartment. This was the point when violence began as a consequence of the wife's complaints about selling the apartment. She suffered severe violence, including murder threats, in spite of the fact that she found a job for him so that from 1998 on he was employed. They divorced on her request in 1999.

One example from Serbia is even more extreme:

> At the request of her violent husband, the wife left her job in order to work in his private enterprise. He killed her after experiencing severe financial crises following his business failure.

Impoverishment and job shortage, as well as the loss of former economic and social security affected a large part of the male population, leaving them feeling powerless and inadequate. Being unemployed is devastating to men in a patriarchal society, since it is a clear indication that they are not fulfilling society's expectations as the family's providers. (Gelles, 1997) A strong connection between men's employment and violence in the family has already been established by research in the West (Gayford, 1975; Prescott&Letko, 1977 and Rounsavill, 1978, quoted by Gelles, 1997; Dobash et al, 2000:109, 183) My research suggests that, apart from unemployment, in a post-communist society, men's feelings of inadequacy are also connected to their inability to earn enough money even when legally and/or illegally employed. The decrease in men's economic position and social status leads to a crisis of male identity.

According to my research findings, a negative change in men's economic position was mainly connected to the fact that they lost their jobs/and or cannot (or do not try to) get new ones, that they failed in private business, cannot earn enough money, became refugees, or were sick or sent on forced leave. If they were socialized in a rigid patriarchal way, violence often represents compensation for the lack of their power in the marriage and is motivated by frustration because of inability to meet unrealized (hegemonic) masculine identity (Cahn, 1996:14; Ferraro, quoted by Messerschmidt, 1993:149)), i.e. as a result of their tendency to overidentify with dysfunctional and stereotypic masculine values and expectations

(Gondolf, quoted by Stordeur and Still, 1989:46). The frustrations are sometimes further aggravated by the wives' complaints about the men's inability to fulfil their traditionally expected role of family providers. This development occurs in cases where both spouses are unemployed and/or do not have any earnings or their earnings are insufficient, as well as in cases where only the wife is employed or earning a living. As Radka Valkova from the *Gender Project for Bulgaria* (interview, 1999) points out:

> "Men are under more stress due to transition stage changes, since when they are unemployed men find themselves in a role which does not fit traditional expectations. Additionally, they may not be prepared to do something other than their profession. When a man is jobless, I am sure that there will be conflict in the family... When a previously employed wife loses her job, this is a more acceptable situation because of cultural attitudes: men are the ones who earn money for the family and women work or do not work. In this country, women were working for many years not because they wished to work but because they had to work."

Similarly, Dicks et al. (1998:293) point out that the focus here is on the damage done to traditional masculine self-esteem when the redundancy occurs and that this is felt "to unleash a whole series of tensions in the family realm". Also, Schechter (1982:226) has drawn attention to the fact that women are often in the uncomfortable position of reminding their husbands that they have financial responsibilities to meet, and if "these men do not want or cannot afford to meet these obligations, women remain easy scapegoats, reminders of his lack of power."

Financial difficulties, economic dependence on others and accommodation problems are inherently the sources of stress, which may cause tensions and conflicts between partners. The presence of stress, both internal and external, has been associated with battering as well (Ganley&Harris, 1978, quoted by Stordeur and Stille, 1989:50). As pointed out by Stordeur and Stille (1989:50), although battering cannot be explained by the presence of stress, stress is a "salient characteristic of most wife assaulters". It is not unusual, having in mind that batterers use violence as a means to reduce stress (frustration, helplessness and anger) and temporarily regain complete control of a stressful or personally threatening situation.

In refugee families in Serbia, the situation is additionally aggravated by trauma caused by war and violent changes in everyday life connected to migration. A special problem exists in families which accepted refugees. Women who had both refugees and violent husbands in their homes report that their husbands became more violent. Also, some women report that their husbands started to be violent after the arrival of refugees. Violence against women in these situations is often connected to an imbalance created in the family by newcomers, as well as to the worsening of their already bad economic situation. For example:

> A woman said that her already aggravated relationship with her husband culminated when his relatives came to live with them as refugees. At one time, nine persons began living together in one apartment. This only added fuel to the conflict which arose as a consequence of a reversed gender division of labor and power imbalance that was created when the wife started to run a private school and became the main breadwinner, while the husband worked only in a state firm and earned only a symbolic amount of

> money. In addition, the husband spent his time going to work (only formally since there was no real work and earnings) and escaping from reality by sleeping. He resisted any discussion about household problems and became especially violent toward both her and their children when she decided to divorce.

This example shows clearly how the accumulation of both different social stresses and gender-related changes increase the risk of violence.

The aforementioned example also shows that the crisis of masculinity as a contributing factor to violence is especially emphasized when social incompatibility is created by the wife's employment and better financial situation. My findings suggest that women who have dependent violent husbands usually have either a private job/business, work in state firms and have additional jobs or earn money otherwise, doing all kinds of jobs regardless of their education and training As pointed out by Albena Koycheva (interview, 1999) an attorney lawyer from Bulgaria, the loss of economic balance is a bigger problem than poverty. This is especially apparent when the wife decides to start a private business. In these cases, violence is obviously connected to the obliteration of the traditional distribution of economic roles in the household, i.e. with men's desire to regain power by any means. Sometimes, it also includes taking and spending all the wife's money, making the wife into a slave, or using the wife's money for alcohol and molesting her after drinking. It may be a part of the man's efforts to retain the picture of his masculinity in front of other people, and, if his wife stands in his way, than the violence is also likely to occur as the expression of his anger because of the shame he experienced. A good illustration of this is the case of an unemployed male respondent from Hungary, who is dependent on his wife and has to cope with a difficult economic situation:

> So I took some of my work mates out for breakfast before work, but when I wanted to pay I saw that there was no money in my wallet. I knew that there had been some money in it from the night before. I was angry and embarrassed in front of my work mates, so I went home and asked my wife what had happened to it. But she said she was sorry because she had forgotten to tell me that she had used it for the bills. And then she just laughed. I got so angry that I hit her as she was standing there, but as a reaction she jumped on me, I tried to stop her by twisting her arm back, but I broke her arm by mistake. It was a big ho-ha and everybody came up to us and asked what happened and, anyway, she was taken away by the ambulance.

Men sometimes use violence to force their economically independent wives to sell their property as well, leaving them without any living accommodation or economic security. This kind of economic violence by men who are economically dependent on their wives is usually followed by physical and psychological violence, as a reaction to women's resistance.

The situation is especially severe when the overall social situation is contrary to the traditional model of married life. In these cases, apart from an inability to fulfill the traditional male role of breadwinner, the contributing factors to men's violent behavior are also their frustrations connected to passivity and spending unusually long hours at home. As stressed by Dicks et al. (1998:296), men's presence in the home is "alien and disruptive", and, because the home is constituted as the woman's realm, it is women who suffer the consequences. The very fact that a man spends an increasing amount of time in the home increases opportunities for violence (Stordeur and Stille, 1989:51). In addition, expectations (and sometimes pressure) by wives that husbands assume at least part of the responsibilities for domestic chores and child care, may further aggravate the situation (Koycheva, interview, 1999). As Feher (interview, 1999) from Hungary points out:

> "The woman is overburdened, because, in addition to working, she must also take care of children and the household since most men are not willing to, even when they are not employed. The men are unwilling 'to take the role of the housewife.' Furthermore, the woman is expected to 'treat the soul' of man who becomes more aggressive, more anxious, and more angry by changing her behavior to try to balance the man's and emphasize his importance. It is a very difficult situation since all the burden is on the woman in such cases."

In situations where men already feel their masculinity is endangered, women's complaints only make the situation worse. In cases where the man is both unemployed and not able to earn a living, he tends to escape from reality through the use of alcohol. This is another factor which increases women's vulnerability to violence. As stressed by Dobash et al. (2000:29) and confirmed by my research, men and women often compete for limited amounts of money to be used for alcohol or food and children' clothing. As well noticed by Waddington et al. (1998:254) "in seeking to understand reactions to unemployment it is apparent that idealizations of gender roles are evident in the words of those experiencing unemployment." And it can even be argued that unemployment "lays bare the vulnerability of these roles, to which the reaction is to rescue and restore rather than revise them." Thus, if a woman is able to protect established male identity in renegotiated terms, "which allows him to feel that he is still a real man, husband and father" (although he is not the breadwinner any more), then the strain may disappear and the relationships may even be ameliorated. If not, the "trouble with men" becomes the trouble for women, often leading to serious conflict and violence. In reality, indeed, this is not very likely to occur because over-burdened women (Dicks et al, 1998:309) are usually under stress themselves and have neither time nor energy to deal with their husband's frustrations. This obviously makes the situation even more complicated and increases the risk of violence.

However, men who feel that their masculinity is in danger also tend to blame the wives on whom they are dependent for not fulfilling their roles of housewives and mothers. "It is always a problem if the woman earns more money or even the same amount of money as her husband", said Maria Minkova, from Animus (Bulgaria). "Or if the woman has higher education. All women from the kind of families I have been working with share that this is always a big problem which causes problems. For example, if the woman earns a lot of money, he blames her for not being a good housewife. Or, when she has higher education, he blames her that she is quite pretentious because she always wants to demonstrate her higher education".[89]

[89] This is also noticed in Western countries. As pointed out by Braithwaite et al, the failure of a dinner to be waiting on the table is a surprisingly common trigger of domestic violence in Australia and this is an effect that "is contingent upon patriarchal values among men who have expectations that cannot easily be met when their partners work (Braithwaite et al, 1998:224).

3.2.3 Theoretical model of economic change, gender and spouse abuse connection
Both my respondents' accounts and other sources of information about domestic violence in countries included in my survey show that instability of social status and income, radical changes in financial situation (impoverishment/ enrichment), housing problems and related changes in gender identities and gender power imbalance, are all strong predictors of spouse abuse. The risk of spouse abuse increases with the increase in the negative impact of any of these factors, and is most likely to occur when risk factors accumulate. Thus the most typical combinations of risk factors allowed me to construct three models of the interconnections between economic change, gender and spouse abuse:

Model 1
Financial problems;
High level of man's employment instability/long periods of unemployment;
Forced return to multi-generational family;
Man's use of alcohol;
Reversed gender roles and gender power relations
(marginalized masculinity/"hard" femininity).

Model 2
Financial problems;
High level of man' employment instability/long periods of unemployment,
Forced return to multi-generational family;
Man's use of alcohol;
Wife's employment instability/long periods of unemployment
Crises of both masculinity and femininity (marginalized masculinity/marginalized femininity).

Model 3
Instability of man's employment and income;
Retraditionalisation of gender role identities (hegemonic masculinity/emphasized femininity/crisis of socialist femininity).

3.3 Elderly, adult children and in-laws abuse

Apart from spousal relationships, changes related to social transition affected the way people live together with other members of the family as well. Both my own and other research findings show that negative effects of economic changes especially affected relationships between parents and adult children and relationships between in-laws. As in other societies, this kind of abuse usually includes either psychological violence, economic violence or neglect, or a combination of one or both with physical violence (Gelles, 1997:116). Since abuse of elderly and adult children prevails, I will address it first emphasizing when necessary the presence of violence against in-laws.

Elder abuse in post-communist society is generally expressed in a similar way as in relatively stable societies. As in Western societies, for example, elder abuse appears as a result of several risk factors, which may exist simultaneously as well: dysfunction of the family relations and psychopathology of the abuser; intergenerational transmission of violence; victim's dependency on the abuser and the offender's dependency on the victim; external stress and social isolation (Brogden and Nijhar, 2000:77; Bennett and Kingston, 1993:17). My research clearly shows the impact of structural changes on all modes of elderly abuse, arguing against abuse studies based on a pathological approach, which fail to locate household victimization within the wider social structure (Brogden and Nijhar, 2000:83).

Elder abuse, but also abuse of adult children and in-lows, in post-communist and post-conflict society is clearly connected to an increase of multi-generational families (and multiple family households) resulting from economic difficulties, housing problems and forced migration. The increase of multi-generational families and multiple family households is often connected with, or the result of dependency of either adult children or parents, or their interdependency in the conditions of scarcity. Difficulties in gaining economic independence, including one's own household, force adult children to stay living with their parents at an age when they are expected to lead life on their own. The very fact that several generations live together is a source of the stress, and economic hardships make the situation more complicated and tense.

Financial dependence of adult children on their parents and related generational identity crises, combined often with gender identity crises, seem to be strong predictor of the abuse of the elderly in post-communist society. One of the most often mentioned motives for elder abuse is related to housing: children and their spouses abuse mothers with whom they live, in order to force them to move from the flat, to sell the flat and give them money etc. For example, a woman living in Serbia took in her son and grandson who came to live with her after escaping from Croatia. Her daughter-in-law, who was a Croat, remained in Croatia. The Serbian woman's son and his child became economically dependent on the mother and beat and eventually expelled her from the apartment.

Alcohol and drug abuse of adult children contribute as well, since drug addicted and alcoholic children are often those who sell property, blackmail and physically abuse parents in order to get money for drugs and alcohol[90]. As in Western countries, available data seem to suggest that abusers are most often sons, while victims are predominantly mothers (Gelles, 1997:117). However, the phenomenon is still largely hidden from the public and there is evidence of daughters' abuse of mothers as well. Thus, it seems that, when elder abuse is in question, the impact of gender is less important as a predictor of abuse in comparison to economic difficulties and pathology.

However, the extended financial dependence of adult children on their parents sometimes makes them vulnerable to their parents' abuse. As noticed by Coffield,

[90] Both drug and alcohol abuse is reported to be increasing in post-communist society (Nikolic, 1998).

(1987:91), the problems in relationships arise in connection with economic dependence of young people on their parents, as well as with their extended presence in an often overcrowded flat/house. The abuse is most often psychological, including control which directly hurts the adult child's age and gender identity, but it may also include physical violence. Most often this kind of abuse involves fathers as abusers and daughters as victims. As well noticed by Coffield (1987:93), when looking at similar problems in Britain, "arguments over money and domestic chores between parents and unemployed daughters who had been drawn back into unpaid work in the home served only to bring out into the open within some families the power relations rooted in gender (and age), and the consequent sexual division of labor within the household".

Also, abused adult children are often those who had to live in the same accommodation with their parents. However, my interviews also stressed the cases where adult daughters and their spouses suffered psychological abuse in spite of the fact that they were living on their own. Their parent's intrusive, insulting and controlling behavior was mostly connected to the fact that the adult children relied on them for financial help so that parents assumed that they maintained the right to interfere in their lives (Coneva, interview, 1999). In some cases, however, a father's physical violence against his adult daughter is only an extension of his earlier abuse of the whole family and sometimes even includes sexual violence after the death of the mother.

The increased dependency of old people in countries in transition is also an important contributing factor to elder abuse. In spite of the fact that they usually have pensions, they are, as I already mentioned, often so small that they cannot live on them. As noticed by McWilliams (1998:131), in societies under stress, where traditional income-generating systems break down, "elderly women are more likely to put pressure on their families for material support." Thus, the fact that their caretakers, usually their children and their spouses, are in very difficult economic situations, make them additionally vulnerable to violence and neglect.

3.4 Vulnerability to domestic violence: the influence of ethnic conflict and war

Apart from direct consequences such as war destruction, war crimes and other forms of direct victimization, ethnic conflicts and war in the former Yugoslavia had serious impact on the way people live together as well. Among the countries included in the survey, they had an impact (in addition to the impact of social transition) on women's vulnerability to domestic violence, primarily in Serbia and to some extent (in relation to forced migration and related economic difficulties) in Macedonia.[91]

War related worsening of spouse and family relationships in Serbia was connected to the disturbance in inter-ethnic relationships, to men's decisions to go to and return from warfare, to difficulties brought on by forced migration, as well as to

[91] Consequently, the discussion in this chapter will be focused on the situation in Serbia, while refugee connected tensions and violence discussed in previous chapters address the situation both in Serbia and Macedonia.

feelings of insecurity, powerlessness and existential fears connected to the NATO bombing of Serbia. My findings suggest that the impact of war is usually combined with the impact of economic difficulties, as well as that the risk for women to become victims of domestic violence increases with an increase in the presence of both sorts of factors in their lives (e.g. often they live in mixed marriages, are refugees confronted with economic hardships, and their husbands spent some time in war and suffer from post traumatic stress disorder and crisis of masculinity).

The disturbance in inter-ethnic relationships connected to ethnic conflicts in the former Yugoslavia affected the lives of spouses who belong to different ethnic groups, whether they lived in territories directly or indirectly (such as Serbia) affected by ethnic conflicts. Domestic violence in these cases is usually connected to the woman's belonging to a different ethnic group. The phenomenon of abstract hatred directed against other nationalities was smoothly transformed into a hatred of very close persons such as wives, children, and relatives. In some cases, violence became more drastic because of the wife's belonging to a different ethnic group, while in some cases nationalism even provoked violent behavior from husbands.

The husband may come to see a woman of another nationality as a concrete symbol of "the enemy" and/or as a part of his property which has become worthless because of her ethnic origin. The woman becomes a source of the man's shame and problems in his interactions with significant persons outside the family. Consequently, the man feels not only that his identity as a man is in danger, but that his ethnic identity is also in danger since his wife's ethnic background is the obstacle to complete social acceptance (Nikolic-Ristanovic, 1996a). Thus his violent behavior is his way to confirm both his masculinity and his ethnic loyalty, i.e. to meet social expectations about them. Sometimes it is a consequence of the hegemonic masculinity of a man from the dominant ethnic group, but sometimes it is an expression of masculinity, marginalized because of economic position, ethnicity or both.

A Croat woman reported that in the last two years she "had been suffering from awful violence committed by her Serbian husband because of her nationality." He had also molested her earlier but with the beginning of war and nationalism he became completely insupportable. He also turned the child against her. One other Croat woman was divorced but because of a bad financial situation had to continue to live in the same apartment with her husband who was Serb. The husband's entire family blamed her for the war and the bad political situation. Her former husband became violent with the beginning of nationalism and beat her several times so that she had serious injuries and had to stay in hospital. One Croat woman said that during 1992 she noticed changes in her husband's behavior. He started to insult her because of her ethnic origin and bring other women to their home. He also threatened to "dig out her eyes with screwdriver"

In addition to beating them, some Serbian men forced their Croat wives to go back to Croatia, although they had been living in Serbia for more than 20 years. Serbian women who lived with Croats as well as Muslims and Albanians married to Serbs reported a similar pattern of violence.

For example, one Muslim woman whose husband was Serb was beaten regularly from the beginning of the war. Earlier she was happy with her husband but when the war broke out friends began to accuse her husband saying:" Why did you choose to marry a Muslim among so many Serbian women". They found her guilty for everything that Moslems did against Serbs. And he started to beat her every night after drinking with his friends. She had serious injuries and tried to flee with their child. However, he would not allow her to bring the child with her saying:" This is a Serbian child and must stay here"(Nikolic-Ristanovic, 1996:207).

But the impact of disturbance in inter-ethnic relations can also be interlaced with financial difficulties and marginalized masculinity connected to that. This is well described by a respondent from Serbia, married to a Croat woman.

> They married in 1987 and, in the beginning, they were living together with his parents. Soon life with his parents became unsupportable, among other things, because of her ethnic origin. Then, they moved to a rented flat and their financial situation started to grow worse and worse, especially when he lost his job. He did not allow his wife to work, in spite of her insistence on it and her dissatisfaction with bad conditions in the flat where they moved. Their arguments then started mostly about financial matters and the flat. At the same time, she was also under pressure from her parents to leave him and come back to Croatia. All that seriously affected their relationship, putting constant pressure on the husband's feeling of inadequacy as the breadwinner and seriously affecting their communication. It finally led to physical violence and the woman divorcing him.

Domestic violence is also connected to family disputes about men's decision to go to war and the ex-soldiers' stresses and desires to regain their status in the family. Also, men who, during the war, went occasionally to see their wives and parents as well as some of those who came back home, were also reported to be violent, tending to show their newly won hegemonic masculinity, often using weapons. More frequent use of weapons in domestic violence is reported by women in Croatia and Northern Ireland as well (Kelly, 2000:59). As observed by McWilliam (1998:132), "the interconnection of militarism and masculinity" means that there is "a much wider tendency to use, or to threaten to use guns in the control and abuse of women within the context of domestic violence."

At the very beginning of the war in the former Yugoslavia some women reported a so-called "post TV violence syndrome" (Fischer, 1994:165). This means that their husbands became very aggressive after watching TV News, Channel 1[92], since the main war propaganda was effected through this broadcasting. Some men made decisions to go to fight after watching this broadcasting and when women started to speak about their worries and fears for them, their violence broke out. Obviously, men became nervous because they were convinced that they should go to fight but, at the same time, they were faced with lack of courage to do it. In such cases every reaction of woman (wives as well as mothers) might be the source of the man's aggression, since it contributed to their frustration related to their difficulty in identifying with widespread cultural images of militarized masculinity. And it is also often connected to their failure to achieve the role of breadwinner One such scene is described by one of my male respondents from Serbia:

[92] Similarly, as pointed out by Kelly, during the Gulf War women told stories of their husbands dressing in army uniforms before beating them, frequently after watching the TV news (Kelly, 2000:59).

"When the war in Croatia started I still had some illusions about "Serbianhood" so that I decided to go to Slavonia as a volunteer. However, I soon realized that it was not the same as I thought, so I came back home after some time... I remember the day when I was leaving. Days before I had arguments with everyone in the home. My parents as well as my wife were against it. I remember that one morning she told me everything: that I am not capable to do anything by my own and, well, that I am a coward since I am escaping from real problems into imagined ones. This latter was the truth, since at that time I had a state job and my salary was extremely small... We were already distant, we did not understand each other. This was one of the uglier scenes and I hit her"

A similar experience was described by female respondent who opposed her son's positive answer to the draft, at a time when her husband was already in the war. She experienced severe psychological violence and pushing, while she was crying and attempting to persuade her son not to go

Moreover, as Women in Black from Belgrade reported, even the rejection of militarized masculinity through avoidance of military service sometimes led to violence committed against the same women who helped men to hide (Zajovic, 1995:174).[93] As noticed in relation to the Vietnam War, men may develop post-traumatic stress disorder even when they refuse to go to war. Faludi has well stated that "these men weren't wrong to feel pain, anger, and a sense that they were incomplete. By the terms of their country's definition of masculinity, they had been 'left out" (Faludi, 2000:311). Apart from the feeling that they are not behaving in the expected masculine way, Serbian men often developed a fear of authority as well, which haunted them even when the danger stopped. This was a source of stress as well. One man, who went for professional help, said:

" I used to sleep at a different place every night. I felt like a hunted beast, I used to jump at every single sound of the doorbell. When the danger disappeared, I though I was saved. However, the fear was still here. I became nervous and could not sleep. I got used to beer and tranquilizers. After my parents insisted on it, I went to see the doctor."[94]

Soldiers and ex-soldiers tended to show their new hegemonic masculinity in different ways: from patrolling the streets of their towns fully equipped with and waving pistols and bombs to bringing mistresses home, insulting and beating their wives and mothers, expelling them from homes etc. (Cetkovic, 1998:105-6). The violence is especially likely to occur when the woman resists the man's attempts to control her, or otherwise frustrates him in his attempts to assume a position of dominance, i.e. strong and "manly" behavior (Matsakis, 1996:183). Ex-soldiers may be incapable of controlling their rage, or may show extraordinarily intense emotions in normal situations. The study of PTSD among Vietnam veterans showed that there are more problems and more violence in families of Vietnam veterans with PTSD than in families of those without it (Kulka et al, 1990:237). Feeling out of control and

[93] Expression of masculinity by men who refused to go to war through aggressive behavior against women working with them on the antiwar campaign was noticed in USA during the Vietnam War as well. As Faludi wrote, when antiwar activist "Marilyn Salzman Webb rose to speak at an antiwar rally in 1969, men in the audience yelled out: 'Take her off the stage and fuck her."(Faludi, 2000:311).

[94] K.Preradovic "Lud je onaj ko je normalan" (The normal one is mad), *Blic News*, 29.3.2000, p.6-9

emasculated (by his own emotions, which, except for the anger, he may view as "feminine"), an ex-soldier may attempt to regain a sense of control and affirm his manhood by battering. And, as Matsakis (1996:183) put it, battering also "helps release the mounting adrenaline caused by his pent-up emotions and inner turmoil". Also, Women's Aid from Dublin, reports on the plight of Bosnian women who were made to seek refuge twice- once from the Serbian army who had displaced them from their homes and again from their husbands who used domestic violence as a means of venting their frustration at their own "powerless" situation. (McWilliams: 1998:128) Similarly, a woman refugee from Bosnia who came as a refugee to Serbia lives with her husband and child in a rented apartment. Both spouses are unemployed. When the husband came back from war he started to consume alcohol, to rape, beat and threaten his wife with a knife. She would like to leave him but does not have anywhere to go.

The men's frustrations are especially emphasized when they are both former soldiers and multiple refugees (e.g. forced to move from one part of Croatia to another and then to Serbia), and if they are dependent on their wives, as in the case of one of my respondents whose husband threatened to kill her several times.[95] Also, violent ex-soldiers often had experiences from several wars and this prolonged war experience created both an enormous "dependence on violence" and an enormous feeling of failure and futility as a consequence of unexpected rejection or ignorance by the society. As a result, their violent behavior in the home progressed over time, so that, as one woman told me, "from every war they became worse and worse". Once again my findings agree with findings of research on wife beating in other wars, which show that the coincidence of war-related risks and negative changes in man's social and economic status is especially likely to lead to violence against women (Matsakis, 1996:195) Additionally, post-war surroundings sometimes transform women into martyrs: they are expected to suffer the consequences of men's post-war trauma. (Andric-Ruzicic, 1999; Corrin, 1999:73) As noticed by a Croatian women's organization, "domestic violence, which has always been considered a minor, women's problem (if a problem at all), has become a woman's patriotic duty...Their duty is to make the pains of 'our soldiers' easier, to be understanding and patient." (Boric and Desnica, 1996:135-6).

Another problem is long term separation of spouses, which may be the source of conflicts connected to men's frustrations because of difficulties to adapt to changed division of labor caused by war. Women's active role and proven ability to undertake both female and male role in the family may additionally lower men's already low self-esteem related to his lost role in the family (Andric-Ruzicic, 1999:15; Mitic, 1997:110; Euler and Welzer-Lang, 2000; Moser, 2001:47) As pointed out by Connell, violence may result from a man's attempt .to re-assert a damaged masculine ego (Connell, 1995a:128).

The crisis of male identity as a contributing factor to domestic violence connected to war is also connected to a man's feeling of helplessness, i.e. marginalization as a man, in relation to oppression done by other men who happen to be much more powerful. As well noticed by El-Bushra (2000:80), in the notion of "hegemonic masculinity" "the differences of power and status between men merge with those between men and

[95] For similar experiences among Vietnam veterans see Matsakis, 1996:183

women, with the result that certain groups of men are allocated characteristics normally associated with women". A similar effect occurred with both soldiers and male civilians during the NATO bombing of Serbia.

Women mainly reported long-term violence, which either continued with the same intensity or became worse during the bombing. Only occasionally, women mentioned that the violence started at that time. Alcohol as a contributing factor to domestic violence increased as well (Nikolic-Ristanovic and Milivojevic, 2000:21). Women often stated that their husbands' and sons' increased consumption of alcohol was caused by their fear of bombing and "long hours", since they stopped working when the bombing started. Also, some women reported that their mentally ill husbands became more violent because of their worsening health under the stress produced by bombing. As in peacetime, abuse by alcoholics and mentally ill men were especially brutal.

As circumstances which precipitated violence, women often mentioned circumstances directly or indirectly related to bombing. A woman said that she was beaten, since, having in mind intensive bombing in close neighborhood and her daughter's fear, she insisted that her husband make the shelter convenient for them. Another woman said that, from the beginning of bombing her husband became more violent than earlier since they did not agree in their political assessments of the situation. In addition to beating, several women were expelled from apartments in the middle of the night, when the bombing was the most intense.

Men's violence also intensified because of difficulties divorced women faced during the bombing in providing visitation. Sometimes, men also used the bombing as a pretext for not bringing children to see their mother.

4. OBSTACLES TO LEAVING THE ABUSER AND GETTING PROTECTION

As in Western society, in post-communist society economic dependence, unsupportive institutions and sex role socialization combine "to make the task of leaving an abusive relationship particularly difficult"(Schechter, 1982:232). Both my own and earlier research findings (Gelles, 1997:88; Schur, 1987:157; Mooney, 2000:148; Zlatanova, 2001:75; Caceva and Coneva, 2000) suggest serious negative consequences from the worsening of women' s economic position, not only for their vulnerability to violence but also for their possibility to leave the abuser.[96] Moreover, as stated by Stanojevic (interview, 1999), economic hardships affect women' s potential to find an exit from violence more than they generate violence itself.

[96] Statistics on divorce in post-communist countries show that divorce rates fell during the initial years of the transition, i.e. during the most severe economic crises, and started to rise recently, following the positive effects of economic reforms. (UNICEF, 1999) It is not unusual since divorce rates in general reflect spouses' ability to support themselves (Brinton, 1983, quoted by Huber, 1991:18).

Many women want to divorce but are not able to provide for themselves and their children.[97] Due to their economic dependence on men and general impoverishment, women often do not have money to pay the legal expenses of divorce. Due to poverty, a deteriorating housing situation and the long duration of divorce and common property division procedures (especially in Bulgaria), women must remain with the men they are divorcing for a significant period of time. In addition, women are aware that their chances to survive on their own are not realistic, since it is well known that divorce is "extremely bad news for women everywhere" (Crompton and Mann, 1994:XVI), and especially in undeveloped countries. In these situations, violence often gets worse, but there are also cases where earlier nonviolent husbands become violent when they are forced to live in the same apartment with their former wives.

As pointed out by experts from Serbia and Macedonia,[98] due to the increase of poverty brought on by the economic transition and war, both women's personal resources and their ability to get aid from others decreased. Since women's capacity to cope is enhanced by support from close relatives in general (Penkower et al., 1988, quoted by Waddington et al., 1998:235), and, having in mind very close ties between relatives in the countries under examination in particular, lack of support is a heavy obstacle to a woman's efforts to leave her abuser. This is especially true when the woman's parents are refugees, as in the case of a woman from Serbia.

The woman wanted to leave her violent husband. However, her economic situation was so desperate that, although she was employed, she did not get any salary for months and did not have money to pay for an abortion. The lack of money for the abortion put the woman in an even worse situation, since it led to having more children and decreasing her possibilities to leave the abuser.

The ability of refugee women to leave violent partners is additionally decreased by the fact that, due to forced migration, they often lose their entire informal support network (Andric-Ruzicic, 1999:17; Mitic, 1997:122).

Sometimes, support is missing even when members of the family are able to help or at least offer the woman temporary shelter. The reason may be fear but also patriarchal expectations for the woman to stay married whatever her relationship with the husband (Bethlen and Minkova, interviews, 1999). In that regard, the *United Nations Development Program* in Sofia reports:

> "It is easy to understand why women beaten by their husbands keep silent on the matter. They feel shame, humiliation and lack of understanding even on the part of their relatives and friends, and finally, the hopelessness of the situation." (quoted from Minnesota Advocates, 1996).

Apart from parents, adult sons are often in a position where they can help their mothers, but they sometimes refuse to do it in solidarity with their father or in fear of losing their own material security.

[97] Dr. Ljubica Coneva says that the arrival of NATO and UN soldiers in Macedonia had an impact on the increase of prices of rented apartments and, in this way, negatively impacted already bad prospects for victims of violence to leave molesters (interview, 1999).

[98] Interview with Nada Polovina, psychologist from Serbia and interview with Dusko Minkovski from Macedonia conducted in 1999.

The importance of a woman's economic independence for her ability to leave the molester is underscored in the rare examples of women who succeeded in this action immediately after they got a job or started a private business and became economically independent from their husbands.

Apart from economic problems and the lack of family support, women also have difficulty leaving violent husbands due to fear that they may take the children or kill them and the children. One important obstacle in leaving the abuser is the inefficiency of the legal system and social services. Women often point out the inefficiency of the police, social welfare agencies, and psychiatrists (in cases of mentally ill husbands).

Apart from the usual refusals of the police to react in cases of domestic violence, which they consider trivial, the refusals are connected to solidarity with the abuser as a colleague or friend, as well as to corruption. In some cases, the police not only refuse to help but also take the abuser's side (Najcevska, interview, 1999) and maltreat the women involved (Nikolic-Ristanovic and Milivojevic, 2000:23). Men often know people who work within the criminal justice system so that, as one woman said, they are usually "more protected than their victims."[99] An especially difficult situation in this regard was reported by partners of new rich and other influential men, who misused their influence to maintain their violent behavior without consequences. [100] Corruption was especially stressed by women victims of violence in Serbia, where police officers refused to intervene after men gave them money or gas, or sold them foreign currencies at low prices.[101] The criminal justice system is also often sympathetic toward a violent man if he spent some time in war[102]. The inefficiency of the legal system is also obvious in relation to violence connected to men's visitation rights as well as in the absence of any protective measures against the abuser. This is particularly true during and after the divorce procedures – women do not feel secure either at home, where they usually live with the abuser, or at work, or on the street. Shelters for battered women either do not exist or there is one or two for the entire country. The case recorded by NANE (a women's organization which supports victims of domestic violence in Hungary) may be a good illustration of how inappropriate legal solutions and a lack of temporary accommodations in transition societies can serve as serious obstacles to women's ability to leave violent husbands, even when they are divorced:

[99] "Pekolen dom" (Hall house), *KISS*, 15 January 1999.

[100] "Semejnata kuka - kuka na strav i uzas"(Family house - house of fear and horror), *Vecer*, 18-19 December, 1999, p.4

[101] Since UN economic sanctions were imposed on Serbia in 1992, the black market started to flourish, including the gas and foreign currency black market. Because selling things and using foreign currency on the domestic market is considered illegal, (although at the same time this is necessity), this created a large space for police blackmails and corruption.

[102] Moreover, even judges from Western countries sometimes sympathize with soldiers who spent some time in the Balkans. For example, the man who was sent to Kosovo as a part of NATO peacekeeping force and who attacked his fiancée, when he came back home, was set free by a judge from Portsmouth Crown Court. The judge told him on that occasion: "Good soldiers are hard to come by. ("Army Brute Freed", *Daily Mail*, November 23, 1999).

> "The woman left her husband with her one year old daughter and went to live in a small apartment which her parents bought for her. She then applied for a divorce. When she moved to this flat, her ex-husband started to come and stalk her. He came every day and molested her, kicked the door, etc. The woman's parents came to live with her, so she would not be alone. The apartment was too small for all of them. She went to the police but they said that they did not want to interfere. Also, according to visitation rights laws, she still had to allow the father to see the child. Once, when she went to pick up the child from the father, her ex-husband raped her. She then called NANE. But the ex-husband still came to the apartment and kicked the door. She did not go to the husband's apartment anymore and, on visitation rights days, they exchanged the child in public places. On one of these occasions, he beat her in a public place. She was also raped again by him. She was a nurse in the hospital and he called the hospital to find out when she was working. Once, when she was going to work, he used a knife and forced her (there were many witnesses) to go to his place, where he raped her very brutally. He also took photos when he was raping her and then made her sign a document that she was engaging in the act willingly and that she did not want anything from him. He also made her sign a document claiming that she owed debts to him. The woman then went to the police. The police came immediately to his apartment and confiscated all the evidence."[103]

As with abused partners, abused mothers and daughters also have problems leaving abusers - due to economic dependence on the abuser and also because they are emotionally tied to them. This latter is especially true for elderly women whose abusive sons are economically dependent on them. However, in spite of that, they only rarely ask for help and try to make them leave home.

Ethnic conflicts, the NATO bombing combined with UN economic sanctions, as well as the almost complete disappearance of the rule of law, and the ensuing long-term political instability of the country, have contributed to make the already mentioned obstacles to women's ability to leave the abuser especially severe in Serbia. As McWilliams stated, referring to the situation in Northern Ireland, in societies under stress, there are fewer options for women and fewer controls on men (McWilliams, 1998:138)[104]Thus, while, on one hand, the beginning or aggravation of domestic violence is connected to a soldier's return home, heightening of interethnic hatred, frustration of refugee status and war and post-war economic hardships, on the other hand, women's options to leave violent husbands and to get protection become significantly lower. And when "women's ability to resist the violence is curtailed, then they become more vulnerable in their homes with fewer options open to them" (McWilliams, 1998:137).

Also, as pointed out by Vesna Stanojevic,[105] even when life with the molester is insupportable, women often postpone the decision to divorce because of general insecurity and uncertainty.[106] However, in spite of the war and the general deteriorating economic situation, during the NATO bombing many women came to *Counseling*

[103] Interview with Anna Bethlen, Hungary, 1999.

[104] Similar is noticed in after-war Bosnia-Herzegovina as well (Andric-Ruzicic, 1999:17).

[105] Interviews conducted on March 5 and August 4, 1999.

[106] This was especially emphasized during NATO threats of bombing Serbia in October 1998, which put severe psychological pressure on ordinary, helpless people. Autonomous Women's Center from Belgrade reported that during bombing women used to take more attention to poverty than to violence. They quote one woman who said: "I don't mind if he beats me up, it is important that I have food for the children" - "Radionice protiv straha" (Workshops against fear), *Glas*, 9 September, 1999.

Service Against Domestic Violence ready for a divorce. A similar development was mentioned by refugee women who made the simultaneous decision to leave both the violent husbands and their country. Ironically, a war can also help women leave violent husbands under the pretext of seeking refuge to protect themselves and their children. (Nikolic-Ristanovic, 1996:208) It is known from other wars that crisis can empower women and sometimes encourage them to rely less on marriage as a means of support. (El-Bushra and Lopez, 1993:25)

5. TOWARD AN EXPLANATION OF SOCIAL CHANGE, GENDER AND DOMESTIC VIOLENCE

As O'Nail and Egan put it, "gender role conflict and violence are both interrelated examples of abuses of power. 'Gender roles mediate power relations' as 'men and women learn different perspectives on power that affect their interpersonal dynamics (O'Neil and Egan, 1992, quoted by Nutt, 1999:119). Similarly, my survey findings suggest significant impacts of both male and female gender role identity changes. It is obvious that a disadvantaged socioeconomic position of both women and man, mediated by changes in their gender identities, has a significant impact on women's vulnerability to violence in the family.

Although hegemonic masculinity has a significant impact as well, it seems that in reality marginalised masculinity is a better predictor of violence against women in the family than hegemonic masculinity. Thus, the high level of oppression experienced by men in connection with social change has a strong impact on their violent behavior against women close to them. However, I do not want to argue that the impact of hegemonic masculinity as a cultural ideal is decreasing in post-communist and post-conflict society. On the contrary, its impact is increasing and since it is strongly associated with aggressiveness and "capacity for violence" (Connell, 1995a:128), violence, especially violence against those even less powerful such as women and children, is often the only kind of hegemonic masculinity they are able to associate with.

As Messerschmidt (1993:147) points out "wife beaters (regardless of their class and race position) presume they have the patriarchal right - because it is part of their 'essential nature' - to dominate and control their wives, and wife beating serves both to ensure continued compliance with their commands and as a resource for constructing a 'damaged' patriarchal masculinity". In addition, Messerschmidt stresses that battering is a resource for affirming "maleness" and, therefore, economically disadvantaged men are more likely to engage in wife beating in order to reestablish their maleness than economically advantaged men (Messerschmidt, 1993:149).

On the other side, the increased oppression of women increases their vulnerability to violence, while at the same time decreases their chances to escape it. However, as shown by research findings about abuse of indigenous women in Australia and abuse of black women in Britain, economic dependence seems not to be central to female abuse in post-communist and post-conflict society, as Western research conducted in white communities often suggests (Mama, 2000:53; Blagg, 2000:5). As my research findings show, many women in post-communist society are economically active, while their husbands are marginalized in different ways. Thus, as within black Western communities and in post-colonial countries, economic difficulties, housing problems, war and oppression of men as a reflection of broader structures of economic, sexual and ethnic inequalities in society (Atkinson, quoted by Blagg, 2000: 4; Schechter, 1982:236; Sanchez-Hucles and Ann Dutton, 1999:189), seem to have a bigger impact on women's vulnerability to violence than women's economic dependence itself.[107]

This is clearly supported by my findings which are consistent with findings of Western research on abusive men, which show that abusive men tend to have following individual and situational characteristics: the gap between dependence on their partners and their rigid patriarchal socialization; alcohol and/or drug use; depression; low self esteem and feeling of inadequacy; "Jekill and Hide" characteristics; isolation; stress and status inconsistency or unemployment (Stordeur and Stille, 1989:37-54; Gelles, 1997:79,80).

Moreover, my research findings show, not only that these characteristics, individually and especially when cumulative, increase the likelihood for violence to occur. They also show that in post-communist, and, especially, in post-conflict society these are characteristics of a large number of men within society, so that social predispositions for domestic violence are widespread throughout society. As Atkinson (1991, quoted by Blagg:2000:4) stressed the significance of the "dynamic interplay between indigenous masculinity 'in crisis' and colonial relationship, I can argue the existence of the same between a crisis of masculinity, (post) communism and war, in the broader context of globalization, i.e. the new social order.

On the other side, women's poor economic situation in general, which does not allow her to live on her own even when she is not economically dependent on her partner, is more significant in terms of being an obstacle to women's ability to leave violent men than as a factor which contribute to violence itself.

It seems that man's transition toward unemployment, i.e. poor socioeconomic status, is a source of risk for women. But, even more, as both my and previous research conducted in Western countries showed (Braithwaite et al., 1998:17; Waddington et al. 1998:234; Rounsavill, 1978, quoted by Stordeur and Stille, 1989:51;Gelles, 1997:85), it is woman's transition toward employment, i.e. better socioeconomic position in comparison to a man. My research findings confirm the findings of other studies dealing with the connection between employment and domestic violence. Such research is Allen and Strauss's (1980:203) survey of 400 couples which showed that "the more the wife's resources exceed those of her husband, the more likely the husband is to have physical force during the referent

[107] It was also stressed by some Western authors but in a different context: the impact of the changing structural relationships between the sexes that occurred during the twentieth century, and which continues, appears to be taking its toll on personal relationships. Thus, although the nature of social change is different, the final result seems to be similar. As well pointed out by Giddens: "A large amount of male sexual violence now stems from insecurity and inadequacy rather than from a seamless continuation of patriarchal dominance. Violence is a destructive reaction to the waning of female complicity (Giddens, 1992, quoted by Walkate, 2001:123).

year." Similarly, Gartner and McCarthy (1991:305) found that married women were at "greater risk of femicide if their employment status exceeds their husbands'", but at lower risk if their husband's employment status exceeds theirs."

As reported by some researchers, violence tends to gravitate toward the partner with the greatest power and toward relationships with the greatest power differential (Finkelhor, 1983, quoted by Cahn, 1996:11). Thus, while egalitarian couples had the lowest rates of conflict and violence, male-dominant and female-dominant couples had the highest rates (Coleman and Straus, 1986, quoted by Cahn, 1996:11). However, although it is clear that family relationships "suffer" very much during social crises, it is also clear that even in these extraordinary circumstances and in the presence of a serious gender power imbalance, a lot of men actually do not use violence in the home.

It seems that we cannot ignore the impact of psychological factors, and especially the connection between identity and relationship concerns. My findings seem to confirm Cahn's (1996:14) suggestion that men's physical violence as compensatory behavior may have been motivated by identity concerns (appearing dominant) to make up for their lack of power (relationship concern). According to Finkelhor and Pillemer (1988, quoted by Brogden and Nijhar, 2000:115), violence as a response to 'a perceived lack of power' can be seen as a common element in family violence, including partner, child and elderly abuse. Or, even more accurate, as suggested by Gadd (2000:103), violence should be seen as indicative of 'emasculated weakness'. Men use violence to assert their difference from and dominance over others when their authority is challenged or exhibits 'crisis tendencies' (Connell, 1995:84-6).

It is also important to note the fact known to those who work with violent men, and that I also learned from my interviewees, that abusers only rarely perceive themselves as those who act in order to maintain or re-establish power. On the contrary, they rather perceive women as powerful sources of the fear and vulnerability they feel in themselves (Gadd, 2000:236). Or, as pointed out by Schechter (1982:219), men are not necessarily consciously aware of their need to dominate, but they are rather socialized to feel uncomfortable when not in control, and they turn to violence as a response to their discomfort.

Abusive men and their victims often construct reality in completely different ways so that it is important, when studying family violence, to examine the meanings members attribute to one another's messages (Cahn, 1996:18). If we want to address men's violence against women in an appropriate way, this is unavoidable in any society, and in a society under stress, where so many men (and women) feel vulnerable, in particular. However, how men will react (by use of violence or otherwise) to the situation where they feel vulnerable depends on many factors, some of which, as Gadd (2000:277) suggests, may be: man's history of anxiety and desire, his socio-economic status, and the ongoing intersubjective dynamics between him and others who lend meaning to his situation. Indeed, there are still many men, who became unemployed as a consequence of social transition and war but are not violent toward their partners and other female family members. Some of them project blame for their redundancy on the government state elite, political change or new world order. Some became more caring and protective in their roles as partners, sons or fathers and, if conflicts occur, they are seen as a part of temporary strains in relationships of intimates who have so many things in common.

But how are we to explain, indeed, the fact shown so clearly by mine (as well as by other research) that men's violent behavior is the expression of both man's power (hegemonic masculinity) and powerlessness (marginalized masculinity)? It seem that it would be impossible without using psychoanalysis and taking into account both tensions between social and psychic and gender roles conflict. As well noticed by Gadd (2000:281), "men's experiences of masculinity are not one or the other. They are both/and. Men who are violent may experience feelings of considerable social power, as well as terrifying fear of powerlessness".

This tension/conflict may well explain why in post-communist and post-conflict society violence is connected to both (apparent) newly won (hegemonic) masculinity and masculinity crises, i.e. frustration because of a widening gap between the cultural ideal and actually achieved masculinity. However, we cannot understand this tension/conflict without bearing in mind gender-role conflict experienced by both women and men under the influence of different macrosocial factors resulting from transition and war. Similarly as in Western society, as stated by Nutt (1999:118), in post-communist society women experience devaluation both because they exhibit power in stereotypically masculine ways or because they express powerlessness that is traditionally associated with the feminine stereotype.

Gender-role conflict experienced by women interlace with the gender-role conflict of men and predisposes the latter for violence. As well noticed by O'Neil and Nadeau (1999:100), and confirmed by my findings, "the documented relationship between men's gender-role conflict and men's negative emotions has implications for understanding men's gender-role identity and their potential for violence. Men's uses of power and control are potentially defensive and self-protective". Thus, on one side, men may believe that demonstrating power and control over others has a meaning of proving their masculinity to others so that they have difficulty giving up power and control during interpersonal conflicts since they are afraid that they would appear unmanly, feminine (O'Neil and Nadeau, 1999:103). On the other side, as the same authors stated, one of men's greatest fears is to be emasculated, and when they fear being emasculated they may use power and control in order to demonstrate their strength and manhood. "Some men irrationally equate loss of power and control with a loss of masculinity. It is well known that when men lose their power, they are more likely to use abuse and violence to compensate for the loss" (O'Neil and Nadeau, 1999:103).

My research findings seem to show that in post-communist society, as in Western society, the main sources of conflict leading to violence may be described as: "Men's possessiveness and jealousy, men's expectations concerning women's domestic work, men's sense of the right to punish "their" women for perceived wrongdoing and the importance to men of maintaining or exercising their position of authority" (Dobash and Dobash, 1992:4). But it also seems that communication skills are an important factor which may contribute either to conflict resolution or to its aggravation. Or as stressed by Waddington et al. (1998:252), the prior nature of the marital relationship will provide mechanisms for conflict resolution or escalation.

Violence is not an isolated event in family life, but is "embedded firmly in the process of interpersonal communication which people use to regulate their daily lives" (Infante, Chandler and Rudd, 1989, quoted by Cahn, 1996:2). Violent men seem to have problems in expressing their opinions, feelings and desires in assertive ways (Ganley&Harris, 1978, quoted by Stordeur and Stille, 1989:41). Abusers, but often victims as well, lack adequate constructive communication, negotiation, problem-solving and argumentation skills (Cahn, 1996:12) or these skills are undermined as a consequence of stress (internal or external). Moreover, as Babcock et al. stressed (quoted by Lloyd, 1996:179), "when both husband and wife are low in communication ability, and when the husband is in a less powerful position, there is an increased risk of physical aggression", or it is more likely that physical violence will be added to earlier psychological violence (Sabourin, 1996:209).

Social stress obviously further deteriorates communication within the family. As many studies show, the likelihood of violence occurring increases with an increase in stressful experiences individuals and families have to deal with (Gelles, 1993:33). However, since the beginning of violence often coincides with the combination of external stress and already bad communication/relationships between victim and offender, it seems that external stress is more likely to influence the aggravation of existing violence than to provoke it (Andric-Ruzicic, 1999:20; Milosavljevic, 1997:15).

It seems that a theoretical model, which is most suitable for explanation of men's domestic violence in post-communist and war affected societies, is the revised multivariate model developed by O'Neil and Harway (1999:214, 215), since it takes into account multiple risk factors (both predispositions and factors which trigger violence against women) for men's violence against women:

a) Macrosocietal factors, i.e. the conditions and values in the larger society that directly or indirectly predispose men to violence against women by oppressing women (during history and in the present) but by oppressing men as well;
b) Relational risk factors (ongoing interactions and interpersonal patterns between partners such as each partner's personal history, family of origin background, personal cognitive and affective characteristics etc.);
c) Psychological risk factors (attitudes, values and behaviors that predispose or trigger violence)
d) Socialization risk factors such as learned roles, primarily gender roles in the family and in the larger society;
e) Psychosocial factors such as the interaction of a man's overall socialization and psychological processes in the context of a larger society.

As may be seen from enlisted risk factors, the multivariate model, similar to my survey findings, shows clearly that multiple risk factors that cause men's violence against women interact, vary and overlap in complex ways. Moreover, it accounts for the way macrosocietal factors, patriarchy as well as other forms of oppression of women as well as oppression of men are mirrored on the micro level, i.e. in gender role socialization, psychosocial characteristics of men and interactions between women and men. Indeed, as my survey findings show, it is not possible to understand domestic violence which occurs in post-communist and war-affected society without taking into account both macrosocial and micro (social and individual) risk factors which either predispose or trigger men's violence against women. Or, in other words, as O'Neil and Harway (1999:216) stressed "men's risk for violence against women can be conceptualized as an interaction between a man's personal, social, and psychological characteristics and societal structure that cause stress, strain, and personal problems".

As I have shown previously in this book, both the transition from communism and war produced rapid growth and a cummulation of negative impacts of macrosocial factors on individual women and men. Consequently, the cummulation of stress, strains and personal problems caused by historical and new macrosocial factors, and mediated by gender-role identity problems, significantly increased the vulnerability of women to violence by partners and other male members of the family. But, similarly as with domestic violence within the black community (and other marginal groups) in the USA, when societal, cultural and individual factors interact, they not only intensify vulnerability to violence but they also leave abused women less able to protect themselves (O'Neil and Harwey, 1999:196).

CHAPTER 5

SEX TRAFFICKING IN WOMEN

1. INTRODUCTION

Since the end of Cold war, the number of women from Central and Eastern Europe working as prostitutes in Western Europe (Bruinsma and Meershoek, 1999:107) and United States (Global Survival Network, 1997:7) increased rapidly. Statistics of STV (Foundation against Trafficking in Women) about women trafficked to The Netherlands, as one of the main destination countries within Europe, may serve as a good illustration for this trend. The number of victims from post-communist countries assisted by STV increased more than ten times since the beginning of transition so that in 1997 they made up two-thirds of the total number of victims who applied to the STV for support. (Bruinsma and Meershoek, 1999:108). A good illustration of the situation regarding trafficking in Europe is given by Thomas Bodstrom, justice minister in Sweden, after he met a woman in Sarajevo, who said she had been sold 18 times:

> "I think it surprised all of us that it was actually slavery going on in Europe. Bosnia has just been in a war - there is not the same possibility to have authority. But what can we say in Europe? In Sweden? Or in Holland? They are selling people. How many people, smuggled by whom? The truth is that we don't know."[108]

Exact figures and statistics are difficult to establish, primarily because of the reluctance of trafficked women to report, i.e. to identify themselves. Thus, in this chapter the overview of the scope of sex trafficking in countries included in the survey will be based on different (mainly non-official) estimations and surveys recently conducted in the region. Also, the analysis of both the characteristics of the phenomena and the main factors which contribute to and facilitate it will be made. I will look at how both changes in everyday life and in gender identities, caused by transition from communism and war, influence women's vulnerability to become victims of traffickers. Also, apart from looking at the impact of factors connected to specific countries, I will explore the impact of globalization and widening of economic inequalities between countries as well. My analysis in this chapter will be based on various data, and especially on case studies and my interviews in countries included in the research. For the reasons elaborated in the

[108] A.Smile "The Dark Side of the Global Economy", *New York Times*, August 26, 2001.

introductory chapter, unlike my data about domestic violence, sex trafficking data are rather secondary than primary.

2. SCOPE AND CHARACTERISTICS OF SEX TRAFFICKING

2.1 Sex trafficking of Hungarian, Macedonian, Bulgarian and Serbian women

Like women from other post-communist countries, women from Hungary, Macedonia, Bulgaria and Serbia are trafficked to and through different Western and East/Central European countries.

According to the Hungarian Central Office for Statistics, the most important countries of destination for Hungarian women are Austria, and then Germany, Italy and The Netherlands, while Croatia and Slovenia might become important in the future (IOM Report, 2000:3). Also, according to Feher, there is trafficking connected to weekend sex tourism to neighboring Austria (Feher, interview, 1999). For example, in 1990 the Austrian police discovered 50, and in 1994/95 751 victims who had arrived from East European countries, from whom 118 were from Hungary, 112 from Slovakia and 133 from the Czech Republic (Forrai, 1999:4). Also, in April 1998 the Austrian police uncovered a ring of traders in Slovak and Hungarian women, some of whom were underage, who were enticed from their home countries by advertisements promising they would earn up to 200,000 shillings a month.[109] According to some sources, women from Hungary are also trafficked to Canada,[110] as well as to Kosovo[111] and Mexico.[112]

A recent survey conducted in Hungary on a sample of 145 women/young girls showed that forced prostitution and trafficking in women are significant problems in this country. The findings of the survey showed that 19 percent of respondents personally know at least one woman who was forced into prostitution through violence or threats. Moreover, 17 percent of respondents personally know at least one woman who was sold abroad. The same survey also identified the most vulnerable group of women/young girls. Thus, girls/young women living in institutional care, with Roma girls and women prevailing among them, are identified as the highest risk group in terms of their vulnerability to trafficking in women. This is confirmed both by their own answers and the answers given by teachers working in institutional care, correctional facilities and

[109] "Austrian police free Slovak and Hungarian prostitutes", APA, 3 April 1998.

[110] T.Godfrey "Strip their Rights: Cop Peelers claim refugee status", *The Toronto Sun*, July 22, 1999.

[111] The message sent to STOP-TRAFFIC@friends-partners.org list on February 10, 2000. by Salamon Alapitvany from Hungary.

[112] The message received through STOP-TRAFFIC @friends-partners.org list on December 21, 1999 says that "the Russian mafia is arranging for Eastern European women to travel to Mexico, where they are obliged to work as prostitutes and nude dancers" and that police have arrested at least 100 Eastern European women, mainly Hungarian, Slavic and Russian, during several raids in the last month.

secondary schools, as well as by the earlier survey conducted by Forrai (IOM Report, 2000:11; Forrai, 1999).

Bulgaria is one of the main sending countries for trafficked women. It is estimated that some 10,000 Bulgarian females have been lured to go abroad as prostitutes. Association Animus reported that there is a trend of an increase in the number of 14-years olds that are illegally transferred abroad[113]. The regions close to the Bulgarian border are at highest risk. From Bulgaria, channels for trafficking lead to many countries such as: to Germany, Belgium and The Netherlands through Serbia, Romania, Czech Republic, Poland and Hungary, as well as through Macedonia to Kosovo, Albania, Italy, Greece, Turkey, United Arab Emirates and Saudi Arabia.

The most vulnerable are women who live in villages near the borders. According to officials and activists from Bulgaria and Poland, Bulgarian women are the largest group of sex slaves in Poland. Also, data of La Strada suggest that at least 3,000 Bulgarian women work the streets in Poland. In comparison to other foreign prostitutes they live in the worst conditions. They usually work at the lowest level and are often victims of violence. Many of them are underage and of Roma or ethnic Turk origin.[114] During 1999, a total of 150 women managed to free themselves and come home after soliciting help from the Association Animus.[115] In 1998 Bulgarian women involved in prostitution in Italy outnumbered Albanian women, who were earlier the most numerous there. Also, they are among the most numerous foreign prostitutes in Germany and The Netherlands as well (Sotirov, 1999:70).

From 1068 Bulgarian women interviewed in the IOM survey, more than a third know of a precise case of trafficking in their surroundings, while 6 percent said that they personally know a woman who was forced into prostitution abroad. Similarly, as in the above-mentioned Hungarian survey, this survey shows that underage Roma girls and women are among those most vulnerable to trafficking (Analytical creative group and IOM, 2000:21). According to Association Animus, risk groups in Bulgaria are also:

1. 14-15 year olds from the countryside, who do not have a prospect to work in Bulgaria;
2. Young, ambitious women who know foreign languages and who are attracted by advertisements about a bright career abroad;
3. Girls from institutions, recruited for prostitution in Bulgaria.[116]

It seems that not so much is known about trafficking of women from Serbia (without Kosovo) and Macedonia. Information available from anti-trafficking organizations from Western countries mainly shows that they are found among victims of trafficking but less often than Hungarian and, especially, Bulgarian women. (Kootstra, 1997:13).

[113] Message received through STOP-TRAFFIC @friends-partners.org list on April 21, 2000.

[114] Message received through STOP-TRAFFIC @friends-partners.org list on November 29, 2000.

[115] Message received through STOP-TRAFFIC @friends-partners.org list on April 21, 2000.

[116] V.Petrov "10 000 Blgarki sa beli robini v cuzbina" (10 000 Bulgarian women are white slaves abroad), *Duma*, May 20, 1999, p.5.

Macedonian woman are mainly trafficked to Italy, The Netherlands, Germany and the Scandinavian countries. Unlike women from other East European countries, they are rarely trafficked trough Greece. One of the possible reasons may be that Macedonian women who are aware that they could work in prostitution avoid being recognized by Macedonian people who often travel or live in Greece (Dokovska, interview, 1999). Women are trafficked by both the Albanian and Macedonian mafia, with the Albanian mafia being more powerful since it has more money and more experience in organized crime (drug and weapons trade as well). However, Roma and Macedonian women still prevail among victims trafficked from Macedonia, with the number of (Macedonian) Albanian women increasing with their emancipation from strong family control (Dokovska, interview, 1999)

Similar to women from Macedonia, women from Serbia are mainly trafficked to Italy, Greece, Cyprus, The Netherlands and Germany. According to the data given by the Italian women's group Casa della Donne, trafficked women from FR Yugoslavia were the third largest group (16%) among those who were assisted by them in 1997 (after Ukrainian-28%, and Albanian women-21%) (Casa della Donne, 1997). Serbian women are trafficked to Macedonia as well but they stay there mainly in transit to Greece and Cyprus. Albanian women from Kosovo as well as Roma women and children from different countries are massively trafficked to Italy

2.2 Sex trafficking of women from other post-communist countries to/through Hungary, Macedonia, Bulgaria and Serbia

Apart from being sending countries, Hungary, Macedonia, Bulgaria and Serbia are also transit countries for women trafficked from other parts of Central and Eastern Europe. In addition, Hungary, Macedonia and Serbia are sometimes also countries of destination.

Owing to their better economic situation at the beginning of transition, both Serbia and Macedonia were for some time among the main destination countries within Eastern Europe. However, later on they both became mainly transit countries - to neighboring territories where the military was large presence (Bosnia, Republika Srpska, Kosovo), and, through them, to Western Europe. Serbia is the country of origin, destination and transit for trafficked women and children. Women from Ukraine, Russia and Romania make up the majority of women trafficked from other countries. Most often they are used as prostitutes in Serbia for some time and then sold further, mainly (through Montenegro) in Italy. Parts of Serbia, which are close to the borders with Macedonia, Romania, Bulgaria, Hungary and Bosnia, are identified as the main parts of Serbia where women from other countries are trafficked to.

Although the economic situation in Macedonia was difficult all the time during the transition, its geographic position, large presence of NATO forces and strong Albanian mafia contributed to it becoming one of the main transit countries, i.e. temporary destination for many trafficked women (Coneva, interview, 1999). Among 152 victims, who were helped by IOM Skopje in the period between August 9, 2000 and February 9, 2001, those of the age 18-24 (59.9%) and 25-30 (19.08%) years prevailed. Fifteen percent of victims were younger than 17, with 3.29 percent of those younger than 15. According to the same source, women with secondary education (50.66%) and those who have only primary school (27.63%) prevail among victims of trafficking. However, the share of those with university education (7.89%) is not low. Also, more than half (57.89%) victims of trafficking were unemployed (Bacanovic, 2001:110). In September 2001, the number of trafficked women assisted by IOM in Macedonia reached 328[117].

Women from Bulgaria, Ukraine, Mongolia, Moldova, Romania and Albania prevail among women trafficked to/through Macedonia, but, according to some of my interviewees (e.g. Dokovska, interview, 1999), there are sometimes even women from Africa. Women are trafficked to the Middle East and Western Europe, mainly via Greece. The increased presence of soldiers in the region, as well as the sudden worsening of the economic situation, made the risks of trafficking women and girls in Macedonia greater than ever.

Serbia and Macedonia are most often transit countries for trafficking women from other East European countries to Kosovo as well. For example, according to the above-mentioned IOM's Kosovo data, 56 percent of women helped by IOM entered Kosovo from Serbia, 30.63 percent from Macedonia, while 8.75 percent did it from Montenegro. Also, women sometimes enter Kosovo from Albania (2.5 percent). The majority of women trafficked to Kosovo and assisted by IOM are women from Moldova (62 %), Romania (19 %), Ukraine (9%) and Bulgaria (8%). Women from Moldova are trafficked through Romania, and they are then sent, either through Hungary and Serbia, or through Bulgaria and Macedonia, to Kosovo. Similarly, Ukrainian women are trafficked through Hungary, Romania or Bulgaria, and then through either Serbia or Macedonia, to Kosovo. Channels for trafficking Russian women mainly go through Ukraine and then through Moldova, Bulgaria and Macedonia. The women are usually sold 3 to 6 times during their journey to Kosovo (IOM Pristina, 2001:6,7). However, after Kosovo's introduction of tough laws against trafficking in 2000, the opposite trend, i.e. the trafficking of women from Kosovo to/through Macedonia was noticed (Bacanovic, 2001:108). Also, the refugee crisis during the Kosovo conflict and NATO intervention was largely used by Albanian mafia for trafficking Albanian and Roma women from Kosovo to Italy and other Western countries (Bacanovic, 2001:106).

Contrary to other countries included in the survey, Hungary was transformed from an almost exclusive sending and transit country at the beginning of transition to a mainly destination and transit country for trafficked women (IOM Report, 2000:4). This is obviously connected with its faster economic development in comparison to the majority of Central and East European countries. Thus, Hungary became the country of destination for women from economically less developed countries such as Ukraine and

[117] Message received through STOP-TRAFFIC @friends-partners.org list on September 11, 2001.

Russia. As noticed by Forrai, the "classic form and structure of prostitution has vanished. Today, instead of the individual pimp and his subservient prostitutes, a pyramid-structured organization has emerged. The possibilities regarding earning a living, offered by prostitution in Hungary, attract Ukrainian, Russian and Polish young women and men like a magnet. They either stay in Hungary or move on to the West". (Forrai, 1999:2). Apart from Ukrainian, Russian and Polish women, there are also Romanian and Bulgarians trafficked there, who, according to some sources, are among the poorest and the worst looking prostitutes in Budapest[118].

Among the countries included in the survey, Bulgaria is the only one that has been a sending and transit country all the time since the beginning of changes. Moreover, as I already showed, Bulgaria has been one of the main sending and transit countries within Eastern Europe as a whole. For example, during 1999, Bulgarian border police have detained (sic!) a total of 1,229 women for whom there was information that they had been sexually victimized. Of those, 561 were Romanians and the rest came from Moldova, Ukraine and Bulgaria. Also, during the first two months of 2000, Bulgarian border police have detained 162 women who were supposed to be transferred abroad.[119]

2.3 Modes of recruitment

There are several most frequent modes of recruitment of trafficked women from Central and Eastern Europe. These are (allegedly legitimate) job offers, kidnapping, false invitations/arrangements for going abroad and recruitment for domestic prostitution. Hence, sex trafficking includes helping women migrate and then directing them into sex slavery (UNICEF, 1999:87; Bacanovic, 2001:111). All available sources suggest deception regarding the nature of work, conditions of work and wages as the most frequent recruitment method, as well as that most often recruiting agents are acquaintances of family, friends and artist agencies (Wijers, Lap-Chew, 1997:98, 99).

Trafficked women often make a conscious decision to go abroad, hoping to find a better life, and the recruitment for prostitution often happens under the facade of a legal activity (Feher, 1995:77). Looking for a job or higher income leads them to rely on tempting offers from job adds in the newspapers or on promises made by people known to them. Unfortunately, this often leads them into the hands of traffickers.

According to a study of job adds in Bulgarian newspapers in the period between May and June 1997, 94 percent of adds offer jobs for women (dancers, au pair, models). They usually require women who are young, nice looking and are not married. Typically, unrealistically high payment is promised (e.g. "Dancers needed in Greece.. no experience needed..earn $3000 per month"). Women who most often answer these job

[118] S.Milanov "Nai-groznoto v Budesa sa blgarskite florci" (The most awful in Budapest are Bulgarian prostitutes), *Nosen trud*, March 23-24, 1999, p.4

[119] Message received through STOP-TRAFFIC @friends-partners.org list on April 21, 2000.

offers are young, ambitious, well-educated who speak a foreign language. They usually need a job to support their families, they are sometimes married and have children (Kojouharova, unpublished).

Apart from job adds, tempting job promises are frequent way of recruitment of women by men and women they know such as boyfriends, family members, acquaintances and even female friends whom they have known for a long time. The latter way of directing women to intermediaries in this process is frequent and methods of recruitment are more informal than is commonly thought (UNICEF, 1999:89). Sometimes, former prostitutes start to work as recruiters of women and actively participate in trafficking (Vintileanu and Babovic, 2001:76). In Hungary, Forrai found that most of the women involved in prostitution are encouraged by their boyfriends in order to solve their financial problems. Some were forced/introduced into it by an older sister or by friends (Forrai, 1999). Also, according to Casa della Donne (Italy), most of the women (63%) came to Italy with the promise of work (in a bar, hotel, factory etc.) and most of them were recruited by a friend or acquaintance from their city or town. Others came with a "boyfriend" (9%), who then forced them to work in prostitution. Only a few were kidnapped (7%) or sold by relatives (2%) (Casa della Donne, 1997).

According to IOM Pristina, 55 percent of women trafficked to Kosovo were promised jobs in Italy. The most often offered jobs are such as baby-sitter, cleaner, waitress or caretaker for old people, i.e. the jobs which normally do not require a high level of education or language skills. Job offers are the most frequent recruitment method among women assisted by IOM - 71.25 percent (IOM Pristina, 2001:6). As well noticed by Corrin, "the deception lies in the fact that many of the women are then forced into prostitution against their will. While some women are actually sold outright, others are so manipulated and exploited by traffickers that only entry into prostitution enables them to survive." (Corrin, 1996:209).

> "One day we were sitting in a cafe shop. A Romanian acquaintance arrived with two men from Kosovo. They offered us jobs as hostesses in their bar in Kosovo for a monthly salary of 2,000 Deutsche Mark. Prostitution was never mentioned" (22 year old Romanian trafficked to Kosovo, quoted by IOM Pristina, 2001:6).

Sometimes, and especially in poor villages, women are recruited through promises of a better life abroad in more general terms. As stated by Kojouharova, after finishing their primary education at the age of 14 and 15, due to financial difficulties, these girls hardly have any opportunity to find a job to continue studying. "Thus", as observed by Kojouharova, "involving them into trafficking becomes very easy by luring them with promises for getting reach, having beautiful clothes, expensive cars, even by offering sweets or chocolates. The girls do not even doubt the promises they receive. They are usually made by a rich man who easily wins their confidence by offering them small gifts and illusions about a better life." (Kojouharova, unpublished). They are brought in some big town in Bulgaria, where they are locked in illegal quarters. At the beginning, they are raped many times by their bosses. The cruel treatment is interlaced with attention such as buying clothes and giving food. Afraid and confused, they slowly become dependent on their bosses.[120]

Another recruitment method is kidnapping. This means that recruitment is done by the use of violence against women who did not have an intention to go abroad. According to Association Animus, for example, Bulgarian women are mainly recruited allegedly for the work abroad but there were also cases of the abduction of girls from schools and directly from the street This method was especially widespread in Kosovo during and after the conflict and NATO bombing.[121] Also, as noticed by Bacanovic, Albanian and Roma girls and women, who escaped Serbian forces and NATO bombs and found refuge in Macedonia, were often "welcomed" by the Albanian mafia who cruelly abused and exploited them (Bacanovic, 2001:106).

> "In a Macedonian town, a 15 year old girl was abducted during the day by a group of traffickers from FR Yugoslavia. After beating her, they put her in a car. When they asked her to get out, she started to cry and asked for help from passerby. The traffickers escaped in fear. This is the group who also kidnapped other girls and forced them to work in prostitution."[122]

> "Romanian citizen Kadres phoned police to report that her friend Marija Diku was kidnapped in the village Grupcin, near Tetovo. He said that the kidnappers asked him 1000$ to free Marija, threatening to sell her in Italy and to force her into prostitution. Later on they phoned and asked for 2000$, promising to free both Marija and the other woman. He accepted the conditions and arranged to meet one of the kidnappers in the hotel "Grand" in Skopje (Macedonia). He informed police about it and they arrested two kidnappers (both from Tetovo, Macedonia). They told police that they bought four Romanian women from the men from Presevo, FR Yugoslavia, for 3600DM. Marija was among these girls. They told girls that they are going to bring them to Greece, but instead, they brought them in the village and asked money to free them. A few days later, one Romanian and one Greek man came to them and bought two women for 2.400 DM. Before the arrest, they gave 50DM to each of these two women and put them on the train for Gevgelia (Macedonia), where a man should wait for them in order to bring them to Greece. Police tried to find the man who reported the kidnapping but he disappeared from Macedonia."[123]

> "After a 24-hour drive from the mountainous Kosovo border, two buses with more than 100 women, children and elderly refugees sputtered to a stop in the dusty speck of a village near the Albanian coast. Out of the evening murk, 50 armed men surrounded the buses. 'You survived the Serbs', a beefy Albanian man with a mobile phone and a Kalashnikov rifle called out. 'Now we will do what we want with you: we are going to take the girls.'..Running high-powered rubber rafts out of Vlore and Durres, the traffickers do a brisk business ferrying desperate Kosovo families illegally across the Adriatic Sea to Western Europe for as

120 V.Petrov "10 000 Blgarki sa beli robini v cuzbina" (10 000 Bulgarian women are white slaves abroad), *Duma*, May 20, 1999, p.5.

121 "Bitka tokom cele noći" (The all night fight), *Glas javnosti*, January 14, 2000, p.2.

122 P.A.L. "Kidnaperite "pokusi" za edna ubava devojka" (Kidnapers "tried" one beautiful woman"), *Vecer*, , February 23, 1999.

123 N.N.S. "Tetovcani preprodavale romanski ilegalki"(Men from Tetovo resold Romanian women), *Dnevnik*, January 11, 1999, p.7.

> much as $800 a head. Ten of the speedy rafts depart the harbor of this port city each night", says Lori Montgomery in the report for the Miami Herald.[124]

Trafficking by family members is similar to kidnapping, as it includes selling young girls into prostitution. This is especially widespread among the Roma population.

One of very typical cases is the case of 17 years old Bulgarian Roma girl. During her 17 years she was sold several times by her own parents. After three years spent in Germany, she returned home after intervention of Association Animus. She was 6 months pregnant, ill and without documents. Moreover, her landlord expelled her when he realized that she used to be prostitute. She fail in depression and attempted suicide several times.[125]

The other recruitment methods are false travel arrangements, false invitation abroad (by friend, acquaintance or official invitation by an agency - e.g. by association for artists) and false marriage promise.

Women who want to work in prostitution in their own country are also often sold to other pimps, first within and later outside the country. As pointed out by Kojouharova (unpublished) "willing or not, sooner or later, they are being trafficked outside the country". But, in spite of the fact that they are aware what they are expected to do, they are denied autonomy and, in this way, exposed to violence and victimized by trafficking as any other victim. In Macedonia, domestic prostitutes are mainly recruited among drug addicts, students and poor girls, as well as among girls from orphanages, while in Bulgaria the most vulnerable are girls accommodated in orphanages and similar institutions. Some pimps first give girls drugs and later a "job" to earn money for drugs. Some girls, mainly Albanians, escape from home and go to live with a pimp.[126]

> "I started to work as a prostitute 6 years ago. I completed secondary education and did not manage to find a job. I grew up without parents, in the orphanage. In the shop they do not ask you who you are and whether you have parents. If you want to buy things, they ask you to pay. I literally did not have food. I found myself accidentally in this profession. Simply, I had to do that. In Skopje, there are a lot of young girls who sell their bodies for money. The majority of them, as myself, need money to survive. The price is constantly going down. Young girls from Bulgaria are coming every day. They are forced by their pimps to go with different types of men for small amounts of money. No one asks them if they want this or not. The conditions for surviving are very difficult. I would be the happiest if I could find some normal job and earn a living for me and my child, who is at the moment in an orphanage. There are also such women who have to support their parents in this way. The parents know about it, even their fathers serve as their pimps." (G.M., 22 years old from Skopje, Macedonia).

[124] L.Montgomery "Albanians sell Kosovo women into prostitution", *Mıamı Herald*, May 30, 1999.

[125] D.Koeva "Beli robini v cerni premini"(White slaves in black changes), *Nıe zenıte*, June 22-28, 1999, p.3.

[126] N.N. "Bugarki za vo motel, studentki za na deloven rucek" (Bulgarians for a motel, students for lunch) , *Makedonıa denes*, August 16, 1999, p.8 and V.Velkova "Izgubena doverba"(Lost confidence), *Jana*, February 1, 1999, p. 24.

"Sometimes, when I need money, it happens to me that I go to sleep with a man. My parents do not know about it. It is very easy to find a man for doing this. You simply need to go to some very good restaurant and you can find a client. I am not ashamed to approach anyone in the crowd and to ask him to buy a drink for me. What can I do when my parents do not have money to buy food, let alone to buy other things for me. Sometimes I am afraid, but it is the risk. When I do it, I get money and can have my pocket money for a few days. I am a good student." (G.P., a student in secondary school, Skopje, Macedonia). [127]

2.4 Forms of victimization

After being trapped in trafficking, women are usually resold several if not many times. Usually, transnational trafficking is interlaced with regional and national, i.e. transnational trafficking is transformed into national and regional and vice versa. For example, Russian women are often resold several times within Serbia (for a price which ranges from 300 to 3000 Deutsche Marks), before they are trafficked to Italy and resold for a much higher price (up to 10, 000 Deutsche Marks).[128]

"Ljudmila, 23 year old Ukrainian girl, was working as a prostitute in Istanbul. She was resold five times before she came to "Night club international"in Slatina (Kosovo), where she used to work together with 15 women. 'Our clients were Albanians and Macedonians, but there are Russian and American soldiers as well', says Ljudmila. Katarina, another Ukrainian woman, 22 years old, said that she had been kidnapped in Bulgaria and that she was forced to work in a brothel in Macedonia, where she was living in bad conditions".[129]

In Macedonian villages near the Bulgarian border there are "black markets" for selling prostitutes from Eastern Europe. Macedonian and foreign citizens organize their transfer and sell them. In Macedonia, they mainly work as dancers and "waitresses" in motels and nightclubs. They are often resold later in Greece, especially on islands where the prices are higher. The girls are usually sold in April and May, before the start of the tourist season. Some of the girls are later resold in Italy, through Albania.[130]According to the study of IOM, Albanians are notoriously brutal. They have been known to punish uncooperative victims with burning cigarettes, underwater immersion and other forms of torture usually associated with wartime paramilitary squads.

" It started in her poor farming village in the former Soviet republic of Moldova, with the promise of a job as a waitress in Italy. It took her on an odyssey of torment through Turkey, Bulgaria, Romania, Yugoslavia and Albania. She was raped, beaten, forced into prostitution, smuggled across borders and sold 18 times from one pimp to the next. It ended 11 months later when police along Italy's Adriatic coast rescued the weeping woman with a miniskirt

[127] V.Velkova "Mirisot na noknite dami" (The smell of night ladies), *Jana*, January 15, 1999, p.24-25

[128] D.Jovanović "Nudaje" (Offerenig), *NIN*, August 13, 1998, p.6

[129] "Zabava košta 100 maraka"(The fun costs 100 DM), *Blic*, January 5, 2000, p.4.

[130] N.N. "Bugarki za vo motel, studentki za na deloven rucek" (Bulgarians for a motel, students for lunch) , *Makedonia denes*, August 16, 1999, p.8.

> and bruised legs and arrested her 21-year-old Albanian captor. 'I had no voice left after all the screaming', she recalls. 'I was one step away from madness."[131]

The survey based on questionnaires filled out by 41 NGO-s from different parts of the world (more then half, i.e. 21 were from Europe) showed that, after being trapped in trafficking, women in Europe (including CEECs) suffer mostly from:

a) Psychological abuse;
b) Constant fear of police arrest;
c) Physical violence;
d) Illegal confinement;
e) Not being paid regularly/paid less then agreed/not being paid at all;
f) Isolation;
g) Sexual assault/rape;
h) More than twelve hour workdays;
i) Debt bondage;
j) Identity paper confiscation (Wijers, Lap-Chew, 1997:92).

As pointed out by Corrin, informal recruitment through known people often lead to women finding themselves "indebted to a trafficker or club owner on arrival in the destination country. In many instances their passports were taken, their freedom was extremely limited and they were threatened with violence". (Corrin, 1996:211). Violence and threats of violence are often used to control women and take away their freedom. Thus, sex trafficking is obviously a new form of slavery. As pointed out by Bales, "all types of slavery depend on violence, which holds the slave in place". Slavery includes the "slave's loss of control over his or her life and an ongoing 'obligation' to the slaveholder." (Bales, 1999:19).

Activists from Association Animus say that there are several mechanisms used by pimps for keeping women in dependence. First, they use serious violence, including rape and beating.

> "Each act of disobedience is severely punished. It can be hunger or beating on the hidden places of the body, like the heels or the kidneys, where it hurts most without leaving any scars. Girls come back to Bulgaria with branded numbers on their skin. Just like being in a concentration camp. In a situation of inhuman torture, the fear of death becomes stronger than pride and dignity and the search for freedom. One is ready to do anything in order to stay alive."(Kojouharova, unpublished)

Physical exhaustion is the second method: 20-hour working days, no privacy, no time to think about self-protection. The third mechanism is total control and complete isolation. The victim stays all the time only with the pimp and her client, and she does not move from a single place.[132]

[131] R.Bourdeaux "Journey into sex slavery", *Los Angeles Times*, August 17, 2001

[132] V.Petrov "10 000 Blgarki sa beli robini v cuzbina" (10 000 Bulgarian women are white slaves abroad), *Duma*, May 20, 1999, p.5.

According to IOM Pristina, the living and working conditions of women trafficked to Kosovo are dramatic. In most of the cases, women are beaten (57%) and sexually abused (60%) by the traffickers and their friends. Fifty-two percent of women were forced into unprotected sex. Also, in most of the cases the shared accommodations are in the bar, sleeping on chairs or sharing a sofa between 3 or 4 women. Hygienic conditions are usually poor and access to food is limited. In 83.75 percent of cases women did not get any payment during their stay in Kosovo. Only few of them received modest occasional allowances (33,75%), which "they had to spend to pay their rent, food, clothes and to buy condoms" (IOM Pristina, 2001:10).

> "After we passed the border to Romania he told me he had bought me from her. I was shocked and scared. From that moment on I was transferred from hand to hand, men bought me and sold me, moving me from apartments and houses to hotels, and making me cross borders illegally. Eventually, I arrived in a bar in Kosovo, where I was locked inside and forced into prostitution. My passport was taken away a long time before. The traffickers passed it from one to the other each time I was sold. In the bar I was never ever paid. I could not go out by myself and the owner became more and more violent as the weeks went by. He was beating and raping me and the other girls. We were his 'property' he said. By buying us he bought the right to beat us, rape us, starve us, force us to have sex with clients" (21 year old girl from Moldova, trafficked to Kosovo, quoted from IOM Pristina, 2001:8)

> "When refusing a client I would be beaten or raped by the owner. It did not matter if I was sick" (26 years Moldavian trafficked to Kosovo, quoted by IOM Pristina, 2001:10)

> "Before I was sold to the bar in Prizren, I was held in an apartment in Gnjilan for four days. I was raped by the guards several times. The women living in that apartment were forced to work as prostitutes One of them was eight months pregnant, but she was not allowed to stop working" (21 year old Moldavian, escaped from a bar in Prizren, quoted by IOM Pristina, 2001:10).

Women who suffered cruel treatment say often that they endured it out of fear of being caught and deported. This fear is much more pronounced among Albanians than among victims of other ethnic origin since the Albanian culture ostracizes sexually abused women, who face rejection by their families.[133] For example, Denisa, an Albanian women who is now living at a Caritas shelter in Udine (Italy) says that she was equally fearful of Artman (the trafficker) and the Italian police. 'I thought the police would send me home', the teenager said. 'That was the last place I wanted to go." [134]

[133] R.Bourdeaux "Journey into sex slavery", *Los Angeles Times*, August 17, 2001.
[134] ibidem

3. CONTRIBUTING FACTORS: THE IMPACT OF TRANSITION FROM COMMUNISM, GLOBALIZATION AND WAR

Similar to sex trafficking from other parts of the world, sex trafficking in women from post-communist countries is influenced by factors existing both within countries of origin of the victims (push factors) and factors which exist in destination countries (pull factors). As I will show later in this chapter, both push and pull factors are strongly related to the post-Cold War structural changes - within post-communist countries as well as in the world as a whole, i.e. in the broader context of globalization. Or, more precisely, the impact of push and pull factors is strongly interlaced, and is intensified by the recent widening of the gap between developed and developing countries as well as by other globalization-related processes. Push and pull factors are connected through the economic, political and military relationships between sending and receiving countries, which serve as bridges between them (Konig, 1997:81). Apart from push and pull factors, which may be considered causes of sex trafficking, it is also important to stress the existence of factors which may be called facilitating factors. These are factors, such as policies and laws in transit and destination countries which are designed in a way which encourages rather than prevents sex trafficking, although it is intended to be vice-versa.

All available findings, both from my own (including the answers of my respondents) and other surveys (Williams, 1999:21), suggest that the following groups of factors related to respective social changes in sending countries should be considered as the main **push factors** for sex trafficking:

a) socio-economic factors;
b) political factors;
c) cultural factors;
d) war/militarism related factors.

In addition, factors such as sexual and domestic violence, are also considered to be strong push factors for prostitution, i.e. sex trafficking. Complementary to the above-mentioned factors are **pull factors**, i.e. the factors existing in or related to destination countries:

a) socio-economic factors;
b) cultural factors;
c) myths about destination countries which exist in sending countries.

In a nutshell, factors which contribute to sex trafficking are mostly the same factors that influence the gendered nature of employment within the sex industry and the feminization of migration.

3.1 Socio-economic, political and cultural factors connected to transition from communism and globalization (push-pull factors)

Unemployment and poverty are among the most important socio-economic changes in the everyday lives of women in post-communist countries as sending countries, which affect women's vulnerability to sex trafficking. As I showed previously in this book, young people and, especially, single mothers and women with children are among those most affected by economic hardships. The feminization of migration is directly linked to a feminization of poverty so that it may be said that "the fact that increasing numbers of women become migrants is evidence of their quest for 'new living strategies'....women are under severe pressure to "search for new perspectives". (Konig, 1997:11) Moreover, there is a link between the feminization of migration and the increased unemployment of men, since reduction in demand for male labor spurs female migration (Wijers, Lap-Chew, 1997:52). Thus, women have a tendency to migrate in order to support their families.

> "My mother is sick and in need of an operation, the family does not have the money. I decided to travel abroad for work. I did not know how and asked a friend to put me in contact with people who could help. Two sisters in Chisinau promised to take me to Italy and arrange for a job as a babysitter or a waitress." (19 year old Moldavian, trafficked to Kosovo, quoted by IOM Pristina, 2001:6).

> "I am 21 years old from Moldova, I have a son, 4 years old. His father left us when he was born, my family cannot support us and the job I had was not paying for our basic needs. My salary was 25 DM per month and lately salaries were not paid at all. Many young women from my town were traveling abroad for work. I thought working abroad was also my chance to earn some money..." (quoted from IOM Pristina, 2001:7)

> "Angela Slobodchuk, the Moldavian woman, says she was seeking a way to escape a drunken, drug-addicted husband who beat her and to earn money for surgery for her 18-month-old son when a half-sister said she could help her find a job. She referred Angela to a stranger named Maria, who was to arrange work in a restaurant in Italy. Instead, Maria took her to the Turkish city of Istanbul and sold her to the first of a string of brutal Albanian pimps"[135].

But even when women do not choose to migrate they may find themselves trapped by sex trafficking when looking for a job within the domestic sex industry. As stressed by Wijers and Lap-Chew (1997:52), "sex work appears therefore as a strategy for many women to cope with painful economic consequences of global capitalism" In addition, it is noticed that apart from poverty and unemployment, disturbed family relationships, sexual and domestic violence are strong push factors for women to enter prostitution. And this is exactly what recruiters use to lure them into prostitution, pretending to be gentle and caring. Thus, it is not rare that in the beginning women get involved in

[135] R.Bourdeaux "Journey into sex slavery", *Los Angeles Times*, August 17, 2001.

emotional relationships with their pimps (Vintileanu and Babovic, 2001:60). Also, it is noticed that women are vulnerable to sex trafficking not only when they try to escape poverty, but misogynist societies as well. For example, many trafficked Albanian women from Kosovo saw sex work as an opportunity to leave behind the oppression of Kosovan men.[136] Thus both traditional patriarchal family relationships and domestic violence are important push factors for prostitution and sex trafficking.

Traffickers make use of the existing market demand and the women's need to find jobs. In that process development of a market (neoliberal) economy plays a major role both by enhancing disparity and inequality between countries and by creating demand for women as sex objects. Disparities and inequalities influence the channels of migration, in general, and the channels of trafficking in particular: they are the consequence of "the world economic order, of the distribution of wealth among nations and the exploitation of persons by others" (Konig, 1997:81).

Thus trafficking channels go from developing countries to the industrialized nations and not vise versa. Trafficking also occurs between developing countries, going from poorer to wealthier countries or from politically unstable to politically stable or more stable countries. However, since economic factors are not the only factors that affect trafficking, all poor countries are not affected in the same way, or to the same degree. This is true with political instability as well. A good example in that respect is the low level of trafficked women from Serbia, in spite of having the worst economic and political situation among the countries included in my survey. In addition, in spite of similar of their economic situations, there is a big difference between the vulnerability of Bulgarian and Macedonian women. As I already showed, Bulgarian women are among those most affected by trafficking within Eastern and Central Europe - disproportionately more in comparison to Macedonian women, for example. The explanation for the differences in vulnerability of women from different countries may partly result from their political differences during the communist time and the specificities of their transition. Thus, myths about the West and westernization[137], as strong pull factors for migration and trafficking, are more emphasized in the countries which were more detached from the West during communism and vise versa. In addition, these pull factors were very weak in Serbia as a consequence of its recent detachment from the Western world due to economic sanctions, isolation and related xenophobia and anger toward West. However, on the other side, in spite of its political instability and bad economic situation, the myth of the good life in Serbia was a strong pull factor for many women from other parts of Eastern Europe. Also, the combined effects of (formal) border opening toward the West and (actual) restrictive European

[136] The message received through STOP-TRAFFIC@friends-partners.org list on September 11, 1999.

[137] One of the very strong pull factors is the myth of independence and emancipation supposedly awaiting women in the West (Wijers, Lap-Chew, 1997:44) The other is connected to a better life and easy access to employment. The picture of the West comes from the global media, cinema, advertisements etc. , where everything seems possible and everyone is happy (Konig, 1997:87).

immigration policy toward poor countries, such as Bulgaria, is an additional contributing factor for sex trafficking (Konig, 1997:22; Williams, 1999:201). Moreover, the rising number of women willing to travel and the short distance between sending and destination countries made Eastern and Central European women very attractive for sex traffickers.

As in any other trade, "supply and demand are inextricably connected in the trade in women and girls" (Konig, 1997:82). Economic hardships and their consequences to women create a potential supply of workers for the sex industry. But this "supply" would never be used for sex trafficking purposes in the way it usually is if demand were not created, which serves as a strong pull factor for trafficking. The increased demand for women as sex objects is evident within both post-communist and developed countries. Thus, as observed by Azize-Vargas, "we need to understand how global capitalism creates conditions for women to sell sexual services at far better rates of pay than the sale of another form of labor" (quoted by Wijers and Lap-Chew, 1997:53).

Enormous profit, which is made within the sex industry, is a strong factor which attracts both potential victims and traffickers. As observed by Bourdeaux, "as Western Europe grows richer and fewer of its women resort to street prostitution, the world's oldest profession is being taken over by immigrant traffickers and their younger, lower-priced chattel. The booming cross-border trade in forced prostitution and sweatshop labor earns traffickers worldwide $7 billion a year, according to the United Nations. It ranks third behind drug running and illicit arms sales in terms of lucrative criminal enterprises."[138] Or, as pointed out by Williams (1999:148), the sex markets will continue to exist "so long as there is demand for commercial sex, so long as there are limited opportunities for women in licit sectors of the economy, and so long as there are individuals who see this as a lucrative area of activity."

As pointed out by Feher (1995:76), the sex industry continuously moves into new territories, where economic and social circumstances create a favorable situation for its business activities. In addition, after the fall of the Berlin wall, the growth of the sex industry was seen as one of the first signs of "freedom" and opening of the borders for Western influence. As a result, there is an obvious increase in demand for sex services within post-communist countries themselves. However, trafficking in women would not exist in its contemporary form (as transnational crime) "if men in the industrialized countries did not create demand for it. This demand for women as domestic servants, wives and sex workers is essential for the trade in migrant women."(Konig, 1997:12) As a result, when recruiting girls for the sex industry, traffickers take care of sexual, power and domination fantasies (hegemonic masculinity ideals) of, primarily, men from industrialized countries, but also of nouveaux *riche* from transition countries.

> "The clients in our escort agency are Swiss businessmen who stay for holiday in Ohrid. Marriage with them is possible as well. The owner of the agency is of Serbian origin. He got

[138] R.Bourdeaux "Journey into sex slavery", *Los Angeles Times*, August 17, 2001.

the idea to open the agency from another men who used to work with Spanish women. He decided to try with Macedonians since the Swiss men wanted innocent girls. We have girls from all parts of Macedonia. There are single mothers among them, who need money so badly. (The woman who works as an agent in the escort agency, Ohrid, Macedonia).[139]

"After 55 years, prostitution started to flourish again in the southeastern part of Macedonia. The price is between 15 and 20 DM. However, for more attractive girls the price is from 50 to 100 DM. The clients are often "small"private businessmen who want to prove their value in their surroundings and show themselves as Don Juans. The majority of prostitutes are from Bulgaria, Serbia and Montenegro, but there are also those from Ukraine.[140]

The influence of economic factors on women's vulnerability to sex trafficking is not exhausted only in them as push factors for migration and prostitution. One of the very important influences of women's marginal economic position is their very small chance to hide from traffickers and start new lives after being released and returning home (Minkova, interview, 1999). Also, socio-economic changes in the everyday lives of both women and men in post-communist countries (e.g. unemployment and/or loss of previous social positions/privileges) play an important role in them becoming involved in prostitution as pimps, i.e. in trafficking as recruiters, traffickers etc, as well (Feher, 1995:76). But labor distribution is strongly gendered so that among recruiters (who get the least profit[141]) women participate in equal measure as men, while men dominate in higher places in the hierarchy. Also, poor and powerless men are usually subordinated to those who lead the "business", i.e. to those having leading roles within the mafia. Thus, as I already stressed , the place which men have within economic structure usually determines the role they have within sex industry business as well (e.g. as street pimps, brothel owners, traffickers or clients). But, whatever their economic position, women who identify themselves as sex objects are always subordinated to men. Thus, although there are differences between different forms of emphasized femininities (e.g. street prostitutes, call girls etc.), and subordinated masculinities, masculinities are always hegemonic in relation to femininities.

"Many pimps would not work in prostitution if the economic situation were better. If they were employed. Many of them are not criminals like in the Western countries. They are unhappy people who are not able to find a job. Sometimes, they live from the prostitution of their wives, girlfriends and daughters. Sometimes, they do not earn anything for several days. Poverty is common for pimps. There are a few who have a network, good car, etc, but the majority live only on the prostitution of their wives or daughters. " (Julija, prostitute from Budapest, interview, 1999).

139 A.Stojanovska "Prostitutki vo Skopje" (Prostitutes in Skopje), *Vecer*, April 19, 1999.

140 Z.Pijanmanov "Prodavanje" ljubov za 20 marki"(Seeling love for 20 marks), *Makedonija denes*, March 9, 1999.

141 For example, criminal gangs buy women from recruiters for small amounts of money such as 50-150 $ and resell them for 5000$ and more.

The East European mafia is known to be extremely violent. They do not restrict themselves to sex trafficking, but usually also sell arms and drugs, which makes them even more dangerous (Altink, 1995:125). For example, according to the findings of Global Survival Network, many members of the Russian mafia are former employees of the Russian national security agency, the KGB, which was replaced after 1991 by the FSB (the state intelligence bureau). As a consequence of this (transition-connected) change, thousands of people, highly skilled in intelligence work and the use of force, became unemployed. Because security police often have "political connections, access to weapons, and knowledge of the banking and business worlds, they are well-positioned to participate in international criminal activities" (Global Survival Network, 1997:33).

Socio-economic and political factors connected to transition from communism and globalization as push/pull factors for prostitution, migration and sex trafficking are further reinforced by retraditionalisation of cultural images about sexuality. This retraditionalisation, as I already showed earlier in this book, is connected to both social changes in post-communist countries and globalization. As a push factor, this new images about sexuality influence women's vulnerability to sex trafficking by widening the gap between cultural expectations and the possibilities for achieving them (e.g. beautiful woman/sex object as an ideal and expensive beauty products, clothes etc.). At the same time, as a pull factor they operate through feeding the myth that working in the sex industry is an attractive job ("pretty woman syndrome", Oleszczuk and Buchowska, 1996:27). Cultural images of women as sex objects became a strong contributing factor for neutralizing and glorifying the scamy side of trafficking and prostitution abroad. But new gender images in post-communist countries media are part of much broader cultural tendencies associated with rapid liberalization of trade and economic activity across the world, especially with "market liberalism," as the "reorganization of economic and political life around the sovereignty of the citizen as a consumer"(Taylor and Jamieson, 1999:264). These cultural tendencies include colonization or commodification of sexuality, which is now playing an increasing role in the public culture of marketised societies throughout the world. But, as Connell found out, the impact of globalization is not limited to cultural images as push/pull factors for sex trafficking, but has an even more significant impact on the world gender order and its consequences on the demand for sex services:

> "Transnational business masculinity differs from traditional bourgeois masculinity by its increasingly libertarian sexuality, with a growing tendency to commodify relations with women. Hotels catering to businessmen in most parts of the world now routinely offer pornographic videos, and in some parts of the world, there is a well-developed prostitution industry catering to international businessmen."(Connell, 2001:65)

3.2 Facilitating factors

An important factor which facilitates sex trafficking is the development of organized crime which is under the significant influence of globalization (Williams, 1999:202), and which developed the sex industry, "based on and perpetuated by prevailing unequal socially and culturally defined gender and power relations" (Nurmi, 1999:10). Immigration laws and policies in destination countries as well as laws, and policies on migrant labor, migration and prostitution, and corrupt officials in both sending and destination countries further contribute to the development of sex trafficking merely by making organized crime possible (Konig, 1997:17). As observed by Wijers (1998:8),

> "While on the one hand the number of women seeking employment opportunities abroad has grown, on the other hand many destination countries, and especially the EU, have put in place more restrictive immigration policies, thereby further decreasing the opportunities for legal migration even when there is a demand for labor in the informal sector. The result is a growing gap between official policies in destination countries and day-to-day practices. This is where organized crime comes in, filling the gap that official policies leave".

In addition, the fact that prostitution is illegal in most of the destination countries makes the women marginalized, stigmatized and unprotected from abusive recruiters, brothel keepers and corrupt officials. Moreover, pimps/traffickers mainly use prostitution laws for blackmailing prostitutes, which makes their situations hopeless since their chances to escape and get protection hardly exist. If they dare to turn to the police, their chances of being arrested and deported are much greater than getting protection and safety. This is especially true in post-communist and war-affected destination countries, where, on the one hand, legal changes are slow and resources are limited, while, on the other hand, border control, criminal justice personnel and other officials are inefficient, corrupt and are not trained adequately. However, even Western countries consular officials seem not to be immune from corruption, which makes the traffickers' plans even more feasible[142].

A good illustration of inefficient and corrupt officials as an obstacle for trafficked women to get protection, even when they manage to return to their own country, owing to the help of non-governmental organizations, are the words of Maria Minkova from Animus Association, Bulgaria:

> "We have a lot of cases of women who are lucky enough to come back. Most of them are quite traumatized. They suffer from posttraumatic stress disorder or depression. The problem is to find a safe place for them to stay when they come back. Usually they are supposed to go back to their families, which they sometimes do not want. And if they do not want to go back, we try to help them to rent a flat or to find a job. But if they are young women, 16

[142] One of the known examples occurred in the French Embassy in Bulgaria, when it was discovered that in a two-year period tens of thousands of illegal visas were issued. As a consequence two members of the Embassy's staff lost their jobs and there were speculations that the French Ambassador in Bulgaria was replaced because of that as well - Dz.Sabljakovic " Prostitutke smenile ambasadora" (Prostitutes replaced ambassador), *Danas*, August 30, 2001, p. 21.

years old for example, they can go either to their parents or to an orphanage. So, there is no safe place for them. If they go to their family, they are not safe there because there is usually no protection from the police. We encourage girls and their parents to explain the case to the police, but sometimes the police do not want to interfere, or sometimes even police are connected with criminals." (Minkova, interview, 1999).

3.3 Militarism and war related factors

Militarism and war are strong factors which influence prostitution and sex trafficking in women and children. Their impact is mostly connected to the war and post-war situation, but may also be a consequence of the very presence of military in the region, regardless of whether there is war going on or not in the precise country. Thus, the impact of militarism on sex trafficking is not necessarily connected to the the war, while war always produces both socio-economic push factors and militarist cultural ideals about gender and, consequently, increases the vulnerability of women to sex trafficking.

During the war, and most often for sometime afterward, there are several ways the push/pull factors for sex trafficking are generated.

The presence of armed forces (including international peace keeping forces) in war-affected territories and their surrounding inevitably creates increased demand for the sex industry and attracts traffickers (Konig, 1997:85; Euler and Welzer-Lang, 2000:17). But, once created, this demand is usually maintained in the post-war period as well. Most often, this is connected to the post-war presence of international peacekeeping forces and, sometimes, as in Bosnia and Kosovo, the expansion of prostitution and sex trafficking is a direct consequence of the arrival of peacekeeping forces and/or building of huge military bases. As pointed out by Kelley (2000:57), the connection between the military and the sex industry does not necessarily need the war to be actively fought. Thus, for example, Jan Austad, a specialized officer from Interpol, says that "before the war in the Yugoslav province of Kosovo, gangs of ethnic Albanians abducted or lured women to Italy, for clients there and to points north. After the war, the gangs set up brothels to cater to the international armed forces stationed there." [143] Prostitution bars were opened in Kosovo in July 1999, immediately after the end of the war and after the arrival of 45,000 KFOR soldiers. Most of the bars were found in the South of Kosovo, between the Albanian and Macedonian border. This is how Kosovo was transformed from a transit to a destination area.[144] In January 2001, in Macedonia, Albania and Kosovo, there were about 50,000 international peacekeeping soldiers as well as about 7,000 workers of different international organizations (Bacanovic, 2001:105)

According to unofficial estimates of non-governmental organizations, there are about 10,000 trafficked women working as sex slaves in Bosnia and Herzegovina. The following is a typical one:

[143] The message received through STOP-TRAFFIC @friends-partners.org list on March 27,2000.

[144] "Zabava kosta 100 maraka" (The fun costs 100 marks), *Blic*, January 5, 2000.

> "Carmen and her friends answered an advertisement for waitresses in Italy.published in their home-town newspaper. They were promised the equivalent of 150 pounds a month and tickets - a small fortune in a country where the average monthly wage is 20 pounds, if you can get a job in the first place. They met their escort in a bar in Moldova's capital, Chisinau, and were driven over the border into Romania, on to Serbia and to an apartment in the capital: 'We were told we would fly from Belgrade.' The driver left with their passports - they never saw him again. Another man collected Carmen and a Ukrainian girl. They were made to lie in the back of a car in the freezing cold and driven over the border into Bosnia." [145]

The violence to which women are exposed is very similar to war violence:

> "The coffee bars springing up in Bosnia bear a chilling resemblance to these wartime rape houses, but the war is now a silent one...Those who cause trouble are easily disposed of. Last year, the naked bodies of two women were found in a river near Arizona Market. Both bore the marks of mafia-style killings - hands tied behind their backs, feet bound to concrete. Tape over their mouth was marked "Organization for Security and Cooperation in Europe". The symbols of protection had been used to stifle their screams. Their identities are impossible to trace"[146].

Having in mind, for example, the Philippines, Okinawa and Thailand[147], there is the danger that the war and/or post-war increase in prostitution will be transformed into peacetime institutionalization of the sex industry as well. Also, it is well known that the sex industry develops and the vulnerability of women to sex trafficking increases with the building of military bases. Thus, prostitution and related trafficking in women may become a long-term problem in the Balkans solely in connection to the emergence of new military bases in the former Yugoslavia, such as Camp Bondsteal (Kosovo), which is expected to be the largest military base in the Europe (Euler, 2000:75). A similar situation exists in Bosnia, where the irony is that Arizona Market, established by peacekeeping forces after the war to foster trade between Serbs, Croats and Muslims, has grown "into five square miles of sinister black facade, where women from the former Soviet Union and elsewhere in Eastern Europe are sold to the highest bidder." The Market is situated near the towns of Brcko and Tuzla, which boast "one of the highest concentrations of the international police force created to establish law and order in Bosnia, one of the largest American army bases and one of the biggest UN-administered aid packages of the post-war years"[148].

[145] K.Holt "Captive Market", *The Sunday Times Magazine*, February 18, 2001.

[146] ibidem.

[147] For example, in the late 1960s, Thailand was used as a place for "rest and recreation" for American G.I.s in Vietnam. After the end of the war, prostitution became one of the main financial resources for Thailand. By developing "mass sex tourism" as a means to pay off its debts, it actually encouraged the peacetime institutionalization of sex industry (Williams, 1999:153). Similar occurred in the Philippines. Also, although 1972 Okinawa returned to Japanese administration, prostitution "continued to be the mainstay of the economy" (Euler and Welzer-Lang, 2000:17).

[148] K.Holt "Captive Market", *The Sunday Times Magazine*, February 18, 2001

As in other countries (Kelley, 2000:58), there is considerable evidences of the involvement of international soldiers in Macedonia, Kosovo and Bosnia both as clients and pimps/traffickers (Bacanovic, 2001:108 and many press reports from Kosovo and Bosnia).

> "In a report broadcast on German television last week (17 December), a 16-year-old Bulgarian girl said she was sold to a nightclub in Tetovo (near Macedonia's northern border with Kosovo) and that hundreds of German soldiers were among her clients. In the televised report, a German soldier acknowledged being with the same girl, and said that he knew other KFOR soldiers who frequented brothels in FRY of Macedonia where underage girls are being kept."[149]

> "In September, six Russians, believed to be SFOR soldiers, allegedly went to a bar near Doboj in northern Bosnia and gang-raped two Moldovan women. It transpired that both women were 'owned' by the club. No charges have been brought against the soldiers, even though the bar owner says he can identify them."[150]

> "A Hungarian sex worker, who worked mainly in Pristina, where we had connections from before the troubles, reported that the Russian KFOR were bringing women in for sex work. This repeated the pattern established in earlier years by the Ukrainian contingent of UNPROFOR in Croatia."[151]

> "For two years, the Chief of Defense Denmark has known that Danish KFOR soldiers frequent prostitutes, who have been kidnapped and held captive by Albanian mafia groups in Ohrid in Macedonia. Despite their knowledge, the army command is still sending Danish soldiers on 60-hour leaves (R&Rs) to Ohrid where they buy sex and thereby support the local mafia. According to the former soldier, around 80% of the Danish soldiers in Macedonia frequent prostitutes"[152].

Lack of prospects connected to the war influenced the demand for paid sex not only by men involved in the army but also by those in the rear. A good illustration is found in Serbia during NATO bombing:

> "While NATO was bombing and destroying Serbian factories and the very foundation of Serbian national economy, the illegal sex market is doing business better than ever. While all other advertisements are rare, those called 'personal contacts' are as numerous as they were in the best of times. Innumerable escort agencies advertise sex services, skillfully adjusting them to the actual moment: 'Young, attractive and unprotected invites real man in her shelter', or 'Two most discrete and bravest women in their own shelter', or 'My shelter is the most comfortable, come, you will not be sorry."[153]

[149] The message received through STOP-TRAFFIC @friends-partners.org list on December 24, 2000.

[150] K.Holt "Captive Market", *The Sunday Times Magazine*, February 18, 2001

[151] The message received through STOP-TRAFFIC @friends-partners.org list on February 10,2000.

[152] The message received through STOP-TRAFFIC @friends-partners.org list on July 21, 2001.

[153] D.Vucicevic "U skloniste sa rasnom plavusom" (In the shelter with racial blond), *Glas javnosti*, June 21, 1999.

Unemployment, poverty and lack of prospects in general, resulting from the war, influence both supply and demand for prostitution/trafficking. Desperate women easily become vulnerable to false promises and deception, as well as to different forms of violence. [154] Traffickers exploit the fact that many persons are in vulnerable situations, undocumented and separated from their families. As stated by Peter Von Behtlemfavy from IOM, the number of illegal prostitutes from the Balkans, where close to a decade of war has wiped out many ordinary jobs, has tripled if not quadrupled from 1995 to 2000.[155]As I already showed, refugees are especially vulnerable, both while fleeing from war zones and when finding themselves in exile. The most widespread in the region was obviously the trafficking of Kosovo Albanian and Roma refugee women (Bacanovic, 2001:106). Apart from their desperate situation as refugees, they were also vulnerable since once raped (either by Serb forces in the war zone or by traffickers while fleeing it) they knew that their families would never accept them back. Thus, they became involved in sex trafficking much easier than raped women in peacetime and those from less patriarchal societies (Nurmi, 1999:6), they become involved in sex trafficking. As Kelley (2000:58) noticed in Bosnia, one of the most common routes into the sex industry is rape, which makes women "unmarriageable." Consequently, armed conflict makes survival even more precarious.

> "Young ethnic Albanian Kosovo refugee women in this camp in Vlora, Albania, are often approached by men promising them work or school, but who actually want to sell them into prostitution...The smugglers sometimes carry another cargo - Kosovo girls, taken by force or persuasion to Italy, where they are sold into prostitution. So far only a handful are believed to have been snared by the Albanian gangs...But with international refugee officials saying they may move 100,000 people out of the northern border camps at Kukes, thousands of women could soon be trucked to the gang strongholds of Durres, Fier and Vlora, where miserable living conditions in filthy camps guarded by corrupt Albanian police would make them easy prey."[156]

> "As the crisis wears on, the Albanian gangs have developed more subtle methods. While Albanian girls are often duped into prostitution by false offers of marriage, the Kosovo girls face false offers of free travel, schooling and jobs abroad. In late April at a camp run by the Italian military near Vlora, five girls aged 16 to 18 were lured away by Albanian men who told their families they would have good jobs and a bright future in Italy. The Italians have since strengthened security at the camp, requiring escorts to accompany visitors. Most camps are not, however, run by NATO. In the facilities run by Albanian authorities, security is often a problem. Many have no fences. 'And', said Sevem Arbana, director of an anti-trafficking association in Tirana, 'the Albanian police who guard them can be bribed with cigarettes and orange juice."

[154] See examples on p.111

[155] J.Smith "Sex Trade Enslaves East Europeans Migrant Women Brutalized in Burgeoning Business", *The Washington Post*, July 25, 2000.

[156] L.Montgomery "Albanians sell Kosovo women into prostitution", *Miami Herald*, May 30, 1999.

> "Alina, who had lived in Pristina until her husband and son were killed in front of her by masked members of a Serbain militia, within days of NATO airstrikes starting, is one of the first known Kosovan refugees forced into prostitution by an Albanian mafia gang. In early April she was approached by a man in Kukas, an Albanian refugee camp she had fled to. He said he would find work and a home for her in Italy. The Albanian drove her to the coast, from where she was smuggled in a speedboat across the Adriatic at night, with other illegal immigrants. She landed somewhere on the coast of southern Italy, to be met by four Albanian men....'I was already mourning the loss of my husband and my son, and now I was forced to sell my body', Alina said. 'The Albanians told me do this or we will beat you, do this or we will kill you."[157]

Lawlessness and corruption, i.e. social disorganization and a state of anomie, have a serious impact on the increase of sex trafficking in war-affected areas as well. The negative impact of war on the functioning of the criminal justice system and the absence of the rule of law in general had obviously influenced an increase of crime, including especially the increase of violent and organized crime. In the Federal Republic of Yugoslavia, i.e. Serbia, the international isolation during the regime of former president Milosevic, which meant that ties with Interpol, other international organizations and other countries' police were severed, was an additional factor which had generated enormous human trafficking.[158] However, it is worth stressing that the links between traffickers "extended beyond the usual boundaries of ethnic hatred in the Balkans. Criminal Serbs, Montenegrins and Albanians collaborated closely to transport the victims and share the profits." [159] After the war, the wartime infrastructure of the mafia was easily transferred to postwar crime and it was able to bring large numbers of illegal immigrants into the country.[160]

4. EXPLAINING SOCIAL CHANGE, GENDER AND SEX TRAFFICKING

Women's vulnerability to sex trafficking is the result of consequences, produced in everyday life and gender identities of both women and men by structural changes in post-communist and war-affected countries as well as in the world as a whole. As I argue in this chapter, microsocial expressions of macrosocial factors, such as transition from communism, war and globalization, serve as strong push factors for women's migration, their employment in the sex industry and vulnerability to sex trafficking. At the same time, as a result of both economic changes, i.e. hardships and changes in

[157] J.Follain and E.Hamzic report on the vise trail from Kosovo, *The Sunday Times*, May 16, 1999, received through STOP-TRAFFIC @friends-partners.org list on May 21, 1999.

[158] "Montenegro to crack down on human trafficking", *The Associated Press*, December 11, 2000, received through STOP-TRAFFIC @friends-partners.org list on December 11, 2000.

[159] J.Smith "Sex Trade Enslaves East Europeans Migrant Women Brutalized in Burgeoning Business", *The Washington Post*, July 25, 2000.

[160] R.Fisk "UK:Immigration - how Sarajevo has become the springboard into Europe", *Independent*, February 5, 2001, p.3

normative heterosexuality, both women and men are also pushed/attracted to take jobs within the sex industry and/or to involve themselves in sex trafficking as organized crime. Thus, both women and men tend to secure economic survival as well as social standing for reaffirming one's gender (Messerschmidt, 1993:122).

As I already mentioned, men's and women's attempts to achieve the traditional cultural model of sexuality are most obvious in the rise of prostitution and other forms of the sex industry in post-communist society. However, the organization of work within the sex industry and sex trafficking "business" is always gendered, reproducing and reworking traditional cultural images about sexuality. These images are largely influenced by imitation of Western images and lead to putting women first in the position of sex object or on lower level within the hierarchy of the sex industry, i.e. the criminal organization dealing with it. Thus, as pointed out by Messerschmidt (1993:120), "gender relations are unequal, reflecting the social structures of labor, power, and normative heterosexuality...the men act as agents and/or companions of these women, substantially profiting from their labor."

While a man is the one who always voluntarily chooses his position within the sex business in order to both secure earnings and assert his maleness, women are those who are much more often forced to use their gender in a traditional way, without even being rewarded for it. Moreover, they are put in slavery conditions and severely abused. As pointed out by Messerschmidt, "pimp violence becomes a means of disciplining the prostitute and of constructing a badass public masculinity...Pimping, then, is a resource for surmounting oppressive class and race conditions and for reasserting the social dominance of men. Moreover, like other men, pimps associate masculinity with work, with authority and control, and with explicit heterosexuality". As a result, pimping and trafficking are not limited to men's doing of hegemonic masculinity. They are also and more importantly a form of social action which facilitates and reproduces all the traditional gender structures (gender divisions of labor and power as well as normative heterosexuality) (Messerschmidt, 1993:124).

But, for understanding sex trafficking as a form of transnational crime, it is also important to take into consideration the relationships between masculinities and femininities themselves worldwide. Sex trafficking would be hardly imaginable without the gap between poor and wealthy countries. Consequently, there is the hierarchy between masculinities of men in these countries with men from poor, i.e. post-communist and war-affected countries being subordinated to masculinities of men they provide women for (e.g. wealthy Western businessmen and soldiers of international forces). In addition, women from sending countries are treated as less worthy in comparison to prostitutes from destination countries, as well as to women engaged in sex trafficking as offenders. Hence, their femininity is treated as subordinate to both the the femininity of prostitutes from destination countries and femininity of female recruiters and pimps. It seems that the place which both women and men have within the economic structure usually determines the role they have within the sex industry business in national as well as international context.

The probability to become a victim of trafficking is greater the younger a woman is and thus more often seen (by herself and/or by potential recruiters) as a sex object, as well as with her marginalization and hopelessness related to the difficulty of her economic, war-related, family or similar situation. Women's desperate state because of their difficult situation and their efforts to find a solution/exit from it both contributes to their inaccurate perception of risks, i.e. of a mistaken cost/ benefit calculation and the failure to anticipate danger.

Bearing in mind the previous analysis, it is possible to identify three groups of factors, which influence the victimization of women as well as men's and women's involvement in sex trafficking as offenders: macrosocietal factors, psychological and psychosocial factors as well as cultural factors and gender role socialization. The following model may be used as a starting point for the development of a theoretical model for an explanation of sex trafficking, social change and gender:

A. Macrosocietal factors

1. Market and war related economy;
2. Expansion of the sex industry;
3. Economic and war-related changes/oppression, which push women to become victims of trafficking as well as both women and men to be involved in trafficking as offenders;
4. An increasing gap between rich and poor countries and an increased presence of military.

B. Psychological and psychosocial factors

1. Victims -women's vulnerability: psychological state resulted from sexual or domestic violence, homelessness, family problems, war-related displacement, economic problems or similar; low self-esteem; poverty; unemployment; social isolation and marginalisation; drug use.
2. Offenders: women's and men's readiness to misuse women's vulnerability in order to solve their own economic problems related to social change/war; lack of empathy; unemployment; poverty.

C. Cultural factors and gender role socialization

Retraditionalisation of normative masculinities/femininities regarding sexuality as desirable cultural ideals for both women and men; patriarchal socialization of both women and men.

As may be seen from the listed factors, as with domestic violence, sex trafficking can be explained only by using a multivariate model which shows that multiple risk factors that cause men's violence against women interact, vary and overlap in complex way. Also, the model accounts for the way macrosocietal factors, patriarchy as well as other forms of oppression of women as well as oppression of men are mirrored on a micro level, i.e. in gender role socialization, psychosocial characteristics of men and interactions between women and men. As my survey findings show, it is not possible to understand the wave of sex trafficking of women from Eastern and Central Europe without taking into account both macrosocial and micro (social and individual) risk factors which either predispose or trigger violence against women. Thus, as shown by Bales's research on new slavery, my survey shows that slavery flourishes in societies under stress and in extreme poverty:

> "Existing power structures are overturned and a battle breaks out to fill the power vacuum. Economies that had been stable, though perhaps poor, are replaced by haphazard development and exploitation. And, as we have seen, in the absence of law, greed can overwhelm human rights" (Bales, 1999:31, 245).

CHAPTER 6

CIVIL SOCIETY, FEMINISM AND INSTITUTIONAL CHANGES

1. INTRODUCTION

As demonstrated in previous chapters, economic hardships and the widening of social differences resulted from the introduction of a market economy, rapid privatization and war. Combined with a renewed traditionalism and masculinity crisis and an upheaval in the traditional gender structure in the institution of marriage, this led to negative consequences in marital relationships. In addition, the widening of the gap between poor and rich countries, ethnic conflicts and war, as well as related migration, led to the commercialization of women's bodies and the expansion of the sex industry in general, and prostitution, in particular. Thus, the costs of changes, in terms of deterioration of interpersonal relationships and violence, seem to be high in all four countries, with people from Serbia and Macedonia being in the worst situation, since they were additionally affected by ethnic conflicts and militarism.

However, positive changes are also obvious. These are mainly related to the democratization of political life, including pluralism, new freedoms and the development of relationships with Western countries, which led to the creation of civil society. In addition, the West's increased interest in investing not only in the economies of these countries, but also in the development of human rights, i.e. including in the improvement of legal systems and policies, is also significant since it offered resources for these new initiatives to develop. Hence, both political and (negative and positive) economic changes functioned as pull/push factors for the development of civil society, the women's movement and legal/institutional changes. In this regard, many long-term positive changes were initiated in the field of protection of human rights for women.

Especially telling was the creation of non-governmental organizations in general, and women's non-governmental organizations in particular, and an increased interest among post-communist states (excepting Serbia before 2000) in showing their democratic face to the world, and in entering international organizations by, among other things, changing laws and policies regarding violence against women. In this chapter I will review the scope and nature of these achievements in order to show how macrolevel changes, produced within a new social context, i.e. their proportions, quality and sustainability, are linked to both micro and macro level changes connected to the transition from communism, globalization and war.

2. WOMEN'S MOVEMENT AND FEMINISM IN POST-COMMUNIST SOCIETIES

Second wave feminism and the worldwide rise of the autonomous women's movement in 1960's and 1970's were certainly significant generators of change regarding women's issues in general and also with regard to violence against women, in particular. However, this development hardly had any impact on women's organizing in the communist countries of Central and Eastern Europe. With the exception of the former Yugoslavia, i.e. Slovenia, Croatia and Serbia, where feminism and the first seeds of women's organizing appeared already in mid-1970's, in other countries women's groups arose only later, after the change from communist regimes was achieved, i.e. during 1990's.

However, the lack of autonomous women's groups during communism does not mean that the women's movement was completely absent in these countries. In Hungary, Serbia and Bulgaria, for example, strong women's organizations existed before the Second World War (Arpad and Marinovich, 1995:82; Bozinovic, 1996:109; Daskalova, 1999:190-192).[161] When communists took power after the war, the earlier women's organizations were banned and replaced by official organizations of the communist party. In this way, the development of the original women's organizations was interrupted and did not continue in most countries before the end of the communist regimes.

Social transformations which occurred after the change in communist regimes offered favorable conditions for the development of women's initiatives and the self-organizing of women, i.e. for the creation of autonomous women's movements. Factors which were especially beneficial in that regard were political pluralism, freedom of speech and self-organizing, i.e. development of democratic institutions in general, as well as increased permeability of borders, especially communication with the West. The impact of these factors, as I will show later, varied in different countries, mainly depending on the degree to which these factors were developed both during and after communism.

In addition, some factors which had negative effects on the everyday lives of women and their social position in general, such as unemployment, poverty, war and women's exclusion from formal politics, had, paradoxically, a positive impact on the development of the women's movement. As pointed out by Watson, the East European revolution, "as the French Revolution two hundred years before, had a dual effect: it consigned women to the domestic sphere, but it also created the necessary preconditions for the emergence of feminism" (Watson, 1993:477). The influence of these factors on the rise of the women's movement is twofold. On one side, the worsening of the economic situation, war suffering and women's exclusion from formal politics motivated women to self-organize in order to defend their interests, help other women and resist war. On the other side, similar factors such as the increase in women's unemployment and exclusion from official political life[162]

[161] Women's organizations existed before the Second World War in Macedonia as well but they were not as strong as in Serbia and other parts of the former Yugoslavia (Bozinovic, 1996:112-115)

[162] Najcevska also stresses that women, who felt excluded from official politics tended to compensate for their exclusion through their activism within NGO's (interview, 1999). However, it seems that traditional gender stereotypes played some role as well since women themselves chose to be involved in NGO's (as connected to less power and less responsibility) rather than in political activities. The best example may be the low level of participation of women not only in state political bodies but also

created spare time, which they did not have earlier and which some used for feminist activism. However, apart from enthusiasm and the time factor as crucial mobilization (people) resources on which any social movement relies (Freeman, 1979:172), women's NGO's, as other NGO's in post-communist societies, in some way became the substitutes for formal employment as well. Thus, although the earnings that women were able to get through activism have been usually very modest, in the difficult economic situation in which they found themselves, it was an additional motivation for some of them to decide to get involved in the women's movement. Therefore, the importance of a possibility for earning and solidarity with other women as selective incentives for mobilization of the women's movement increased as much as the living conditions of women worsened. Thus, as occurred with other social movements, the decision to join the women's movement was based on both the collective good and self-interest, i.e. a cost benefit consideration (Fireman and Gamson, 1979:27). This latter was especially pronounced in those countries which were seriously affected by economic difficulties and did not have autonomous women's groups during communism, such as Bulgaria and Macedonia.[163] In Serbia, feminist activism also had an additional psychotherapeutic dimension since many women tried to heal themselves from the feeling of powerlessness, i.e. to escape from their own desperate reality, by helping other women.

Opening toward the West was very important as a precondition for East European women's access to feminist ideas and Western women' s experiences of self-organizing, but the emergence of Western financially and other support was also crucial for East European women's initiatives. Even in Serbia, which in the 1990's was more isolated than before, foreign financial support for women's NGO-s was present, more or less, all the time. Moreover, in the most difficult years, this support came almost exclusively from international women's organizations. As Blagojevic points out, "at the moment when Serbia was cut off from the rest of the world, perhaps the only thing that worked smoothly and was a 'normal' connection with the world were women's organizations (Nikolic-Ristanovic et al, 1998:51)

Among the countries included in my survey, the impact of Western feminist ideas on the development of women's organizations seems to be the strongest in Serbia, less strong in Hungary, and the weakest in Bulgaria and Macedonia. The strongest impact of Western feminism in Serbia is not surprising, since during communism Serbia was much more open toward the West than other countries which enabled feminism to start developing in mid-1970's.[164] Feminist ideas,

---

as members of political parties. Also, as Blagojevic points out, by accepting "the women's victim story," women's groups accepted traditional gender roles (Blagojevic, 1998:26).

163 Interviews with Tatyana Kotzeva (Bulgaria) and Mirjana Najcevska (Macedonia). Also, Blagojevic points out that the move from volunteer to paid work was a special challenge for the women's movement in Serbia and it speeded the process of transformation of feminist activism into a profession (Blagojevic, 1998:31). This latter was also noticed in other post-communist and some Western countries. For example, as Lang points out, both East and West German women's movements have metamorphosed from overarching movements into small-scale professionalized organizations (NGO-s) (Lang, 1997:102.)

164 Feminist panels, meetings and other events with participation of feminists from Western countries have been organized in Belgrade on a regular basis from 1975 to 1992 when the war and international isolation of Serbia prevented from continuing.

developed during communism through intensive contacts and exchange of information with Western feminists, resulted in the creation of the first Belgrade feminist group as early as in 1979, which in 1986 was transformed into the group Zena i drustvo (Woman and society) (Blagojevic, 1998:47-59). This was decisive for the developments in 1990's, when political pluralism and increased possibilities for self-organizing created favorable conditions for the creation of nongovernmental organizations in general, and women's NGO's in particular. At the beginning of 1990's, new women's organizations derived from the feminist group Woman and Society, and this is how development of the autonomous women's movement in Serbia started.

Since the free exchange of information with Western countries was an important precondition for the development of feminist ideas, other countries, which were much more closed during communist times, mainly came in touch with the ideas of second wave feminism only after the change of the former regimes.

In Hungary, the first feminist group, Feminist Network, was established soon after the changes - in 1990. As Woman and Society in Serbia, Feminist Network's main aim was to disseminate feminist ideas and raise women's consciousness and it served as the root organization from which other autonomous women's groups were created. Thus, Western feminist ideas in both Serbia and Hungary obviously shaped the development of autonomous women's groups created in the post-communist period, even when some of them refused to declare themselves feminist.

However, the development of the women's movement in Macedonia and Bulgaria was significantly different. The first women's organizations created in both Macedonia and Bulgaria immediately after the political changes were successors of massive women's organizations from communist times, i.e. official organizations of the former communist party. [165] In both Macedonia and Bulgaria, feminist ideas became available later than in Serbia and Hungary and the impact of Western feminism on development of women's initiatives was much less present, especially at the beginning. However, later on, within these large organizations or under their auspices, autonomous women's groups started to emerge, such as SOS hotlines and refuges for battered women, as well as different interest and professional women's organizations. Although these large organizations, like similar organizations in Hungary and Serbia, mainly tend to maintain traditional gender stereotypes and patronizing attitudes toward women (Daskalova, 1997:163;Hochberg, 1997:107; Bejkova, interview 1999), they are also, especially in Macedonia and Hungary, ready to co-operate with autonomous women's groups in order to struggle for women's common interests.[166]

165 Although the Association of Hungarian Women has the same origin, and was the first Hungarian women's organization established as an NGO after the political changes, its impact on further development of women's groups in Hungary was less than the impact of similar organizations in Bulgaria and Macedonia.

166 The exception is the Association of Women of Yugoslavia who never accepted cooperation with autonomous women's groups. This was a consequence of its complete political instrumentalisation and loyalty to the ruling party, who considered all NGO's its enemies. Paradoxically, even the former communist party's official women's organization was more friendly toward feminists. For example, I

Thus, in Hungary, Macedonia and Bulgaria, as in the Western feminist movement, there are large membership organizations of women as well as small organizations. As in the West, there is also a distinct age difference between them, i.e. they represent different political generations (Freeman, 1979:168). However, small organizations, especially in Bulgaria and Macedonia, often tend to become professional organizations.

As already mentioned, the Association of Hungarian women, established in 1989, was the first women's organization registered as such after the political changes in Hungary. In both Serbia and Hungary, several new organizations were established between 1989 and 1991.In Macedonia and Bulgaria, however, 1991 was the year when the first women's organizations based on self organizing were established, with successors of former communist women's organizations, as in other countries, being among the first.[167]

The development of women's groups was gradual in both Hungary and Macedonia. However, in Bulgaria, the raise of NGO's was rather slow until 1995[168], when it started suddenly to flourish. In Serbia, the development of women's NGO's was especially evident during the wars in Croatia and Bosnia (between 1992 and 1995) and, even more, after the end of these wars (1995-1999), and after the Milosevic regime fell in 2000.

Differences in the dynamics of development of the women's movement seem to be connected with both the external and internal incentives and, especially, with differences in resource mobilization priorities. For example, feminist ideology, solidarity and commitment were the main incentives for the autonomous women's movements in Serbia and Hungary. Hence, especially at the beginning, they relied primarily on people as a resource, while money had a marginal role. This could explain the fact that the first autonomous women's groups were established in Serbia and Hungary soon after the political context changed, i.e. when neither international nor internal funding was yet available. This "first wave" in the development of the women's movement continued in Serbia during the wars in neighboring Bosnia and Croatia as well. However, after the end of the wars, and with both a decrease in the standard of living and an increase in international funding, new women's groups started to flourish in Serbia. Thus, this "second wave" in the development of the

---

was invited to make a presentation about domestic violence at one of the last meetings of the official Yugoslavian women's organization held in 1989. Other feminist activists were invited as well and in conclusion, there was an assessment that changes of laws regarding marital rape and domestic violence were necessary. However, the worsening of situation in Serbia as a whole made the achievement of these conclusions much less realistic at the end of 1990's than 10 years earlier.

167 This is not unusual, having in mind that, unlike completely new organizations, these organizations did not have problems with resources since they simply continued to use the resources of the organizations from which they originated.

168 Kotzeva explains this trend by the fact that the establishment of NGO's in general has been seriously hindered by the re-emergence of nationalistic and regional politics. She also considers that in the context of a weak 'pro civil society' ideology, during the first years of transition, rare women's organizations were elitist, their influence in society was very constrained and their mobilization role was slight (Kotzeva, 1999:88).

women's movement in Serbia was more influenced by the availability of money than the first one.[169]

For some Macedonian and most of the Bulgarian organizations the situation was different from that in Serbia and Hungary. It seems that, especially in Bulgaria, money and expertise had priority as resources. After the political changes, most of the introductory knowledge about discrimination against women in general and violence against women in particular was transferred to women from these countries through Western and international NGO's, who organized conferences, researches, trainings and inquiries about potential partner organizations.[170] As a result, the transfer of both ideas and money is most obvious in these countries, and particularly in Bulgaria. This may explain, for example, both the high level of professionalism of women's organizations in Bulgaria and the rapid development of the women's movement after 1995. As Bulgarian feminist historian Daskalova puts it, "the appearance of women's NGO's in Bulgaria was a consequence of the appearance of foreign funding organizations rather than of women's interests to deal with their own problems" (interview, 1999).

At the time of the survey, women's groups were the most numerous in Serbia (49 plus 10 groups in Kosovo[171]), while in the other countries the number of women's groups was smaller, such as 21 in Hungary, 24 in Macedonia and 23 in Bulgaria.[172] The largest concentration of women's groups in all countries was in their capitals, with Serbia having the largest and Hungary the smallest network of organizations in other parts of the country. It seems that only in Serbia was it possible to speak about the existence of a kind of autonomous women's movement, even if co-operation among groups was still on a low level. Apart from women's groups who advocated around different aspects of women's rights and the autonomy of women, in all

[169] It is even more pronounced in the "third wave" of the development of the Serbian women's movement, which started after the fall of Milosevic in 2000, coinciding with the increased interest of international foundations to fund NGO's in Serbia.

[170] Transfer of ideas was most obvious through research, publications, training and conferences organized by Minnesota Advocates for Human Rights and ABA CEELI in both Macedonia and Bulgaria, after which American ideas about violence against women became very popular there.

[171] All groups in Kosovo were run by Albanian women, while Serbian women's groups (as well as other Serbian NGO's) did not exist at all. This may be explained by the extremely good social and economic position of Serbs in Kosovo during Milosevic's regime, so that they were not motivated to self-organize (Milenkovic, Maletin, unpublished). Also, it is worth mentioning that the ethnic conflict in Kosovo and the NATO bombing cut off all relationships between Serbia and Kosovo. This made it impossible for me to get details about the work of Albanian women's groups. Also, possible analysis of Albanian groups from Kosovo in the survey which examines the situation in Serbia would pose both politically sensitive and methodological questions which I tried to avoid by abandoning my previous idea about doing it.

[172] I took into consideration only those groups which are clearly established as NGO's. Thus, the groups which are parts of political parties and trade unions were not considered. However, the given numbers should not be taken for granted, since, especially in Bulgaria and Hungary, it was difficult to make a clear distinction between different forms of women's organizations. Determination of the precise numbers was especially difficult since different sources use different criteria and as a consequence give different information.

countries, but far more often in Hungary, Macedonia and Bulgaria, there were also other groups such as:

a) Women's interest groups, professional associations of women and minority women's groups, concerned mainly to lobby for their own group interests;
b) Groups of women who are struggling for broader social interests rather than for the autonomy of women (for example, the environmental group Women for Balaton in Hungary or Women's Federation for World Peace in both Hungary and Macedonia).

In Hungary and Bulgaria women's interest and professional groups were more frequent than in Macedonia and Serbia. In all countries, there were also a number of women's organizations within trade unions and political parties, but less often in Serbia than in other countries. Also, in all countries, there were some newly created groups who tended to promote traditional values and gender stereotypes.

The majority of women's groups in all four countries deal in some way with issues of violence against women.[173] However, only few of them deal predominantly or exclusively with violence against women. Other women's organizations deal with issues such as: discrimination against marginal women, economic, social and political rights and empowerment of women, antiwar activism, network building, women's studies, etc. They deal with these issues mainly through panels, training, lectures, research, publications, by providing a free information service and legal aid to women in cases other then violence as well as through lobbying for law changes.

Groups involving marginal women who struggle for their own autonomy exist in all countries. However, while in Serbia these groups include refugee, lesbian, disabled and ethnic minority women's groups, in Macedonia, Hungary and Bulgaria there are only groups of ethnic minority women.[174] A large part of the activities of women's groups, especially in Serbia and Macedonia, include humanitarian aid and support of refugees. Because of ethnic conflicts, the large number of refugees and constant and rapid impoverishment, the latter was an additional activity for almost all women's groups in Serbia, regardless of their main focus. In addition, some organizations in Serbia, such as "Lastavica", the house for refugee women from Krajina, were established specifically for supporting refugee women.

Only a small number of women's organizations deal with economic and political issues. Some groups deal with the economic empowerment of women as their main activity (for example, Gea and Women in Action in Serbia and Association of Business Women in both Serbia and Bulgaria). Women's House in Hungary organizes training for both women managers and housemaids, and also mediates between women who need help in housekeeping and those who offer this service (Nemeskesy, interview, 1999). However, it seems that most efforts in Serbia are

[173] The activities of these groups are discussed in more details later in this chapter.

[174] For example, in Macedonia there are organizations of Albanian, Serbian, Walach and Turkish women, while in Bulgaria and Hungary there are only Roma women's groups.

made to promote self-employment of women as well as to try to secure the sustainability of women's groups through their own economic activity. [175]

At the time of the survey, the only autonomous women's political organization in the region was Women in Black in Serbia. [176] The organization was established in 1991 as a response to the beginning of the war in the former Yugoslavia. Its main aim was to make visible women's resistance to the war and to broaden the anti-war network of solidarity of women from the former Yugoslavia. The main activities of Women in Black included: anti-war protests, including regular weekly vigils in downtown Belgrade, publications in several languages, annual meetings of Women's solidarity network against war and support for refugees.[177] Through all these activities, Women in Black also dealt with the issue of violence as a consequence of militarism and cooperated with other women's groups whose main activities are related to domestic and sexual violence.

Feminist academic work has partly developed within the universities and partly within non-governmental organizations. The latter was especially the case in countries such as Serbia, where the material conditions for the development of new courses barely existed within the universities and other academic institutions. An exception is a women's studies course established in 1993 and not so regularly thaught in the Department of Sociology of the Arts Faculty in Belgrade. Thus, most women's studies courses, feminist researches and publications in Serbia emerged under the auspices of women's NGO's. [178]

[175] For example, only in Serbia are there several women's second hand shops, women's safe houses and houses for refugee women that support themselves mainly through different forms of women's work (e.g. farming, catering service for women's and other NGO's, etc.).

[176] At the end of 1980's and the beginning of 1990's there were several political women's organizations in Serbia (Women's Lobby, Women's Party and Women's Parliament). Since the beginning of the war in the former Yugoslavia, "pure" political projects were replaced by anti-war activism concentrated in the activities of Women in Black, in which women from almost all women's groups took part. As stated by Blagojevic, it seems that unsuccessful attempts in preventing the war resulted in women's organizing in order to resist the war (Blagojevic, 1998:25). Later on, almost all women's groups were involved in some kind of political struggle against Milosevic's regime, resulting in its end in 2000.

[177] They found the model for their activities in the countries where the Women in Black network was established previously, such as Italy, Israel, Spain, Germany and USA.

[178] At the time of the survey three autonomous women's studies centers were active (Belgrade, Novi Sad and Subotica). The Belgrade Women's Study Center was established in 1992 as the first women's studies center in Serbia. Later, the Belgrade Center became one of the best-developed women' studies grassroots initiatives in Eastern and Central Europe as a whole. Also, since 1999, Gender and Culture have been taught as a postgraduate program, within the Alternative Academic Network in Belgrade. The development of women's and gender studies in Serbia is also reflected in numerous publications, i.e. journals and books that are hardly comparable with the small amount of published work in other countries. Women's and gender studies as well as feminist activism periodicals include *Zenske studije* (Women's Studies), *Temida*-journal on victimization, human rights and gender, *Profemina*-journal on women's writing, *Femisticke sveske* (Feminist Notebooks), *SOS bilten* (SOS Bulletin), *Zene za mir* (Women for Peace), and *Zene protiv rata* (Women against War). Also, only Serbia has a feminist publishing house ("94"), which publishes books about women (including books about domestic violence, sexual violence, incest and women's human rights). Articles published by feminist academics have a significant place within general academic journals as well, especially in those dealing with sociology, literature, criminology and law.

In Bulgaria, gender studies exist as individual courses within the University, established mainly due to efforts made by feminists from the Association of University Women as well as by Animus Association. Gender studies were established in the Departments of English language of the Philology Faculties in Sofia and Veliko Trnovo and in the Department of Sociology of the Faculty of Arts in Blagoevgrad. There is no grassroots women's studies center at all, but several victim support organizations, such as Nadja Center and Animus, offer educational programs and lectures for students, scholars and professionals. The only grassroots women's journal in Bulgaria is *Zharava*, edited and published by WaD (Women's Alliance for Development). [179]

In Hungary, women's studies courses exist within universities such as Budapest University of Economic Sciences and at Janus Pannonius University, in Pecs. Also, there is the Program on Gender and Culture at Central European University. [180] On a grassroots level, lectures, panels and public discussions are organized by women's organizations such as MONA, Feminist Network, Ombudswoman and Women's Rights and Children's Rights Research and Training Center. Also, there is a journal published by Feminist Network which is called *Noszemely* (Female Person) as well as series or articles on feminism in academic journals (Ascady, 1999:407).

Women's and gender studies seem to be least developed in Macedonia. However, the establishment of the Research Center for Gender Study in 1999 seems to be promising in terms of development of feminist thought and gender studies in Macedonia, which is, together with promotion of women's rights and ideas of civil society, one of its main goals. The only autonomous women's periodical in Macedonia is the monthly magazine *KISS*, edited and published by the Alliance of Macedonian Women' s Organizations.

As shown above, the possibility for self-organizing of women brought by social change led to the creation of a number of women's groups in all four countries included in my survey. However, the number of groups as well as the level of their co-operation and readiness to join their efforts in order to achieve their common interests is still very low. The inability of women's groups to attract more women and to enlarge network of women's groups, especially out of capital cities, is more or less evident everywhere. Women's organizations are rather small groups, with the same women often involved in activities of different organizations. Also, the level of both the co-operation between groups and their openness for communication with women from the larger society is rather low. Thus the lack of national co-ordination and a well-structured movement is evident. However, in spite of the fact that the number of women's organizations in post-communist countries is far below the number of similar organizations in the West, my findings suggest many similarities between autonomous women's movements in Western and post-communist countries (Freeman, 1979:184).

[179] Also, some organizations such as Gender project for Bulgaria, Association of University Women and Women for dignity as well as Nadja Centre publish newsletters. Occasionally general academic journals on literature and culture publish articles written by feminists as well (Daskalova, 1997:163).

[180] It is worth mentioning that this University as a whole, and the Program on Gender and Culture in particular, was initiated and established from outside Hungary, i.e. from USA.

Women's groups in all countries included in my survey mostly failed to formulate their common demands. It is only in Serbia where women's groups, sharing a general political mobilization for change, formulated their common demands during the pre-election campaign leading to the final defeat of communism in October 2000. [181] However, some attempts at network building, joint campaigns and support for women's initiatives outside capital cities[182] may be a sign of more energetic steps in the direction of the development of larger and more efficient women's movements in the near future. It is worth mentioning that the most efficient common actions of women's groups are those related to issues, such as abortion, laws on rape, pornography and prostitution, which most easily united Western feminists as well (Bouchier, 1983:106; Rowbotham, 1992:74-76). Obviously, these actions were most efficient in terms of preventing negative or advocating for positive legal changes, since these are issues around which women's groups found high level of agreement and interest for advocacy. This is not unusual since, as Fireman and Gamson stressed, mobilization is more likely when collective action is more urgent. And "collective action is most urgent when there is no reason to believe that collective goods will be preserved without collective action"(Fireman and Gamson, 1979:28). And this is exactly the kind of urgency, which most easily managed to unite women in collective action when their rights were threatened by announced changes of laws. Thus, for example, this is how we can explain the fact that in Hungary, where networking among women's organizations seems to be at the lowest level of the countries included in the survey, examples of some very successful campaigns were found, such as those organized as a reaction to a new abortion law, reform of the pension system and legalization of prostitution (Ascady, 1999:406).

3. CIVIL SOCIETY AND WOMEN'S INITIATIVES REGARDING VIOLENCE AGAINST WOMEN

Violence against women seems to be the issue that is most frequently dealt with by women's groups in post-communist countries. Thus, the development of the women's movement is supposed to have an important role in the production of changes regarding the public, and, especially, state attitudes and approaches toward the problem of violence against women. Moreover, violence against women is a subject of interest for some mixed (male-female) NGO's, whose activities are

[181] These common demands included: equal division of labor and responsibilities, equality in education, employment, earnings and pensions, life without war politics, fear and violence against women, right to safe abortion, free contraception, appropriate and accessible health service as well as education for peace, equality, solidarity and respect for difference.

[182] Main networking organizations in countries included in my survey are AWIN (Serbia), WaD and Bulgarian Gender Research Foundation (Bulgaria), ESE and Alliance of women's organizations (Macedonia) and MONA (Hungary).

significant as well.[183] Consequently, in addition to the development of the women's movement, the rise of victim advocacy and victim support organizations in general, i.e. as a part of the much broader context of the development of civil society is also very important.

The dynamics of the development of NGO's dealing with violence against women is mainly in accordance with the dynamics of the development of the women's and victim's rights movements in general. Thus, in Hungary and Serbia the first women's advocacy and victim support organizations were already established in the late 1980's and at the beginning of the 1990's[184], while in other countries similar organizations were established several years later. However, the first SOS hotline for battered women and children in Hungary (NANE) started several years later, in1994. That was also the year when the first women's organization dealing with violence against women was established in Macedonia (SOS hotline for battered women and children, Skopje). The development of organizations dealing with violence against women in Bulgaria followed Program against Violence, launched in 1995 by the Bulgarian Women's Union so that the first organization of that kind (Animus) in Bulgaria was established one year later (1995).

As with the development of the women's movement, the development of women's groups and other NGO's dealing with violence against women was either gradual and continuous (e.g. in Hungary and Macedonia), or had periods of rapid growth, connected to some macrostructural change (e.g. in Serbia and Bulgaria). In Serbia, for example, development of women's NGO's dealing with violence was accelerated during the wars in Croatia and Bosnia (between 1992 and 1995) and even more after the end of these wars (after 1995). In the period between 1995 and 1999, the number of women's groups and other NGO's dealing with violence against women more than doubled in the comparison to the end of 1994 (34 versus 14).

In Bulgaria, the increase in NGO's dealing with violence was rather slow until 1995, when it suddenly started to flourish. Until the end of 1994, there were only three NGO's dealing with violence against women, while at the end of 1999 they reached fourteen. This kind of development in Bulgaria seems to be primarily connected to an increased interest of Western human rights and funding organizations to support civil society's initiatives that address the problem of violence against women in this country. In the beginning, Western organizations were those who initiated research and organized seminars and training for women - first in the capital, Sofia, and later on, in other cities. These seminars and trainings encouraged women's initiatives and, consequently, led to the establishment of new organizations. Thus, in contrast to Hungary, Serbia and Macedonia where the establishment of women's NGO's (in general and those dealing with violence)

[183] Ester, Escape and White Ring - Hungary, SOS for Families in Disgrace and Society X - Bulgaria, I.A.N.- SOS telephone and counseling service for victims of war and violence, Victimology Society of Serbia, Group for Women's Human Rights-YUCOM, Society for Protection of Mental Health of Families Endangered by War, Center for Non-Violent Conflict Resolution-Nis-Serbia and Journalists for Rights of Women and Children-Macedonia

[184] For example, White Ring and Association of Hungarian Women were established already in 1989, and Belgrade's Women's Lobby and two SOS hotlines for battered women and children were established in1990.

resulted primarily from women's original grassroots endeavors, Bulgarian NGO's were inspired instead from outside the country.

Organizations that deal with violence against women mainly focus on one or more of following activities: awareness raising, victim support, advocacy and education/research.

Table 1. The types of activities of NGO's dealing with violence against women

	Victim support		Advocacy		Education Research		Awareness raising		Total (100%)
		%		%		%		%	
Hungary	6	50	3	25	3	25	8	66.1	12
Bulgaria	7	53.1	7	53.1	6	46.1	8	61.6	13
Macedonia	2	14.3	6	42.1	6	42.1	12	84.2	14
Serbia	14	41.2	8	23.5	8	23.5	27	79.4	34

As Table 1 shows, in all countries included in the survey awareness raising is the prevailing activity among organizations that deal with violence against women. For some organizations, awareness raising was, initially or for a longer time, the main or one of main activities, while for others (e.g. victim support organizations) it was only an additional activity.

It is not unusual that so much effort was made in post-communist countries merely to reveal the incidence and seriousness of violence against women, i.e. to show that it is a serious social problem rather than a trivial or private matter. During communism, violence against women was mostly hidden from the public so that awareness-raising activities were usually intended to make it visible. Thus, as in Western countries, these activities include media campaigns, publication and distribution of journals, brochures, posters and other materials, as well as organization of workshops, courses, lectures, etc. In Macedonia, unlike other countries, in addition to women's groups who have been making efforts toward awareness raising, two professional organizations were created by journalists. Their main aim was to raise public awareness about gender relations (Center for Urban and Media Actions in Macedonia) and the human rights of women and children (Journalists for Rights of Children and Women and for Protection of Environment). Both organizations made serious efforts, alone or in cooperation with women's groups, to change media images about violence against women (especially about domestic violence, sexual harassment in the workplace and trafficking in women).

In Hungary, Bulgaria and Serbia, victim support takes to second place in terms of frequency among activities of NGO's dealing with violence against women, while in Macedonia victim support is less frequent than advocacy and education. In Bulgaria, victim support and advocacy are activities dealt with by the same number of organizations, while education and research are slightly less frequent than the former two activities. In Serbia and Hungary, the same (the smallest) number of organizations is dealing with advocacy and education/research. However, if we consider both quantitative and qualitative data, we can see that, apart from awareness raising, the most developed activities are victim support and research/education in Bulgaria, advocacy in Macedonia, victim support in Hungary and victim support and education/research in Serbia. Although there are not a lot of NGO's in Serbia dealing with education and research on violence against women, the contribution of those that exist is significant, because it often includes serious academic work and original research, which is only rarely found in other countries included in the survey.[185]

When looking at the kind of violence against women the organizations are dealing with, one can see that they turn most often to domestic violence, while prostitution and trafficking in women are still the least developed fields of interest. Moreover, the majority of women's victim support organizations are primarily dealing with domestic violence with only a few of them helping victims of sexual violence and trafficking in women on a regular basis.[186] Thus, for example, the activities regarding trafficking in women in Serbia and Macedonia mainly consist of activities regarding awareness raising and advocacy, while only rarely, as we will see later, of supporting victims. Hence, at the time of the survey, victim support to trafficked women and prostitutes was offered on a regular basis only by Animus in Bulgaria and Escape in Hungary.

Table 2. The kinds of violence against women NGO's are dealing with

	Domestic violence		sexual violence		prostitution trafficking		total (100%)
		%		%		%	
Hungary	7	58.3	7	58.3	2	16.7	12
Bulgaria	13	100	9	69.2	5	38.5	13
Macedonia	14	100	2	14.3	1	7.1	14
Serbia	27	79.4	16	47	7	20.6	34

As Table 2 shows, all NGO's in Bulgaria and Macedonia, and the majority of NGO's in Serbia, that deal with violence against women, deal in some way with domestic violence. In Macedonia, the great interest of women's NGO's in domestic violence was mainly the consequence of the awareness raising campaigns organized by the women's group the Humanitarian Association for Equality, Solidarity and Emancipation of Women (ESE), which served as a generator for an increase in the number of NGO's dealing with domestic violence (Mehmeti, interview, 1999). Although in Hungary the same number of organizations answered that they deal

[185] Answers about research as an NGO activity should be considered cautiously, since, when answering questions about research, some organizations (especially victim support organizations) obviously had in mind sporadic analysis or their own (nor so regularly collected) statistical data.

[186] See the analysis of activities of victim support organizations later in this chapter.

with domestic as well as with sexual violence, domestic violence is still the prevailing field of interest for the majority of organizations, while sexual violence is addressed only occasionally. The exception is Eszter, an organization specializing in support for victims of sexual violence, as well as the Foundation for Sexual Education which deals with sexual education and prevention of sexual violence and prostitution.

There are only two women's organizations in Serbia established specifically to support women victims of sexual violence (Incest Trauma Center and Autonomous Center against Sexual Violence). While the Incest Trauma Center offers support to sexually abused children and children victims of war, the Autonomous Center against Sexual Violence in Belgrade (Serbia) was originally established with the main goal to support women victims of war rape and other kinds of war victimization. However, later, for different reasons, sexual violence was left on the margins of the Center's work and, as recognized in the information brochure of the Women's Center, it was planned to be developed in the future. Thus, in spite of the fact that the Center was established to support victims of sexual violence, their clients are both victims of domestic and sexual violence. The Center offers an SOS hotline as well as direct psychological counseling and free legal aid. Also, the Center offers humanitarian aid to refugee and Roma women and children.[187].

Organizations in Serbia, answering that they deal with trafficking in women only sporadically offer victim support to trafficked women (SOS hotlines and the Autonomous Women's Center). When sex trafficking is in question, at the time of the survey, advocacy and public awareness campaigns done by the Group for Women's Rights (panels, publications and media campaigns), the Association for Women's Initiatives (translation, presentation and distribution of video "Bought&Sold) and the Victimology Society of Serbia (advocacy for legal changes) were more important. But during 2001 the women's group ASTRA was established with the specific purpose to organize information and support for victims of trafficking as well as prevention campaigns.

In some countries, there are also groups specialized in dealing with violence against particular groups of women, such as adolescent girls, disabled women, battered women who kill and women in prison. For example, in Serbia there are groups dealing with problems of girls, including violence against them. They mainly deal with awareness raising, education and support of victims. Sometimes, as in the case of the Incest Trauma Center in Belgrade and the Center for girls in Belgrade and Nis, they are specialized for the problems of girls, but more often they address problems of girls equally with problems of adult women (Women's Center in Uzice and Center "Mila" in Novi Sad). Center for girls in Belgrade, which seems to be the most developed organization dealing with violence against girls, offers: SOS

[187] During NATO bombing of Serbia, they offered psychological support by telephone to the number of women from different part of Serbia, including Albanian women from Kosovo while the telephone lines were functioning. Because of the circumstances, this time they did not wait for women to call them but instead called first and asked women how they were doing and tried to empower them. (S.Stanimirovic "Radionice protiv straha"(Workshops against fear), *Glas*, 9 September 1999, p.6).

Hotline, meeting place, workshops on sexual violence, visits to institutions, training on child abuse prevention for professionals, legal aid, medical help, computer classes and tutoring. Also, the Center opens the possibility for girls who don't recognize themselves as feminists to become acquainted with feminist ideas and put special emphasis on supporting refugee girls.[188]

In Bulgaria, Society X, from Rousse, deals equally with problems of girls and boys. Society X runs the Preventive Counseling Center in order to provide qualified psychosocial aid and legal advices to victims of violence. Also, they organize (on an annual basis) Children Against Violence Campaigns - an exhibition of children's drawings and essays showing children's attitudes toward violence.

As already mentioned, a women's group dealing with discrimination and violence against disabled women only exists in Serbia (Iz kruga...- From the circle..). The group was established by disabled and non-disabled women at time when they became aware that there was neither women's groups dealing with problems of disabled women nor organizations of disabled persons dealing with problems of violence. Their activities include an SOS hotline, direct psychological counseling, counseling via mail for deaf women, legal aid as well as education (seminars), media campaigns, advocacy and development of databases. They also support disabled refugee women and mothers of disabled children and try to educate women who work in institutions on how to deal with violence against disabled women.

Women in prison and battered women who kill were supported in a systematic way only in Serbia, by the Group for Women's Rights and the Victimology Society of Serbia. The Group for Women's Rights is the only NGO in the countries included in the survey who organized women's rights and legal literacy training for women in prison. In Macedonia, SOS Kumanovo also dealt with a few cases of battered women who kill, while in Hungary, well-known feminist lawyer and academic Kristina Morvai is campaigning for release of battered women who kill.

In all countries included in the survey, Roma women's organizations deal with education and awareness raising of Roma women and girls, including prevention of domestic violence. They also participate in activities organized by other women's groups, such as awareness raising and advocacy campaigns. However, these groups only rarely offer practical support to Roma women victims of violence (for example, Nadezhda in Bulgaria). Organizations of other minority women also only occasionally deal with violence against women.

[188] SOS Hotline and Center for Girls, Belgrade, Annual Report, 1998.

Table 3. Model used in the activities of NGO's dealing with violence against women

	Foreign model		domestic model		developed model		total (100%)
		%		%		%	
Hungary	4	33.3		-	8	66.7	12
Bulgaria	6	46.1	1	7.7	6	46.1	13
Macedonia	4	28.6		-	10	71.4	14
Serbia	11	32.3	5	14.7	18	52.1	34

According to the statements of their representatives, the majority of NGO's that deal with violence against women rely mainly on their own experience, i.e. they are developing their own original models for dealing with violence against women. However, in the beginning, the influence of foreign experiences was much stronger. This was usually the consequence of both the low level of NGO's knowledge about the problem and their dependence on foreign funding organizations which also tended to impose their own ideas on them. Also, some organizations, such as NANE in Hungary, were established and coordinated for a long time by Western women which also had an obvious influence on their model of functioning (Adamik, interview, 1999).

Uncritical acceptance of Western models as a characteristic of the first phase of development of women's groups was especially emphasized by my interviewees in Macedonia. They stressed the negative impact that the training offered by foreign organizations had on advocacy for legal changes regarding violence against women, since it often led to uncritical acceptance of Western solutions, even when it was obvious that they did not fit the completely different cultural context (Bejkova and Najcevska, interviews, 1999). However, later on Macedonian as well as organizations in other post-communist countries became more critical toward Western models and thus relied more on their own knowledge and experiences.

The foreign models used by NGO's in the countries included in the survey are usually those from European countries, USA and, only rarely, from Canada. For example, UK and Canadian experiences are used in Serbia in the work with battered women who kill, i.e. women in prison. UK and US experiences are used in advocacy, i.e. in drafting laws regarding domestic violence. The Minnesota (Duluth) model seems to be popular among organizations dealing with domestic violence in all countries.

Victim support organizations in Serbia use models from different European countries (mainly from the Netherlands, Slovenia, Croatia, France, Italy, Sweden and Germany) and USA. Bulgarian victim support organizations use experiences from Austria, Germany, Switzerland, USA and UK. US and UK experiences are used by Eszter in Hungary as well. NANE from Hungary and SOS hotlines in Macedonia used the experiences of SOS hotlines from Serbia, Croatia and Slovenia, as well as some models from USA and The Netherlands. Whose models, i.e. the experiences, are used is mainly determined by previously established contacts, availability of information, foreign experts/trainers and funding organizations, as well as, but not always, by a similarity of social context and women's needs. As Table 4 shows, domestic models (models developed on the basis of the experiences of domestic NGO's) are used only in Serbia and Bulgaria. This is not unusual, since in these countries the initiatives for creation and training of groups on the local level are the most developed.[189]

Table 4. Whether women's organization identifies itself as a feminist organization?[190]

	YES		NO		total (100%)
		%		%	
Hungary	4	22.2	14	77.8	18
Bulgaria	5	45.5	6	54.5	11
Macedonia	2	11.8	15	88.2	17
Serbia	16	47	18	52.9	34

As Table 4 shows, data about feminism and women's NGO's that deal with violence mainly confirm my earlier statements about the impact of Western feminism on the development of women's movements in the respective countries. Women's groups which declare themselves feminist are the most numerous in Serbia, less numerous in Bulgaria and Hungary and rare in Macedonia. However, it seems that in reality the groups accept feminist principles more often than they are ready to recognize. In all countries, women's groups that did not declare themselves as feminist organizations either answered that some of their members considered themselves feminists, or said that they are not feminists since they struggle not against men but for equality between them and women. As well noticed by Molyneux (1996:245), "women who by any definition would qualify as feminists, avoid identifying themselves as such in order to maintain their credibility". This is not unusual bearing in mind strong anti-feminist feelings in post-communist society which affects not only men's but also women's attitudes toward the women's movement. Thus, even women's group activists often reject declaring themselves feminists since they do not want to be considered as "enemies of men". Also, as Rowbotham puts it, many of them do not identify at all with socialism or with feminism because they connect both with the lack of freedom and democracy that

[189] These initiatives and trainings are very important since experiences of organizations from the capitals were disseminated through them in other parts of the country, and served as an inspiration for the establishment of new organizations.

[190] Total number of organizations in Table 5 differs from total number in previous tables because the question about feminism was posed only to representatives of women's organizations, while all other questions were posed to other (male-female) organizations which deal with violence against women as well.

existed under the communist party (Rowbotham, 1992:269). As pointed out by Najcevska (interview, 1999), it seems that they prefer to introduce themselves as women's rights activists. Indeed, as Heitlinger says, "whether or not the women's groups call themselves feminists is much less important than the opportunity they offer for gaining political experience in agenda setting, building coalitions, lobbying, writing submissions" etc. (Heitlinger, 1996:88).

3.1 Victim support

Victim support is the main activity of those women's NGO's who exclusively or predominantly deal with violence against women: four organizations in Hungary (SOS hotline NANE, Escape, Eszter and Center for Legal Assistance to Women and Children), six in Bulgaria (Animus, Demetra, Nadja Center, Support, New Beginning, SOS to Families in Disgrace), two SOS hotlines in Macedonia[191] and seven NGO's in Serbia (four SOS hotlines, the Counseling Service Against Domestic Violence, Women's Safe Houses and the Autonomous Women's Center Against Sexual Violence). Some other organizations, such as Women's House and Women's Rights and Children's Rights Research and Training Center in Hungary[192] as well as I.A.N., Center for Girls, Group for Women's Rights and Victimology Society in Serbia also offer support to women victims of violence, as part of their broader range of activities. Woman's House offers both legal and psychological aid, while IAN offers psychological aid to victims of war violence. Also, Women's line, as part of Ombudswoman (Hungary), is a hotline for women which offers information and advice. Women's Line established a circle of experts who are able to provide women with appropriate assistance and, in this way, i.e. by trying to resolve conflicts before they escalate into violence, it works on prevention of violence against women.

Animus from Bulgaria is a rare organization in the region which developed programs suitable for equal support of victims of domestic violence, sexual violence and trafficking in women and which has a 24-hours help line (Center for Rehabilitation of Women Victims of Violence). Unlike Animus, other SOS hotlines (in Bulgaria as well as in other countries) are accessible only several hours a day and mainly oriented toward supporting victims of domestic violence.

Since June 1998,[193]Animus, as a Bulgarian partner, joined the La Strada Program for Prevention of Trafficking in Women in Central and Eastern Europe. The Women and Development (W.A.D) is a partner organization with Animus in the La Strada

[191] At the time of the survey the opening of third SOS hotline in Macedonia was announced by the women's group Iskra (Bitola).

[192] The Centre established Domestic Violence Legal Clinic in Hungary, which, at the time of the survey, was unique in the whole region.

[193] The program has been functioning for several years in the Netherlands, the Czech Republic, Poland and Ukraine. Bulgaria joined it in its third phase (1998-2001). As stated in Animus information leaflet, it is not accidental that Bulgaria joined La Strada at exactly this moment. Bulgaria became one of the leading origin countries for trafficked women and in 1998, women's NGO's became developed enough to deal with delicate trafficking issues.

project and, while Animus offers emotional and social support to trafficked women and work on prevention, W.A.D. conducts media and lobbying campaigns. The work of Animus is done on a professional basis, mainly by psychologists. Some women friendly lawyers work as external associates and are engaged occasionally when women need legal aid. In cooperation with the International Organization for Migration (IOM), Animus also works on action research and prevention campaigns among various groups of women at risk of being involved in forced prostitution in other countries – young women, students, unemployed and poor women, orphan girls etc. Moreover, Animus runs a women's club called "Who is Margaret" and a Correspondence program for women from other parts of the country. The "Who is Margaret" club connects victim support with the community. This means that women who participate in it already have support in the care programs and are ready to share their knowledge on violence and to develop activities against violence in society. However, in spite of the programs developed, and both professionals and volunteers trained to deal with all kinds of violence, the majority of women who seek help from Animus are victims of domestic violence. For example, during1998, 63% of their clients were victims of domestic violence, while 12% were victims of sexual violence and only 5% of trafficking (Annual Report of Animus Association Foundation, 1998:17).

While Animus, together with Nadja Center, mainly supports women from the capital Sofija[194], SOS to Families in Disgrace, Demetra and Support are operating in small towns within Bulgaria.[195] SOS to Families in Disgrace, for example, offers telephone and direct (legal, psychological and psychiatric) counseling to victims of domestic violence and has developed good cooperation with and training for police. At the time of the survey, Demetra was a new organization (founded in 1999) that offered psychological aid to women victims of domestic and sexual violence. Support from Gabrovo offers both telephone and direct psychological counseling to women and children victims of domestic and sexual violence and also works on prevention programs in schools.

In Macedonia and Serbia, SOS hotlines usually provide telephone counseling to women and children victims of domestic violence and offer free legal aid and direct psychological counseling. While SOS hotlines mainly provide help by telephone, the Counseling Service Against Domestic Violence in Serbia primarily offers direct psychological counseling and legal aid.

Shelters for battered women and children exist in all countries, except Macedonia. However, there are no more than one shelter in each country except Serbia where a second shelter was opened in 2000. All shelters are located in the capitals and do not have enough space for everyone in need.

In Serbia, the only shelter that existed at the time of the survey was run by Women's Safe Houses. The organization was established in 1994 and for some time

[194] Both Animus and Nadja Center also support women from other towns who turn to them. Sometimes, even when they have a similar organization in their own towns, women feel it is more confidential to call an organization in Sofia. It is understandable since in a small town people know each other very well so that women are afraid of being recognized and prefer to stay anonymous.

[195] At the time of the survey, several local women's organization, offering help to victims of violence, just started to work.

was running three shelters in different parts of Serbia. Due to financial problems, two shelters were closed and, at the time of the survey, only one shelter (near Belgrade) was still active. Later on, at the end of 2000, Counseling Service Against Domestic Violence opened a new shelter with the purpose of serving battered women exclusively. From April 1, 1994 to February 23 1999, Women's Safe Houses accommodated in their shelters 70 women and 91 children. Women are not supposed to stay longer than six months, but since it is impossible for them to solve their problems in such a short time, they are allowed to stay longer so that in reality their stay is not limited. Apart from battered women, shelter also accommodates women victims of war (raped women, refugees, etc.), who made up 22, 4 per cent of women who spent some time in the shelter between 1994 and 1999 (Cetkovic, 1998:24).

In Bulgaria, Nadja Center runs both a SOS hotline and a shelter for women and children victims of domestic and sexual violence, and also offers direct psychological and legal aid as well as psychotherapy to women and couples. The only shelter in Bulgaria was established in 1997 (one year after the establishment of Nadja Center). The shelter accepts women and children and can accommodate 18-20 persons who are allowed to stay up to six months. Since its establishment, 47 women and 26 children have been accommodated in the shelter. Apart from its main activity connected to victim support, Nadja Center also advocates for legal changes regarding domestic violence and offers education in high schools, medical college and work on public consciousness raising.

In Hungary, there is only one shelter which specifically serves battered women. The shelter is run by the Salvation Army and was originally set up for homeless mothers. Consequently, it is available only to battered women with children. Battered women may also use some of the other shelters for homeless people but the conditions there are even less convenient. In Macedonia, there are no shelters at all. Journalists for Rights of Children and Women wants to establish a shelter and, at the time of the survey, was seeking funds for it.

Specialized organizations who offer support to victims of sexual violence are rare. As mentioned above, such an organization is found only in Hungary (Eszter). while Animus, Nadja Center and Demetra in Bulgaria, SOS hotlines in all countries and the Autonomous Women's Center in Serbia also deal with it but only occasionally or as part of a broader scope of activities.

Eszter was established on 1991 by the criminologist Gyorgy Virag. The organization provides crisis intervention telephone counseling, comprehensive and confidential face-to-face counseling and long-term psychotherapy to survivors of sexual assault and abuse. Eszter offers support to both women and men, while the majority of their clients are women, girls and young boys. Also, the majority of their clients are those who were sexually abused in the past, while recently the number of rape crisis cases has increased.

Prostitution and trafficking in women is the main field of interest only for Escape in Hungary. The Escape Association was established in 1996 with its main aims to communicate with prostitutes, to offer support and to help them to leave prostitution and reintegrate into society. The organization consists of a social worker group, research group and expert group. Social workers visit prostitutes on a regular basis and, together with the expert group (lawyers, doctors and psychologists), help and support them. The research group is responsible for the creation of a database and raising public and professionals awareness. The Escape Association was a co-organizer of two international conferences on prostitution and trafficking in women (1996 and1997).

As already mentioned, trafficking in women is also an important part of the activity of Animus and Society X in Bulgaria, as well as of Journalists for Rights of Women and Children and Protection of the Environment in Macedonia. Society X is involved in prevention of trafficking in women which is very important since Rousse is located on the Danube river, the location for several channels of trafficking in women. Their volunteers meet with prostitutes and truck drivers, talk to them about HIV/AIDS and give them condoms and brochures translated into different languages. Also, they offer medical aid to them. Only sporadically, SOS hotlines in Macedonia and Serbia as well as the Autonomous Women's Center in Belgrade support trafficked women.

The average yearly number of calls from women who seek help from victim support organizations varies significantly from one to another group, regardless of the specific country. It ranges from 100 (Eszter-Hungary) to 3000 (Counseling Service Against Domestic Violence-Serbia). However, data obtained from the organizations, with rare exceptions, must be taken with caution. Women's groups records are only rarely reliable since they are usually not kept systematically, and relate to the number of calls rather than to the number of women asking for and receiving support. Women's groups sometimes also tend to exaggerate the number of cases reported to them and often refuse to make their documentation available to researchers. Even if they are willing to cooperate with researchers, it is extremely difficult to make use of their records due to the lack of systematization, regular data analysis and case files.[196] On the other side, the documentation of male-female victim support organizations, although sometimes better systematized, do not always show the ratio between female and male victims.

3.2 Advocacy for legal changes

Advocacy for change of laws and legal practice was one of the important activities of NGO's in all countries included in the survey. The majority of women's groups who offer support to victims of violence have been in some way involved in advocacy from their very beginning, while the advocacy campaign was the main or one of the main activities of several groups.

In Serbia, the Group for Women's Rights and the Victimology Society of Serbia lobbied for changes of several laws relevant for women victims of violence. The Group for Women's Rights was successful in lobbying for both changes of the Law on Implementation of Criminal Penalties and practice in women's prison. The Group was successful in campaigning for release/fair punishment of several battered

[196] The records are usually handwritten which additionally makes use of them difficult.

women who killed or committed other crimes under coercion from their violent partners. The same Group also organized a successful awareness raising and advocacy campaign through publication of brochures and posters on domestic violence as well as through media events and panels on domestic violence and trafficking in women. The Victimology Society of Serbia made a proposal and lobbied for changes in laws regarding sexual violence (marital rape and rape as a crime regardless of the sex of victim and perpetrator), domestic violence and trafficking in human beings. The proposal of a New model for legal protection of domestic violence victims, created by the Victimology Society, was largely accepted and supported by all women's groups in Serbia. The Victimology Society also monitors cases of domestic violence and domestic murders and advocates for changes in legal practice as well as for data about victims to be included in official statistics. The advocacy of the Victimology Society also includes addressing courts as *amicus curiae*, which is not found in other countries.[197] Also, the Center for Women's Human Rights-YUCOM was very active in the advocacy campaign for legal changes regarding sexual violence.

In Bulgaria, the Bulgarian association of women in the legal profession is an important advocacy group whose main activities are to monitor legislation and practice and lobby for changes. Also, the Bulgarian Gender Research Foundation (BGRF) is working on advocacy for free legal protection in cases of domestic violence. However, advocacy is obviously not among the priorities of Bulgarian NGO's that deal with violence against women.

The main advocacy group in Macedonia is ESE. ESE was established in 1995 with the main aims to work on protection of women's human rights, increase women's participation in politics and among decision makers, educate and establish self-help groups. ESE's activities include five programs: program against domestic violence; legal education and action; health education; participation of women in politics and creation of databases about women. The main activity regarding violence against women is advocacy for changes in laws and practice regarding domestic violence. An advocacy campaign, which was organized during 1999, resulted in a proposal for legal changes submitted to the Parliament at the end of the same year. The campaign was actually started in 1996 with the establishment of a group of volunteers consisting of lawyers and representatives of governmental and non-governmental organizations dealing with domestic violence. During 1997 ESE organized a domestic violence survey among students (the first survey of its kind in Macedonia) and published the survey results in the book *Rea Silvia* (in Macedonian, Albanian and English language). From 25 November to 10 December 1997 (16 days of activism against violence against women), ESE initiated and organized a campaign against domestic violence throughout the country, followed by a public awareness campaign in 1998. During its public awareness campaign, ESE published several brochures offering useful practical information about domestic violence to the larger public. At the end of 1998 and during 1999, ESE organized a number of seminars for lawyers, social workers, researchers and other professionals dealing

[197] In the time of the survey, Ombudswoman from Hungary had plans to start it as well.

with domestic violence as well as other interconnected advocacy activities aimed to change laws and practice regarding domestic violence. The series of advocacy activities was finalized by the drafting of new laws on domestic violence.

A strong advocacy group is, however, obviously missing in Hungary, where advocacy campaigns for legal changes are mainly organized by victim support organizations such as NANE, White Ring and Escape. However, although advocacy is only an extra activity, their campaigns appear as the most effective among the respective countries. For example, NANE organized a successful campaign for inclusion of marital rape and regarding the Law on Prostitution. They opposed the Government's proposal for legalization of prostitution, which was partly accepted so that the prostitution is now partly legalized, i.e. it is legal out of areas such as those near schools, churches etc. (Bethlen, interview, 1999). White ring proposed the establishment of the Fund for compensation of victims of bodily injuries which was accepted by the Parliament. Also, White Ring advocated for better protection of victims as witnesses and some of their suggestions were accepted and included in the draft of the Law on criminal procedure. Escape was working on awareness raising about victimization of women through prostitution and trafficking as well as on advocacy for the new law on trafficking in human beings which was passed in 1999.

3.3 Education and research

Violence against women has been an important part of the curricula of women's studies centers in Serbia from their very beginning. It included lectures and courses on domestic violence, battered women who kill, women in prison, sexual violence, prostitution, pornography and trafficking in women. In addition, several NGO's in Serbia were also organizing panels, seminars and lectures from the field of women's and gender studies on a more or less regular basis, with the violence against women issue being specially emphasized.[198]. Also, within the Group for Women's Rights and the Victimology Society of Serbia several feminist action researches about violence against women in war, domestic violence, battered women who kill and women in prison were carried out.

In Bulgaria, the women's group Dialog does research and education on women's problems, including violence against women. Apart from research, Dialog tends to include abused women in the education for equal opportunity on the labor market and offers them qualification courses and motivation training free of charge.

The gender project for Bulgaria, whose main aims are awareness raising and prevention of violence, has for its main activities human rights research and education, as well as publication of popular brochures about different kinds of violence. On the initiative and in cooperation with Minnesota Advocates for Human Rights, they carried out research on domestic violence and sexual harassment. Their

[198] Such organizations are Women's Research Center-Nis, Group for Women's Rights-Belgrade, Society for protection of mental health of families endangered by war-Novi Sad, YUCOM-Center for Women's Human Rights-Belgrade, Women's Center-Uzice, "Luna"-Vrsac and Center for non-violent conflict resolution-Nis.

work is an interesting combination of human rights research, education, media campaigns about violence against women and lobbying for establishment of national mechanisms in the interest of women. It includes organization of workshops and lectures in schools ("Gender education in schools") and for journalists. Similar organization is Bulgarian Gender Research Foundation (BGRF), whose activities mainly focus on gender research, including violence against women. The organization strongly cooperates with the Gender Project for Bulgaria. BGRF was especially successful in helping to create new women's organizations dealing with violence against women in small cities, as a result of research and workshops they organized throughout the country.

Several victim support organizations in Bulgaria, such as Nadja Center and Animus, offer educational programs and lectures on violence against women for students, scholars and professionals. Gender studies courses that are taught in the Department of Sociology of the Faculty of Arts in Blagoevgrad also address violence against women. "The majority of last year's students took violence against women as the topic of their essays", says Tatyana Kotzeva, feminist and professor of sociology (interview, 1999). Moreover, Animus introduced the topic of violence against women and trauma to the social work students of the bachelor program of Burgas University. An increased interest in the problem of violence against women resulted in creation of courses on violence for the MA Social Work Program of Burgas Free University and for the MA Social and Clinical Work Program of New Bulgarian University. In sum, three academic courses are taught by the Animus team (Annual Report of Animus Association Foundation, 1998:28).

In Macedonia, education on violence against women is mainly done through panels and seminars, organized by ESE (Skopje), the Alliance of Macedonian Women's Organizations (Skopje) and Iskra (Bitola). Similarly, the Women's Rights and Children's Rights Center in Hungary organizes public lectures on violence against women for lawyers, journalists and the general public. However, violence against women is mainly sporadically included in existing women's studies courses at Hungarian universities. At the time of the survey, ESE in Macedonia and the Women's Rights and Children's Rights Center in Hungary were the only NGO's that dealt with research on violence against women in their respective countries.

4. LAWS AND POLICY CHANGES REGARDING VIOLENCE AGAINST WOMEN

Legal and policy reforms, although still partial and mostly in the form of drafts, represent, together with the development of civil society, one of the best proofs that, social changes in post-communist countries have produced positive as well as negative impacts on the life of the people. Positive changes regarding legal reforms are mostly the result of women's groups public awareness and advocacy campaigns, research and education, reviewed previously in this chapter, as well as of the public pressure resulting from them. At the same time, even more powerful and effective pressure came from the West which urged post-communist countries to harmonize their legal systems with European Union standards in order to become eligible to join the EU and other European organizations.

One of the first and so far the only legal change regarding violence against women in the countries included in the survey are the changes which made marital rape punishable in Hungary (since 1997) and Macedonia (since 1996), as well as new legal provisions regarding trafficking in human beings in Hungary (since 1999). In addition, in both Hungary and Macedonia, the gendered definition of rape (offender and victim) has been removed as well. However, marital rape is still not considered a criminal offense in Bulgaria, while in Serbia the long and continuous efforts of women's advocacy groups has resulted in the inclusion of marital rape in the draft of the new Criminal Code of Serbia.

Trafficking in women is not a special criminal offense in Serbia, Macedonia or Bulgaria. This does not mean it is not possible to prosecute it, since some existing provisions regarding procuring and transport of people held in slavery may be used. For example, article 156 of the Criminal Code of Bulgaria provides a "penalty of up to 10 years imprisonment for the abduction of a female for the purpose of making the woman available for lechery"(Women 2000, 2000:18). However, in spite of the fact that in the last years these provisions began to be used more frequently and led to more frequent prosecution of offenders, there are still not enough effective measures for the protection of victims. For example, one report states that during the first two months of 2000 alone, the Bulgarian Border Police detained (sic!) 162 women who were supposed to be transferred abroad, while in 1999, 786 offenders were convicted of sex trafficking.[199] Also, even the Hungarian law is not in accordance with the most recent international documents (e.g. with the Palermo Convention and the additional Protocol on trafficking in human beings). However, some additional mechanisms for the prosecution of offenders, protection of victims as witnesses and the prevention of trafficking are expected to be implemented soon as part of the Hungarian Government's broader plan for improving the position of crime victims as provided in Government decision No. 1074 of July 7, 1999. In addition, in 2000, Hungary introduced a new law on prostitution, which made prostitution legal everywhere outside restricted areas such as near churches and schools. Thus, as part of the package passed by Parliament with the purpose to fight sex trafficking, the Government decided to crack down on the criminals who organize prostitution, while allowing individual men and women to sell sex in special zones to be designated by local authorities. [200] Also, at the time of writing of this book, the drafting of new legal solutions on trafficking in human beings was just started by an expert group of the Victimology Society of Serbia, which was coordinated by the author of this book.

In spite of intensive advocacy by women's groups and the public awareness campaigns related to it, there is no country included in my survey where domestic violence laws were changed in a way that would assure better protection of women.

[199] Bulgaria: Roundtable on fight against trafficking of women kicks off, the Message received through stop-traffic@friends-partners.org on April 20, 2000.

[200] P.Finn "Hungarians Say 'Stop' to red-light Districts Officials Befuddled By New Prostitution Law", *Washington Post Foreign Service*, March 12, 2000.

In all countries, both criminal and family laws still have regressive provisions, which guarantee neither prosecution and treatment of the abuser nor protection of the victim. In all countries, possibilities for prosecution of the abuser are available only by using general provisions on assault, injury and similar offenses (Women 2000). However, since domestic violence is only rarely considered a crime by criminal justice officials, there is no possibility for issuing a protection order and no clearly defined role for the police in domestic violence cases, these provisions are used only rarely. In addition, police are still not trained properly to deal with domestic violence cases and in most cases of domestic violence, the victim must proceed through the court system without the assistance of a prosecutor. Moreover, police are reluctant to interfere in these cases based on the idea of a "sanctity of private life" brought by the restoration of capitalism (Wirth, forthcoming; Toth, interview, 1999; Morvai, 1994:68). Thus, knowing that there is little they can get and a lot they can lose by reporting abuse, women choose not to ask for help from the police and court.

However, although legal changes regarding domestic violence have not yet been achieved, at the time of the survey in all countries included in the survey draft laws had been developed or were scheduled to be developed in the near future. In Hungary, for example, it was part of the above-mentioned broader efforts made by the Government in order to improve the position of crime victims. As Lenke Feher (interview, 1999) noted, "it is very important that the Government wants to fulfill international norms and it is the reason why the Ministry of Interior took an interest in the issues. The Meeting of European Forum for Victim Services, organized and highly publicized in Budapest, also played an important role. Police representatives were invited and all documents of the European Forum were translated into Hungarian."

It is obvious that, apart from the pressure made by women' s advocacy groups and victimologists, the willingness of the Hungarian government to adjust legislation to international standards coincided with Hungary's strong commitment for EU membership and had a significant impact on the development of the proposal.

Over the last several years, owing to the women's group *ESE*, a major campaign for legal reform regarding domestic violence was organized in Macedonia as well. The campaign included media events and a series of seminars for professionals of different occupational backgrounds who deal with domestic violence. The campaign also included a proposal for changes of relevant laws, proposing harsher penalties for domestic violence, including domestic homicide, as well as witness protection and protective orders. The proposal was handed over to the Macedonian Government and, at the time of writing this book, it was being seriously considered. Similarly, during 1998 the *Victimology Society of Serbia* developed a comprehensive model of new legal approaches to domestic violence, including new criminal offences specifically addressing domestic violence, protective orders and the counseling of batterers in addition to penalties, as well as arrest and other sanctions for violation of protective orders. The former Serbian government did not show any interest in it. However, there is hope that the new Government will have more understanding and willingness to accept proposals made by NGO's and feminist scholars.[201] Also, there is an additional motivation in its urge to fulfill international requests in order to overcome the consequences of long-term isolation.

Bulgaria is the slowest in developing legal changes, which may be explained by the fact that legal reform in general is still at the beginning stages and there is still no consensus among women's advocacy groups about appropriate legal solutions to domestic violence. Also, in spite of public awareness campaigns, it seems that the level of awareness in general is still very low in comparison to strong patriarchal attitudes. "Regarding the law, the situation is the same and the legal system is not very friendly for women who are victims of violence," says Maria Minkova (interview, 1999) from *Animus Association*. "In Bulgaria, violence against women in the family is not considered criminal activity. So, our biggest goal is to change this situation. I think it will be hard and it will not happen until the society also changes. The existing law only represents what people think in Bulgaria. And what people think here about family violence is that it is the woman's fault." Similarly, Irina Moulechkova (interview, 1999) from the Bulgarian Association of Women in the Legal Profession says:

> "I do not think for the time being that the protective order will be accepted because there is no public awareness about the problem and I do not think that such a change can go through the Parliament at this moment. In the future, it depends on education. I do not think it is realistic for rape in marriage to be accepted as a crime. People are not sensitized in these issues Their main concern is with the economic structure - nothing else is important. Even new legislation on children's rights has been waiting more than one year after the first vote in Parliament. It is not considered something important. All the changes are about economic problems here. "

However, on the other side, Bulgaria, together with Hungary, was among the first post-communist countries where training for police was organized in a systematic way. Thus, some positive changes in police reaction to domestic violence have been noticed in Bulgaria and Hungary, while representatives of women's organizations in Macedonia and Serbia said they have good relations with a few police stations or with some individual police officers. As pointed out by Kozuharova (interview, 1999):

> "People from police now better understand women who were beaten in the family. This is something which is connected to recent social changes. Police have instructions to ask the abuser to sign that he will not be abusive again. We just signed an agreement with police for the training we are going to do for them to teach them how to recognize domestic violence, and how to distinguish between forced and voluntary prostitution and migration..We discussed with police how to get passports for sex trafficking victims in Sofia instead of in small towns where they are afraid to return.."

However, apart from seminars organized by grassroots women's organizations, changes in police attitudes toward violence against women in both Bulgaria and Hungary could partly be the result of the establishment of associations of

[201] It is worthwhile mentioning that after the NATO bombing, the prospects of the state's acceptance of any NGO initiatives became poorer than ever. Although the government was hostile toward NGO's before the NATO attack, after the bombing, NGO's were openly called traitors and terrorists allegedly paid by NATO to complete the destruction of the country. However, the changes which occurred in October 2000 opened a more optimistic perspective for changes in that regard.

policewomen. The associations have made many efforts to raise awareness of police staff about violence against women, and, in some ways, have been serving as mediator between women's organizations and police. As part of the European Network of police women, both associations declared that active help to specialized institutions and non-governmental organizations in their efforts to prevent crime, drug addiction, prostitution and violence against women are among their main objectives (European Network of Policewomen-Bulgaria, 1999:9; Magyarorszagi noszervezetek kiadji, 1998:15).

In Hungary, a very important step in changing attitudes of the police came from the Government. The Ministry of Internal Affairs initiated the action to change the behavior of the police toward the victims. It included the training of police officers and the establishment of a Victim Protection Office in the Ministry. Also, in every police office there is at least one officer responsible for victim protection who is supposed to ensure that victims are well treated by the police. Recently, police stations have designated special rooms for interviewing victims of domestic violence, where other persons do not have access. Also, experimental psychological tests for policemen have been introduced, screening their ability to work with victims (Feher, interview, 1999). In January 1999, the Ministry of Internal Affairs gave instructions to all police stations to deal in an appropriate way with cases of family violence, which also included the obligation to arrest abusers (Bethlen, interview, 1999).

In all countries[202] there was increasing cooperation between the governments and NGO's, especially regarding domestic violence and sex trafficking issues. The Beijing Declaration and Platform for Action as well as the Palermo Convention and the additional protocols had an obvious impact, leading to the creation of national plans for action and the establishment of special departments or committees for women's issues as part of either the Government or the Parliament. National plans mainly included schedules for public awareness campaigns, for education, international cooperation, ratification of international documents, legal reforms, establishment of state commissions or committees on women's issues, and development of victim support. In Serbia, this kind of cooperation was developed especially in relation to sex trafficking after the establishment of the National team for the struggle against trafficking in human beings in 2001. This cooperation is the result of the increased willingness of the Government to cooperate with non-governmental organizations as well as of the request made to the Government by international organizations such as OSCE, EU, the Stability Pact for Southeastern Europe, etc[203].

[202] At the time of the survey, Serbia was an exception in that regard, but at the time of writing this book, cooperation between the Government and non-governmental organizations was much better there as well. Cooperation developed especially regarding sex trafficking.

[203] "EU urges Yugoslavia to tackle illegal immigration", Reuters, ltd, Message received through stop-traffic@friends-partners.org on April 11, 2001.

5. LINKING MICRO AND MACRO CHANGES: EVERYDAY LIFE, ACTIVISM AND REFORMS

Political change, i.e. political pluralism, freedom of speech and self-organizing, as well as an increased permeability of borders (for both transfer of ideas and money), was a *condition sine qua non* for the emergence of social movements in post-communist countries in general, and the feminist movement in particular. As pointed out by Freeman, the group can do no more than its resources and its environment permit (Freeman, 1979:167), and this is exactly why the development of social movements was not possible during communism (Szabo, 1994:287). But deterioration of the social and economic position of women, as a result of social transition and war, especially unemployment, re-domestication and poverty, contributed as well. These were significant push factors for women's activism in post-communist countries since they motivated women to join newly established women's organizations in order to spend their newly acquired time in useful ways and to earn a living. In some ways, this is similar to the way in which, after WW II, the withdrawal of a large number of women from active participation in the labor force and their return to traditional women's roles pushed the re-emergence of Western feminism in the 1960's (Bouchier, 1983:40). Moreover, the availability of Western knowledge and experiences as well as an increased interest of international foundations to fund projects in post-communist countries had significant impacts as well (pull factors). Thus, as the dramatic rise of private philanthropy was important for development of Western social movements in the 1960's and 1970's (Perow, 1979:192), women's movements in post-communist countries developed in large measure owing to the financial support of international foundations.

However, both internal circumstances in post-communist countries and the broader (international) social context in the 1990's were less favorable than the social context within which second wave feminism emerged in the West. This created serious obstacles to the success of women's initiatives and the sustainability of their activities.

For example, contrary to Western women[204], East European women did not have or had only limited experiences (e.g. in Serbia) of self-organizing and were not in a position to use the immediate experiences of their own civil rights movements simply because such movements did not exist before the collapse of communism. Women's groups emerged as part of the broader human and civil rights struggles led by NGO's, which became possible only when the political changes were achieved. Lacking their own experience, they mainly relied on the experiences of the Western women's movement, with achievements of the battered women's movement being among the most important among them. [205]

[204] As Rosalyn Fraad Baxandall says, many women involved in the 1960's women's movement in the US came from the civil rights movement and the New left, so that their aim was "to build a mass movement to end segregation and discrimination based on sex" (Rowbotham, 1992:259).

[205] This is not unusual having in mind that during communism violence against women, especially domestic violence was among the most hidden violations of women's human rights. In addition, Western experiences regarding violence against women were among the first Western feminist experiences that women from post-communist countries became familiar with.

The social context in which women's movements in post-communist countries emerged was less favorable also because, unlike Western feminism, it was not part of a general protest against global processes, but was instead part of a general excitement about them. Women's organizations are situated within a seemingly paradoxical context: on the one hand, there is a welcome turn towards democratization, while on the other hand the situation of women has continued to deteriorate (Molyneux, 1996:232). This is why it was much easier for women in Serbia than those in other countries to put their own requests in the broader context of criticism of the political regime, they did it by connecting their demands for change regarding women's social position with more general demands regarding war and militarism. Another difference in comparison with Western feminism lay in the fact that East European feminism emerged in societies severely hit by both poverty and emerging consumerism, while Western feminism had mainly to deal with the consequences of consumerism in generally affluent societies.

Unlike Western women in 1960's, who struggled for equal rights in general, and for maternity leave rights, reproductive rights, equal education and employment opportunities as well as for child care, in particular (Bauchier, 1983:46), East European women were quite surprised that the long awaited changes led to their loss of exactly the same rights they at least formally enjoyed at a time when their sisters in the West struggled for them so hard. Women in Eastern Europe found themselves in a position not only to oppose the deterioration of women's everyday life, but also to struggle to retain rights they had already gained, to make them more realistic and to expand them.

One of the greatest obstacles to the struggle of East European women came from widespread anti-feminist attitudes. These were partly inherited from the communist era, when feminism was regarded as "Western ideology," alien to the East European tradition (Ascady, 1999:407; Arpad and Marinovich, 1995:91) and was considered a selfish movement of "pampered women in a consumer society" (Arpad and Marinovich, 1995:87). Feminism was considered inappropriate since it was largely accepted that during communism women had gained all rights, which were denied to women under capitalism. In addition, after the change, feminism was discredited as just another utopian philosophy, like communism (Arpad and Marinovich, 1995:91). The other part of anti-feminist attitudes, similar to those in Western countries (Bauchier, 1983:149, 156), is connected to the lack of knowledge about feminism and equating it with the perceived anti-male line of radical feminists and lesbians, this latter being seen as even less acceptable than feminism itself.[206] As in the West, feminists in Eastern Europe blame the media for contributing to the negative image of feminism within society - they either avoid addressing feminist issues or address them in inappropriate ways (Bouchier, 1983: 165; Acsady, 1999:407).[207]

[206] Interviews with Virginia Zaharjeva an Tatyana Kotzeva (Bulgaria), Maria Adamik and Elekes Iren Borbala (Hungary), Biljana Bejkova and Mirjana Najcevska (Macedonia) and Vesna Stanojevic (Serbia).

[207] Also interviews with Virginia Zaharjeva (Bulgaria) and Biljana Bejkova (Macedonia). In Serbia, Blagojevic points out the positive exception regarding media presentation of feminist activities on violence against women. The same may be applied to other countries. As argued by Blagojevic, it

An additional obstacle to the efforts made by women's organizations in post-communist countries lies in the fact that the new democracies of the 1980's and 1990's were established in an international policy environment, which is very different in comparison to the situation in the 1960's and 1970's. Apart from "backlash" campaigns advocating restriction of reproductive rights and relocation of women within subordinate positions in the economy and family, the obvious difference lies in the changed economic climate, i.e. the prolonged global recession that led to a sharp diminution of the resources which made possible the advances of the 1970's (Molyneux, 1996:233-35). Moreover, the economic crisis challenged the viability of existing development and welfare models in which the state had played a central role, which led to the loss of existing rights rather than to gaining new ones. The situation where external financial factors urge the withdrawal of the state from its former areas of responsibility (Molineux, 1996:240) leaves little space for women's advocates demands for the state to fund their projects. In that way, after the initial generous aid of Western foundations, the young women's movements in post-communist societies are usually left with scarce resources and with unclear prospects for their future development and sustainability.

Bearing in mind all these obstacles, it seems that the concern of some Western authors about the slow emergence of feminism in post-communist countries (Dolling, Rosenberg and Kennedy, quoted by Watson, 1993:472; Einhorn, 1991:175) is based on unrealistic expectations. In spite of strong civil rights and democratic tradition, second wave feminism emerged in the West more than ten years after women lost what they had gained during WWII. It is, however, not unusual, since, as Bouchier points out "social movements are rarely sudden things, but emerge when a long process of change has caused some part of the population to expect and demand better life chances" (Bouchier, 1983:42).

I conclude that the development of a women's movement in post-communist countries in general, and a battered women's movement in particular is proof that their very existence reflects enormous change in the lives of women in general, and especially in the lives of those who are endangered by violence. As shown in this chapter, ten years of development of civil society initiatives regarding violence against women led to slow but certain changes in all four countries included in the survey. As in the US and Britain in the late 1970's, campaigns against violence against women in post-communist countries seem to be the most highly visible issues of the women's movement (Bouchier, 1983:144). Thus, the findings about the achievements of the battered women's movement in both Western (e.g. Dobash and Dobash, 1992) and post-communist countries seem to confirm Alder's statement that "it needs to be recognized that planned social change may have important effects as well". (Alder, 1999:119). Or, to put it otherwise, it is obvious that the women's groups main achievements regarding violence against women are those realized through activities intended to increase public awareness. However, although there are some similarities between awareness raising in post-communist societies and

---

may be that it confirms a well-known fact that problems arise when women begin to gain power, while dealing with problems considered marginal is still seen as acceptable (Blagojevic, 1998:40).

consciousness raising as a central activity of women's groups in the West in the 1960's, their aims are in some way different as well. While consciousness raising seemed to be oriented initially toward changing women themselves, awareness raising tends rather to educate the general public and professionals in order to change their attitudes toward violence against women, as well as to inform women about where they can get help.

Women's organizations put the issue of violence against women on the public agenda suggesting clearly that domestic violence is not a private matter but a serious social problem which needs serious discussion and solutions[208]. Also, they offered new images of violence against women, where deconstruction of traditional stereotypes (putting blame on the offender (man) instead of on the victim (woman) and concern about victims and their rights) prevail (Nikolic-Ristanovic, 2001:291). Although often facing obstacles and without proper understanding, these changed images of women, which dominate in articles initiated, written by, or as interviews with women's group activists and feminist scholars, obviously have had an increasing impact on media images about violence against women. i.e. on their messages to women, men and those dealing professionally with violence. Professionals and women's group activists also agree that this is the main change achieved so far in terms that women victims feel they are not alone and that they have information on where to turn for help. As stated by Tatyana Kmetova from Bulgaria, it was very important to show "that cases of violence are real, i.e. that they do not exist only in American movies. The change which was achieved owing to women' s groups was also that women are now more willing to speak about violence and to ask for help. When examples of battered women trying to find somebody who can help them are available, that means the situation is completely changed", says Kmetova (interview, 1999).

Dr Gyorgy Virag, psychologist and director of Eszter has a similar opinion:

> "The changes are slow but they exist. The media speaks about persons who work in NGO's, i.e. about the assistance that NGO's offer so that now victims know, they are informed that there are organizations which can help them. From my experience at Eszter, I can say that women are more willing to speak openly about sexual crimes, and more and more of them come to ask for help from victim support organizations" (interview, 1999).

Women's studies and research, the development of which in some countries such as Serbia and Bulgaria is rather impressive, also made a significant contribution to increasing public awareness. This is especially important because of the difficult and unstable political situation (Serbia), as well as the late emergence of NGO's dealing with violence against women (Bulgaria).

The second important change is that, although still rare and far from being able to meet all the needs of battered women, organizations offering help and support have started to become a reality of post-communist society. As I showed in this

[208] Before changes violence against women was seriously discussed only in Serbia, which is not strange bearing in mind Serbia's earlier openness toward the West as well as the fact that the women's movement and feminist ideas, including those developed by feminist scholars just in the field of law and victimology, started already in the 1980's.

chapter, the existing organizations offer either telephone aid (SOS hotlines) or both telephone aid and direct counseling (usually psychological and legal). Only rarely do they also accompany women to court. The biggest problem these organizations face is lack of shelters and women's friendly lawyers. As mentioned before, the number of places in shelters in Serbia, Hungary and Bulgaria are far from sufficient to meet the needs of all battered women, while in Macedonia there are no shelters at all. Only shelters in Serbia and Bulgaria are run by women's organizations and they are established specifically for battered women. In Serbia the only shelter for battered women is used also to accommodate refugee women and other women in need. New governments are not yet willing or able to invest in women's victim support organizations,[209] so they are mainly dependent on funders who usually fund them for some time and then leave.[210]

However, on the other side, NGO's report that one of their important achievements was the improvement of cooperation with state institutions. Concrete results of grassroots organizations' advocacy are limited and include provisions for marital rape as a criminal offence in Hungary and Macedonia, the introduction of the Law on trafficking in human beings in Hungary and legal changes regarding the women's prison in Serbia. Also, in Serbia, the longtime advocacy of women's groups and feminist lawyers resulted in the inclusion of marital rape in the draft of the new Criminal code. One important achievement in terms of changes of legal practice is related to release and lighter punishment of battered women who kill their abusers and harsher penalties for violent husbands who kill their wives, which is especially evident in Serbia and Hungary.

Apart from women's and general victim support organization advocacy, in both Serbia and Hungary, development of proposals for legal change is also related to victimology theory and research, started in both countries in the early 1980's. However, it is obvious that, apart from advocacy of grassroots organizations and victimologists, the willingness of the Hungarian Government to adjust legislation with international standards (which coincided with Hungary's strong commitment for EU membership) had a significant impact on the development of the above-mentioned proposal. This latter is exactly the condition which, until the changes in 2000, was missing in Serbia. For example, in spite of serious efforts made by the Victimology Society of Serbia to develop a comprehensive model of new legal approaches to domestic violence, sexual violence and trafficking in women, the Government did not show any interest in making changes.

209 However, some positive examples are found in Bulgaria, where Sofia municipality has provided a buildings for both shelter (Nadja Center) and Center for rehabilitation of women victims of violence (Animus). Sofia municipality also supported Animus in giving it an opportunity to advertise its activities on public places. In 1998 Animus received official permission to put stickers of the help-line in the public transport (Annual Report of Animus Association, 1998:34).

210 For example, few years ago Serbia had three shelters but two of them had to be closed recently because of lack of funding. Although foreign funding of NGO's in Serbia was always poor, for some time women's groups managed to cover their expenses and continue their activities thanks to the solidarity of women's groups from different countries. After the NATO bombing funding became even more limited and selective than earlier, often negatively affecting the activities of women's victim support organizations. As already mentioned, the situation improved again after the changes in 2000.

The connection between the success of women's group' advocacy and requests from the international community is also obvious in the fact that legal changes regarding marital rape and trafficking in women, in relation to which international pressure was especially pronounced in all countries included in the survey, were faster and without a lot of confrontation as those related to domestic violence. Moreover, in spite of significant public awareness campaigns, legal advocacy, seminars and trainings for professionals, it seems that the level of both public and professional awareness about domestic violence is still very low in comparison to strong patriarchal attitudes. Thus the current situation regarding violence against women in post-communist countries seems to be best described by Molyneux (1996:253), who says that, although the current policy environment in Eastern Europe is in many ways unfavorable with respect to women's rights, "its overall effects are contradictory, undermining some forms of protective rights, but promoting others. It may well be that the very process of integration into the international economy acts as a check on the adoption of legislation influenced by the more extreme forms of national communitarianism. The bid for membership of 'the West' to some degree rests on leadership claims that countries are modern nation states". On the other side, however, the fact that lawyers from women's organizations are involved in expert groups working on drafting new laws (e.g. family and criminal law) may be promising in terms of prospects for positive achievements in the near future. Also, although newly created departments on women's issues in all countries are still mainly the expression of the Government's formal fulfillment of its international obligations rather than its real commitment to improvement of women's situation, they seem to be a good starting point for future developments. It is promising that feminists, at least some in Hungary, have realized that in order to produce real change they should not separate themselves from the state but need to try to intervene, i.e. to be a part of it. [211] This may also be a good path for women's organizations to secure both a recognized place within society and the sustainability of their activities once international support/interest for their countries is concluded.

[211] Anna Bethlen, counselor for women's issues in the Ministry of Social Affairs-Secretariat for Women (Hungary), who is also a volunteer with NANE, gave a good example of this. In the interview conducted on May 1, 1999, she said: "I think that Government does not have a real interest in our actions - it was their obligation toward international bodies to establish that department and they did it because of that. So we have to fight a lot to be visible. We are now on a lower level than we were before the most recent change of Government. Now we are a department with less competence than before. Our staff was changed too, so we now have new people who do not know the problem very well. We have seven persons who are professionals but they are not trained to deal with women's issues. We also have a fund for helping women's NGO's but it is seven million forints and that is too little for us to help in an effective way and it makes our actions ineffective. And we have a very limited function so that we do not have a real impact on solving women's problems. Because of that, I made a proposal for the establishment of a special state institution, which can help NGO's dealing with violence against women. Also, this institution would deal with the reactions of state bodies (court, police) to violence against women and help finance organizations that can provide help to victims - urgent help, psychological help, legal help, help to get access to the social system, etc. This institution is also going to deal with raising awareness of women victims, who do not know how to reach those who can help them, and it should build a network of both governmental and non-governmental organizations.

CONCLUSION

Social change, gender and violence: from understanding to prevention of violence against women in a globalized world

> "...What is particularly effective in increasing the amount of violence in the world is to widen the gap between the rich and the poor....Relative poverty - poverty for some groups coexisting with wealth for others - is much more effective in stimulating shame, and hence, violence, than is a level of poverty that is higher in absolute terms but is universally shared."(p.238-39)
>
> " If humanity is to evolve beyond the propensity toward violence that now threatens our very survival as a species, then it can only do so by recognizing the extent to which the patriarchal code of honor and shame generates and obligates male violence. If we wish to bring this violence under control, we need to begin by reconstituting what we mean by both masculinity and femininity."(p.267)
>
> "If cleaning up sewer systems could prevent more deaths than all the physicians in the world, then perhaps reforming the social, economic, and legal institutions that systematically humiliate people can do more to prevent violence than all the preaching and punishing in the world" (p.239)
>
> James Gilligan, Violence: Reflections on a National Epidemic (1997)

The argument underlying this monograph is well expressed in Gilligan's words quoted above. Research findings seem to confirm both Gilligan' s and Kurtz and Turpin's theories on violence. Thus, violence is to be considered a result of "causal connections between personal-level and global-level structures, processes and behaviors" (Kurtz and Turpin, 1997:208), with both "cross-cut by gender" (Moser, 2001:39). It is evident that an understanding of the role of structural violence in both the creation of situations in which violence against women occurs and in the development of effective social responses and prevention measures to it is necessary in any society, and in a society under stress in particular. Indeed, although social change is the reality of almost all countries in the contemporary (globalized) world, the speed and accumulation of changes and related stresses in everyday life are more pronounced in developing and war-affected societies. Thus, doing research on interconnections between social change, gender and violence in post-communist and war-affected societies has allowed me to identify a multitude of causes of violence against women in the post-Cold War world.

This is important for many reasons, two being especially significant. First, although micro/macro linkages were ignored before as well, individualistic solutions to the violence problem that ignore larger structural causes became dominant on the policy scene especially after the collapse of communism (Kurtz and Turpin, 1997:208). Moreover, these same approaches in day to day decision-making in post-communist (and other developing) countries are strongly encouraged by the fragmented (project) funding policy of the West. As a consequence there is no comprehensive prevention strategy regarding violence against women in general, and in relation to domestic violence and sex trafficking, in particular. Thus, an understanding of violence against women which draws a complete causation scheme, or as Gilligan (1997:7) puts it "the whole story of violence," which includes the lives of both victims and victimizers, is crucial for building effective prevention strategies as well. Or, to borrow Gilligan's words again "until it is understood, it cannot be prevented - that is, brought under individual and societal self-control" (Gilligan 1997:9).

As my survey findings suggest, global economic and political changes and war produce microlevel changes, i.e. changes in everyday life and gender, generational and ethnic structures/identities. Obviously, the impact of macrosocial changes on economic and gender structures and interconnections between them are especially important to take into account when women's vulnerability to violence is considered.

As shown by my findings, the establishment of a capitalist economy in post-communist societies contributed to the reinforcement of patriarchy as well. Privatization and a market economy led to the development of both a traditional gender ideology and re-traditionalization of gender structures. This is not unexpected since a patriarchal gender structure is inherent to capitalism. War, militarism, dissatisfaction with the quasi-equality of women and men, emasculation of men and "masculinization" of women during communism as well as antifeminism contributed as well. Moreover, "capitalism generates massive inequalities in the social structure" (Mooney, 2000:216) and privatizes family and women's secondary status within it, which, as observed by Schechter (1982:225), is dangerous "because it allows violence to accelerate while everyone says 'Mind your own business. This is a family problem." Moreover, a market economy also limits women's body to a sexual object and marketable good. Thus, patriarchy, structural violence brought by capitalism and macroviolence may be considered the main macrostructural factors which affect women's vulnerability to violence.

However, while reinforcing traditional patriarchal expectations, a market economy and militarism contribute to a decrease rather than to an increase in the chances for large numbers of men and women to achieve ideal masculinity and femininity. When violence against women is in question, the inability of men to achieve the ideal family class model, i.e. hegemonic masculinity in terms of the gender division of labor and consequently gender power relations, is especially risky. Thus, as noted by Alder (1999:117), "an understanding of the implications of economic change on violence entails consideration of the interactions between masculinity and economic status." Similarly, as in the third world (Schechter, 1982:235), in post-communist and war-affected societies oppression rather than domination of men is an important contributing factor to male violence in the home.

Structural violence oppresses men in a way that they are not able to perform the expected male role and, consequently, the gender role order generates violence by shaming them for not being able to express their gender. Also, as pointed out by Gilligan, "the male gender role generates violence by exposing men to shame if they are not violent and rewarding them with honor when they are". On the other side, the female gender role stimulates violence by restricting women to "highly unfree sex objects and honoring them to the degree that they submit to those roles or shaming them when they rebel." As a consequence, men are encouraged to treat women as sex objects and women to conform to that. Moreover, a man is encouraged also to be violent against a woman "to whom he is related or married when she 'dishonors' him by acting in ways that transgress her prescribed sexual roles" (Gilligan, 1997:233).

It seems that Gilligan's theory of shaming is applicable to the explanation of both domestic violence and sex trafficking in post-communist and war-affected societies. Both forms of violence against women seem to be connected also with what Gilligan calls the "horror of dependency." In the case of post-communist and war-affected societies, the horror of dependency culminates in the fact that large numbers of both women and men find themselves trapped in poverty so that it is not unusual that in some countries fear of life is more widespread than fear of death. As a result of men's dependency or lack of sufficient earnings to fulfill the role of breadwinner, in general, and especially of men's dependency on women, domestic violence is either generated or becomes worse, while women's dependency is much more important as an obstacle to leaving violent men, i.e. for finding an exit from violence. On the other side, however, women's dependency is an important contributing factor for sex trafficking, although dependency of men should not be ignored (e.g. most perpetrators involved in sex trafficking are poor men, while only a small number of them are really powerful). Thus both a high level of structural violence and few resources for social programs result in a large part of the population in post-communist and war-affected societies being vulnerable to interpersonal violence - as victims but also as perpetrators.

It seems that structural violence contributes to gendered interpersonal violence both by causing it and by preventing society and victims from confronting it effectively. Therefore, it is not surprising that, in spite of all the positive political changes, and despite the efforts made by civil society and women's movements, not much has changed in terms of legal and institutional reforms regarding violence against women in post-communist countries. A significant obstacle even in more developed post-communist countries, such as Hungary, is the obvious lack of material resources. Expansion of neoliberal capitalism, deepening of the gap between poor and rich countries as well as dependent development (Sklair, 1991:233) of post-communist countries do not promise much chance for a strong (welfare) state in the near future. Moreover, the costs of economic change are very high, especially in countries where the economic situation was bad at the beginning of the transition and in those affected by war.

High costs in terms of a dramatic decrease in the standard of living, and an increase in uncertainty, overall fluidity and instability have led to continued production of violence. This is also an important reason why even those changes which have been achieved do not produce the expected results in terms of increased safety of women who suffer from male violence. As observed by Cunningham (2000:7), "if the society's structural dynamics continue to produce violence, anti-violence policies and programs are bound to fail." But, when social conditions are altered, "the exposure of the human population to shame is dramatically reduced - and so is violence". Hence, as argued by Gilligan (1997:226), a close connection between the welfare state and a decrease of both shaming and violence is obvious. The problem is, however, that, because of the global expansion of neoliberal capitalism, the welfare state is presently difficult to build even in developed countries, let alone in developing ones.

Moreover, in post-communist societies the contradictions of capitalism are interlaced with the mostly negative relics of communism, while the positive aspects of former communist society are usually removed very quickly. As a result, contradictory processes in post-communist society have led to a rather paradoxical result: political pluralism and a capitalist economic system generate both violence against women and a women's movement, albeit not the conditions for a reduction of violence. This is where the answer to the question about the low level efficiency of rather active and growing women's initiatives in post-communist society can be sought. Hence, prevention of violence against women in societies under stress as in any other society, and even more, have to take into account the dialectic interaction of macro- and microlevel changes. Moreover, as well observed by Kurtz and Turpin, "solutions to the problem of violence must address all levels - as well as interactions among them" (Kurtz and Turpin, 1997:209). But, in the conditions of "a new international division of labor" (Sklair, 1991:34), expansion of militarism and other negative consequences of globalization, as in other developing countries, it is not realistic to expect post-communist ones to be successful in reducing violence.

Policies which underlie the global dimensions of violence against women are most visible in the example of sex trafficking. The pressure of the international community toward post-communist countries to undertake decisive (mainly repressive) measures is in obvious contradiction with global processes which generate structural violence on the world level, leaving no room for appropriate protection of victims, let alone for reduction of violence. In addition, even feminism is misused for the creation of fragmented images and solutions, which led to a restriction of the violence against women problem to the interpersonal level and to male to female relations only. This is what Watson (2001:43) called "a kind of American state feminism for abroad".

CONCLUSION

As far as violence against women is considered out of context, i.e. regardless of its connection to macrosocial processes which produce it both within individual countries and globally, and by oppressing both women and men, we cannot expect any substantial change to be achieved whatever enthusiasm and ideas are involved in efforts to reduce it. Changes are necessary on all levels of society - in social conditions, patriarchal gender roles as well as in economic and legal institutions, nationally and internationally.

REFERENCES

Alder, C. (1999) "Violence, Gender and Social Change" in M.B.Steger and N.S.Lind *An interdisciplinary Reader - Violence and its alternatives*, London: MacMillan Press LTD, p. 114-120.

Altink, S. (1995) *Stolen Lives*, London:Scarlet Press.

Allcock, J. (1999) »Macedonia« in D.Turnock and F. Carter (eds) *The States of Eastern Europe*, Vol.II: South-Eastern Europe, Aldershot: Ashgate, pp.141-166

Allen, Craig M. and Strauss, A.M (1980) "Resources, power, and husband-wife violence". In M.A. Strauss and G.T. Hotaling (eds), *The Social Causes of Husband-Wife Violence.* Minneapolis:University of Minnesota Press.

Analytical creative group and IOM (2000) "Information Campaign for the Prevention of Trafficking in Women in Bulgaria", Sofia:IOM.

Andric-Ruzicic, D. ed.(1999), "Ne/ziveti sa nasiljem" (Not/Living with Violence), *Drugi pogled*, 2, Zenica: Medica Zenica

Andersen, L. M. (1988) *Thinking about women: Sociological Perspectives on Sex and Gender*, New York :Macmillan.

Animus Association Foundation (1998) Annual Report, Animus Association Foundation , Sofia.

Ascady, J. (1999) "Urges and Obstacles: Chances for Feminism in Eastern Europe", *Women's Studies International Forum*, 4, pp.405-409.

Arpad, S. S., Marinovich, S. (1995) "Why Hasn't there Been a Strong Women's Movement in Hungary?", *Journal of Popular Culture*, 2, p. 77-96.

Attwood. L. (1996) "The post-Soviet woman in the move to the market: a return to domesticity and dependence?", in R. March (ed) *Women in Russia and Ukraine*, Cambridge: Cambridge University Press, p. p. 255-267.

Bacanovic, O. (2001) "Zeni zrtvo na trgovija so luge" (Women victims of traffick in people), *Annual Edition of the School of Security*, Skopje, p.104-116.

Bales, K. (1999) *Disposable people*, Berkley, Los Angeles, London: University of California Press.

Barett, M. (1997) "Ideology and the Cultural Production of Gender" in R.Hennessy and C.Ingraham (eds) *Materialist Feminism*, New York and London:Routledge, p.88-95.

Blagg, H.(2000) "Crisis Intervention in Aboriginal Family Violence", Summary Report, Commonwealth of Australia

Blagojevic M., (1994) "War and Everyday life: Deconstruction of Self/Sacrifice", *Sociologija*, 4, p.469-482

Blagojevic, M. (1997) *Roditeljstvo i fertilitet – Srbija devedesetih* (Parenthood and Fertility - Serbia in 1990s), Beograd: Institut za socioloska istrazivanja Filozofskog fakulteta u Beogradu.

Blagojevic, M. (ed) (1998) *Ka vidljivoj zenskoj istoriji – zenski pokreti u Beogradu 90-ih* (Toward Visible Women's History - Women's Movement in Belgrade in 90s) , Beograd,Centar za zenske studije, istrazivanja i komunikaciju.

Blagojevic, M. (2000) Preface, in Nikolic-Ristanovic, V.(ed) (2000) *Women, Violence and War*, CEU Press, Budapest, p. IX-XV.

Bod, P. (1998) "The social and economic legacies of direct capital inflows: the case of Hungary" in J. Bastian (ed) *The Political Economy of Transition in Central and Eastern Europe*, Aldershot: Ashgate, p.13-45.

Bolcic, S. (1995) "Izmenjena sfera rada" (Changed Sphere of Work), in Bolcic, S.(ed) *Drustvene promene i svakodnevni zivot: Srbija pocetkom 1990s* (Social Changes and Everyday Life: Serbia at the Beginning of 1990s), Belgrade: Insitut za socioloska istrazivanja Filozofskog fakulteta u Beogradu, p. 79-108.

Boric, R. and Desnica, M. (1996) "Croatia:Three Years After" in C. Corrin (ed*) Women in a Violent Word, Feminist Analyses and Resistance Across "Europe"*, Edinburgh:Edinburgh University Press.

Bouchier, D. (1983) *The Feminist Challenge*, London: Macmillan Press

Bozinovic, N. (1996) *Zensko pitanje u Srbiji u XIX i XX veku* (Women's Questions in Serbia in 19th and 20th century), Beograd: Devedesetcetvrta i Zene u crnom .

REFERENCES

Braithwaite, J., Chapman, B. and Kapuscinski, C. A. (1998) "Unemployment and crime:resolving the paradox" American Bar Foundation Working Paper #9201.

Browne, A. (1987) *When battered women kill*, New York and London :The Free Press and Collier Macmillan Publishers.

Brogden, M. and Nijhar, P. (2000) *Crime, Abuse and Elderly*, Devon:Willan Publishing

Bruinsma, G.J.N., Meershoek, G. (1999) "Organized Crime and Trafficking in Women from Eastern Europe in the Netherlands"", *Transnational Organized Crime*, Special Issue "Illegal Immigration and Commercial Sex - the New Slave Trade" (ed. P.Williams), Vol. 3, 4., p.105-117.

Burgoyne, J. (1987) "Change, gender and the life course" in G.Cohen (ed) *Social change and the life course*, London and New York: Tavistock Publications, p.33-66.

Caceva, V. and Coneva, Lj. (2000) *Semejno nasilstvo* (Domestic Violence), Skopje:ESE.

Carter, F. (1999) "Bulgaria" in D.Turnock and F. Carter (eds) *The States of Eastern Europe*, Vol.II: South-Eastern Europe, Aldershot: Ashgate, pp.71-109.

Casa delle donne "Project against Forced Prostitution" (unpublished report).

Cahn, D.D. (1996) "Family Violence From a Communication Perspective" in Cahn, D.D. and Lloyd S.A. (1996) *Family Violence from a Communication Perspective*, Thousand Oaks: Sage. p.1-20.

Coneva, Lj. and Darkovski, D. (1995) "Kriznite sastojbi kaj naselenieto vo Republika Makedonija - nacini i formi za nivno nadminuvanje" (Crises events in the life of citizens of Republic of Macedonia - Ways and Forms of their Reduction), Skopje, unpublished research report.

Coneva, Lj. (1998)"Socijalnata sigurnost i tranzicijata"(Social security and transition) in B. Nanevski and V. Stojanova. (eds) *Socijalnata sigurnost na naselenieto vo Republika Makedonia vo uslovi na tranzicija*, Skopje: Friedrich Ebert Stiftung and Economski institut, p.133-136.

Connell, R.W. (1993) *Gender and Power – Society, the Person and Sexual Politics*, Cambridge:Polity Press.

Connell, R. (1995) *Masculinities*, Cambridge:Polity Press.

Connell, R. (1995a) "Masculinity, Violence and War" in M.Kimmer, M.Messner (eds) *Men's lives*, Meedham Heights:Allyn and Bacon, p.125-131.

Connell, R. (2001) "Masculinities and Globalization" in M.S.Kimmel and M.A.Messner *Men's Lives*, Meedham Heights:Allyn and Bacon, p.56-71.

Corrin, C. ed. (1992), *Super women and the Double Burden – Women's experience of change in Central and Eastern Europe and the former Soviet Union*, London, Scarlet Press.

Corrin, C. (1996) (ed) *Women in a Violent Word: Feminist Analyses and Resistance Across "Europe"*, Edinburgh: Edinburgh University Press.

Corrin, C. (1999) "Rethinking Citizenship: Analyses and Activism in Central and Eastern Europe", *The Journal of Communist Studies and Transition Politics*, 1, p.64-82.

Cook, K. (1991) "The Microfoundations of Social Structure: An Exchange Perspective" in J. Huber *Macro-Micro Linkages in Sociology*, Newbury Park, London and New Delhy:Sage, p.29-45.

Cetkovic, N., (1998) *U traganju za sigurnim zenskim mestom* (In the Search of Safe Women's Place) Belgrade: SOS telefon za zene i decu zrtve nasilja i Sigurne zenske kuce.

Coffield, F. (1987) "From the celebration to the marginalization of youth" in G.Cohen (ed) *Social change and the life course*, London and New York: Tavistock Publications, p. 87-106

Cohen, G. (1987) "Introduction: the economy, the family, and the life course" in G.Cohen (ed) *Social change and the life course*, London and New York: Tavistock Publications, p.1-29.

Crompton, R. and Mann, M. (1994) *Gender and Stratification*, Cambridge:Polity Press, p.VII-XXIV.

Cunningham, S.(2000) "What we Teach about When We Teach about Violence", *The HFG Review*, 1, p.4-9

Dainov, E., Garnizov, V. (1995) *Politics, Reform & Daily Life, Evolution of popular attitudes to key issues in the reform process in Bulgaria* (1993-1994), Sofia:Centre for Social Practices-New Bulgarian University Centre for Liberal Strategies.

Daskalova, K. (1997) "The Women's Movement in Bulgaria After Communism", in: Scott, W.J., Kaplan, C., Keates, D. *Transitions, Environments, Translations, Feminisms in International Politics*, New York:Routledge, p. 162-175.

Daskalova, K. (1999) "Bulgarian Women in Movements, Laws, Discourses (1840s-1940s)", *Bulgarian Historical Review*, 1-2, p.184 -199.

Dakova, V. and Indshewa, R. (1999) "Transition: Gains and Losses", *Social Watch*, 3, p.119-122 .

REFERENCES

Deacon, B. (1992) "East European Welfare:Past, Present and Future in Comparative context" in B.Deacon (ed) *The New Eastern Europe:Social Policy, Past, Present and Future*, London: Sage, p.1-31.

Dempsey, G. (2000) "Headaches for Neighboring Countries", in T.G. Carpenter *Nato' Empty Victory*, Washington.D.C: Cato Institute, p.59-77.

Dicks, B., Waddington, D. and Critcher, C. (1998) "Redundant Men and Overburdened Women" in J.Popay, J.Hearn and J.Edwards (eds) *Men, Gender Division and Welfare*, London and New York: Routledge, p.287-311.

Dimitrievska,V. (1998) »Poimot siromastija i moznosti za nejzino merenje« (The Notion of Poverty and Possibilities for its Measuring) in B.Nanveski. and V. Stojanova (eds) *Socijalnata sigurnost na naselenieto vo Republika Makedonia vo uslovi na tranzicija*, Skopje: Friedrich Ebert Stiftung and Economski institut, p.19-31.

Dimitrievska, V. (1999) "Kvalitativna analiza siromastva u Republici Makedoniji"(Qualitative Analyses of Poverty in Republic of Macedonia), in *Ostvarivanje ekonomskih i socijalnih prava*, Belgrade: Beogradski centar za ljudska prava, p. 180-190.

Dinkic, M. (1999) *Zavrsni racun* (Final Account), Beograd, Stubovi kulture.

Dobash R.E. and Dobash R.P. (1979) *Violence against Wives: a Case Against Patriarchy*, New York: The Free Press.

Dobach, R.E. and Dobash R.P. (1992) *Women, Violence and Social Change*, London: Routledge .

Dobash, R.E and Dobash, R.P. (1998) *Rethinking Violence against Women*, Thousand Oaks: Sage.

Dobash, R.E., Dobash, R.P., Cavanagh, K., Lawis, R. (2000) *Changing Violent Men*, Thousend Oaks, London, New Delhi: Sage

Dobrinski, R. (2000) "The Transition crisis in Bulgaria", *Cambridge Journal of Economics*, 24, p. 581-602.

Dowler, L. (1997) "The Mother of all Warriors:Women in War, Belfast, Northern Ireland" in R.Lentin *Gender and Catastrophe*, London and New York: Zed Books, p.77-92.

Drezov, K. (2000) "Transition Comes Full Circle, 1989-1997" in G. Pridham and T.Gallagher (eds) *Experimenting with Democracy: Regime Change in the Balkans*, London &New York: Routledge, p.194-218.

Drezov, K. (2001) "Bulgaria and Macedonia: Voluntary Dependence on External Actors" in J. Zielonka and A. Pravda (eds.) *Democratic Consolidation in Eastern Europe:International and Transnational Factors*, Volume 2, Oxford:Oxford University Press, pp. 413-436.

Earle, J. and Sakova, Z. (2000) "Business Start-ups or Disguised Unemployment? Evidence on The Character of Self-Employment from Transition Economies", *Labour Economics*, 7, p. 575-601.

Einhorn, B. (1993) *Cinderella Goes to Market – Citizenship, Gender and Women's Movement in East Central Europe*, London, Verso.

El-Bushra , J. and E.P.Lopez (1993) "Development in Conflict:the Gender Dimension". In Report of an Oxfam AGRA East workshop held in Pattaya, Thailand, February 1-4, 1993. Oxfam.

El-Bushra, J. (2000) "Transforming Conflict: Some Thoughts on a Gendered Understanding of Conflict Processes" in S.Jacobs, R.Jacobson and J.Marchbank (eds) *States of Conflict*, London-New York: Zed Books, p.66-86.

ESE (1997) *Rhea Silvia*, Skopje: ESE.

Efremov, B. (1998) "Nerabotenosta i sivata ekonomija" (Unemployment and Shadow Economy) in B.Nanevski and V.Stojanova (eds) *Socijalnata sigurnost na naselenieto vo R Makedonija vo uslovi na tranzicija*, Skopje: Fridrich Ebert Foundation, p. 137-142.

Euler, C., Welzer-Lang, D. (2000) "Developing Best Professional Practice for Reducing Sexual Abuse, Domestic Violence and Trafficking in Militarised Areas of Peacetime Europe", Project No. 98/043/WC Report, Leeds: Leeds Metropolitan University.

Euler, C. (2000) "Razvijanje najbolje vojne profesionalne prakse u pogledu nasilja nad zenama na i u blizini vojnih baza" (Developing Best Professional Military Practice With Regard to Violence Against Women on and Near Defense Estates), *Temida*, 2, 75-79.

European Network of Policewomen , Sofia (informative brochure).

Faludi, S. (1991) *Backlash: The Undeclared War Against American Women*, New York: Anchor Book.

Faludi, S. (2000) *Stiffed: the Betrayal of Modern Man*, London:Vintage.

REFERENCES

Feher, L. (1995) "Forced Prostitution and Traffick in Persons" in M. Klap, Y.Klerk and J.Smith *Combating Traffick in Persons*, Utreht: SIM, p.67-79.

Fireman, B. and Gamson, W. (1979) "Utilitarian Logic in the Resource Mobilization Perspective" in M.N.Zald and J.D.McCarthy *The Dynamics of Social Movements*, Cambridge: Winthrop Publishers, p.8-44.

Fisher, E. (1994) "War, Women and Democracy" in *Test the West:Gender Democracy and Violence*, Vienna:Austrian Federal Ministry of Women's Affairs.

Forrai, J. (1999) "Strange Form of Poverty and Crime on the Streets of Budapest: Male and Female Prostitution", *International Review of Home Affairs*, 2.

Freeman, J. (1979) "Resource Mobilization and Strategy: A Model for Analyzing Social Movement Organization Actions" in M.N.Zald and J.D McCarthy *The Dynamics of Social Movements*, Cambridge: Winthrop Publishers, p.167-190.

Frey, M. (1998) "Szemelyi szolgaltatasok fejlesztese a foglkoztatas bovitesere" (Development of services for improvement of work engagement) in *A szemelyi szoltatasok eselyei a munkahely - teremtesben*, Budapest:Nok haza, p.2-10.

Gadd, D. (2000) "Deconstructing Male Violence: a Study of Male Workers and Clients on an Anti-Violence Programme", Keele University (England), unpublished PhD theses.

Garnizov, V. (1995) *Politics, Reform and Everyday Life*, Sofia; Center for Social Practices.

Gartner, R. and McCarthy, B. (1991) "The Social Distribution of Femicide in Urban Canada, 1921-1988", *Law and Society Review* 25, p.287-312.

Gelles, R. (1993) "Through a Sociological Lens" in R.J. Gelles. and D.R. Loseke (eds). *Current Controversies on Family Violence*, California:Sage, p.31-62.

Gelles, R. (1997) *Intimate Violence in Families*, Thousand Oaks, London and New Delhi:Sage.

Gilligan, J. (1997) *Violence: reflections on a national epidemic*, New York:Vintage Books.

Global Survival Network (1997) "Crime and Servitude - An Expose of the Traffic in Women for Prostitution from the Newly Independent States", Washington D.C: Global Survival Network.

G17Plus, 2000 *Bela knjiga Miloseviceve vladavine* (White Book of Milosevic's Regime) Belgrade: B92.

Hatty, S. (2000) *Masculinities, Violence and Culture*, London: Sage.

Hagan, J. (1988) *Structural Criminology*, New Brunowich, New Jersey: Rutgers University Press.

Hague, E.(1997) "Rape, Power and Masculinity: The Construction of Gender and National Identities in the War in Bosnia-Herzegovina" in R.Lentin *Gender and Catastrophe*, London and New York:Zed Books, p.50-64.

Hearn, J. (1987) *The Gender of Oppression*, Sussex: Wheatsheaf Books.

Hearn, J. (1998) "Troubled Masculinities in Social Policy Discourses: Young Men" in J.Popay, J.Hearn and J.Edwards (eds) *Men, Gender, Divisions and Welfare*, London and New York:Routledge, p. 37-63.

Heitlinger, A. (1996) "Framing Feminism in Post-Communist Cheque Republic", *Communist and Post-Communist Studies*, 1, pp. 77-93.

Helsinki Committee Report "Izbeglice sa Kosova govore"(Refugees from Kosovo Speak), *Vreme*, 26 February, 2000.

Hochberg, A. (1997) "The Feminist Network" in T.Renne *Ana's land:Sisterhood in Eastern Europe*, Colorado:Westview Press, p. 106-112.

Huber, J. (1991) "Macro-Micro Links in Gender Stratification" in J.Huber *Macro-Micro Linkages in Sociology*, Newbury Park, London and New Delhi:Sage, p.11-25.

IOM (2000) "Information Campaign for the Prevention of Trafficking in Women in Hungary" (unpublished report).

IOM Pristina (2001) Return and Reintegration Project, situation report - February 2000 - May 2001.

IHF (2000) *Women 2000*, Vienna:IHF.

Jamieson, R.(1998) "Towards a Criminology of War in Europe" in V. Ruggiero, N. South and.Taylor (eds) *New European Criminology*, London: Routledge p .480-506.

Jakimovski, J. (1998) "Socijalno raslojuvanje i potrebata od socijalno obezbeduvanje na naselenieto vo Republika Makedonija"(Social Stratification and the Need for Social Security of People in Republic of Macedonia) in B.Nanevski and V.Stojanova (eds) *Socijalnata sigurnost na naselenieto vo R Makedonija bo uslovi na tranzicija*, Skopje: Fridrich Ebert Foundation, p.9-19.

REFERENCES

Jefferson, T. (1997) "Masculinities and Crime" in M.Maguire, R.Morgan and R.Reiner (eds) *The Oxford Handbook of Criminology*, Oxford:Clarendon press, p.535-549.

Jelkic, O. (1996) "Post-traumatski poremecaj i krivicna odgovornost - sindrom ratnog stresa (vijetnamski sindrom) " (Post-Traumatic Disorder and Criminal Responsibility - War Stress Syndrom (Vietnam syndrom) in *Teorijski i prakticni problemi jugoslovenskog kaznenog zakonodavstva*, Belgrade: Institut za kriminoloska i socioloska istrazivanja.

Jovanovski, J. (1998) "Socijalnata sigurnost na graganite korisnici na socijalna pomoc vo Makedonija"(Social Security of Citizens who are Users of Social Support in Macedonia) in B. Nanevski and V. Stojanova (eds) *Socijalnata sigurnost na naselenieto vo Republika Makedonia vo uslovi na tranzicija*, Skopje: Friedrich Ebert Stiftung and Economski institut, p. 85-95.

Karstedt, S. (1993) "The Impact of Social Crises on Dissocial and Problem Behavior of Women: Effects on Sex Differences Across the Life Course", *Soziale probleme*, 4, p.139-166.

Karner, T. (1998) "Engendering Violent Men" in L.H.Bowker (ed) *Masculinities and Violence*, London: Sage, p.197-234.

Kelly, L. (2000) "Wars Against Women: Sexual Violence, Sexual Politics and the Militarised State" in S.Jacobs, R.Jacobson and J.Marchbank (eds) *States of Conflict*, London-New York: Zed Books, p.45-65.

Knezic, B.(2000), "Stari ljudi-posebno ugrozena kategorija izbeglica"(Old people-specially endangered category of refugees), *Temida*, 2, str.41-47.

Kocsis, A., Szauto, A. (1997) "The Economic State of the Nation", *The Hungarian Quarterly*, 145, p.20-26.

Konig, I. (ed) (1997) *Trafficking in women*, Vienna: Federal Chancellery.

Kootstra, T. (1997) "I Thought I would be the Lady-Companion of One Man" - the Background of Victims of Traffick in Women in the Netherlands", in *One year La Strada* (report), p. 12-24.

Kostova, V. *Nasilieto nad zeni- Problem ot purvostepenno znacenie v socialnata rabota v Bulgarija* (Violence against Women - Significant Problem for Social Work in Bulgaria) (unpublished)

Kotzeva, T. (1999) "Women's Business: Outline of the Portrait of Women in Private Business", *Fair Play*, Digest of the Women's Alliance for Development, 2, p.8-9.

Kotzeva, T. (1999a) "Re-imaging Bulgarian Women:The Marxist Legacy and Women's Self-Identity", *The Journal of Communist Studies and Transition Politics*, 1, p.83-99.

Kojouharova, N. "Bulgarian Trafficking in Women: the Starting Point of La Strada Bulgaria" (unpublished).

Korac, M. (1994) "Representation of Mass Rape in Ethnic Conflicts in What Was Yugoslavia", Sociologija, 4, p.496-512.

Kulka, R., Schlenger, W, Farrbank, J., Hough, R., Jordan, B.K., Marmer, C, Weiss, D. (1990) *Trauma and the Vietnam War Generation*, New York: Brunner/Mazel Publishers.

Lang, S. (1997) "The NGOization of Feminism", in: Scott, J.W., Kallon, C. and Keates, D. (eds) *Transitions, Environments, Translations,* New York and London : Routledge, , p. 101-117.

Lazic, M.(1995) "Osobenosti globalne drustvene transformacije u Jugoslaviji" (Characteristics of Global Social Transformation in Yugoslavia)., in Bolcic, S. (ed) *Drustvene promene i svakodnevni zivot: Srbija pocetkom 1990* (Social Changes and Everyday Life: Serbia at the Beginning of 1990s), Belgrade: Insitut za socioloska istrazivanja Filozofskog fakulteta u Beogradu, p. 57-77.

Lloyd, S.A.(1996) "Physical Aggression, Distress, and Everyday Marital Interaction" in D.D. Cahn and S.A. Lloyd *Family Violence from a Communication Perspective*, Thousand Oaks: Sage, p.177-199.

Lobodzinska, B. (1996) "Women's Employment or Return to Family Values in Central-Eastern Europe", *Journal of Comparative Family Studies*, 3, p. 519-533.

Lentin, R.(1997) "Introduction: (En)gendering Genocide" in R.Lentin *Gender and Catastrophe*, London and New York:Zed Books, p.2-18.

Mama, A. (2000) "Violence against Black Women in the Home" in J.Hanmer and C.Itzin (eds) *Home Truths about Domestic Violence*, London and New York: Routledge, p.44-57.

Mateeva, M. (1998) *Sabitiata v iztocna i centralna Evropa: hronologicen pregled* (Events in East and Central Europe:Hronological Review) , Sofia: Akademicno izdatelstvo "Prof. Marin Drinov".

Matsakis, A. (1996) *Vietnam Wives*, Lutherville:The Sidran press.

McWilliams, (1998) "Violence Against Women in Societies Under Stress", in R.E.Dobash and R.P. Dobash (eds) *Rethinking Violence against Women*, Thousand Oaks, Sage, pp.111-140.

Milenkovic, N. and Maletin, B. (2000) "Kosovo-Unmikland", unpublished.

REFERENCES

Milic, A. (1994) *Zene, Politika, Porodica* (Women, Politics, Family), Belgrade: Institut za politicke studije.

Milic, A. (1995) "Svakodnevni zivot porodica u vrtlogu drustvenog rasula: Srbija, 1991-1995.godine"(Everyday Life of the Family in the State of Social Disintigration: Serbia, 1991-1995), in S. Bolcic (ed) *Drustvene promene i svakodnevni zivot: Srbija pocetkom 1990* ((Social Changes and Everyday Life: Serbia at the Beginning of 1990s), Belgrade:Insitut za socioloska istrazivanja Filozofskog fakulteta u Beogradu, p. 154-180.

Milivojevic, S. (1999) "Nasilje u porodici za vreme agresije NATO na SRJ" (Domestic Violence during NATO aggression on FRY), *Temida*, 2, p.45-48.

Milivojevic, S. and Vukobratovic, T. (1999) "Tribina: Trgovina zenama i decom i savremeni drustveno-ekonomski kontekst u SRJ" (Panel: Trafficking in Women and Children and Contemporary socio-economic context in FRY), *Temida*, 3-4, p.53-60.

Milosavljevic, M. (1997) "Socijalni aspekti izbeglistva" (Social Aspects of Exile) in J. Vlajkovic (ed) *Psihologija izbeglistva* (Psychology of Exile), Belgrade: Nauka, p. 9-20.

Milosavljevic, M. (1998) "Socijalne posledice drustvenih kriza"(Social Consequences of Social Crises) in Group of authors *Socijalne tenzije i drustvene implikacije*, Beograd: Fakultet politickih nauka, p. 13-26.

Millett, K. (1977) *Sexual Politics*, London:Virago.

Minnesota Advocates for Human Rights (1996) *Domestic Violence in Bulgaria*.

Minnesota Advocates for Human Rights (1998) *Semejno nasilstvo vo Makedonija* (Domestic Violence in Macedonia).

Mitic, M. (1997) *Porodica i stres – izmedju poraza i nade* (Family and Stress - Between Defeat and Hope), Belgrade: Institut za psihologiju.

Moeller, R. (1993) *Protecting Motherhood: Women and the Family in the Politics of Postwar West Germany*, Berkley and Los Angeles: University of California Press

Molyneux, M. (1996) "Women's Rights and the International Context in the Post-Communist States" in M. Threlfall *Mapping the Women's Movement*, London-New York:Verso, pp. 232-259.

Mooney, J. (2000) *Gender, Violence and the Social Change*, London: Macmillan Press ltd.

Morvai, K. (1994) "Continuity and Discontinuity in the Legal System: What it Means for Women: A Female Lawyer's Perspective on Women and the Law in Hungary, *UCLA Women's Law Journal*, 1, p. 63-70.

Morvai, K. (1998) *Terror a csaladban, a falesegbantalmazas es a jog* (Terror in the home and the law), Budapest:Kossuth Kiado.

Moser, A. (2001) "The Gendered Continuum of Violence and Conflict: An operational Framework" in C.Moser and F.Clark (eds) *Victims, Perpetrators or Actors?*, London&New York:Zed Books, p. 30-51.

Mrsevic, Z. (1999) "Mesto i uloga domaceg nasilja u kriznim periodima"(The Place and the Role of Domestic Violence in the Periods of Crises), in *Ostvarivanje ekonomskih i socijalnih prava*, Belgrade:Beogradski centar za ljudska prava, p. 462-445.

Mrvic-Petrovic, N. (2000) "Problemi zbrinjavanja i socijalne adaptacije izbeglica"(Problems of Help and Social Adaptation of Refugees), *Temida*, 2, p.101-109.

Mrvic-Petrovic, N., Stevanovic, I. (2000) "Life in Refuge - Changes in Socioeconomic and Familial Status" in V.Nikolic-Ristanovic (ed.) *Women, Violence and War*, Budapest: CEU Press, p. 35-41.

Muleskova, I. (1999) *Vlijanie na privatizacijata vurhu zenite v procesa na ikonomiceski prehod v Bulgarija* (The Impact of Privatization on Women in the Process of Economic Change in Bulgaria), Sofija:BGRF.

Messerschmidt, J. (1993) *Masculinities and Crime*, Lanham, MD: Rowman and Littlefield Publishers.

Messerschmidt, J (1995) "From Patriarchy to Gender:Feminist Theory, Criminology and the Challenge of Diversity" in N.Rafter and F.Heidensohn (eds) *International Feminist Perspectives in Criminology*, Buckingham-Philadelphia: Open University Press, p. 167-189.

Messerschmidt, J. (1997) *Crime as Structured Action: Gender, Race, Class, and Crime in the Making*, London:Sage.

Mies, M. (1997) "Colonization and Housewifization" in R.Hennessy and C.Ingraham (eds) *Materialist Feminism*, New York and London:Routledge, p.175-186.

Nanevski, B. (1998) "Ekonomski i finansiski aspekti na sociajalnata sigurnost na naselenieto" (Economic and Financial Aspects of Social Security of People in Macedonia), in B. Nanveski. and V. Stojanova (eds) *Socijalnata sigurnost na naselenieto vo Republika Makedonia vo uslovi na tranzicija*, Skopje: Friedrich Ebert Stiftung and Economski institut, p. 49-69.

REFERENCES

Novkovska, B. (1998) "Zivotni standard na naselenieto vo Republika Makedonija vo periodot na tranzicija" (Living Standard of People in Republic of Macedonia in the Period of Transition) in B. Nanveski. and V. Stojanova (eds) *Socijalnata sigurnost na naselenieto vo Republika Makedonia vo uslovi na tranzicija*, Skopje: Friedrich Ebert Stiftung and Economski institut, p.77-84 .

Nikolic, D. (1998) "Bolesti zavisnosti u Jugoslaviji i svetu" (Addiction Illnesses in Yugoslavia and in the World) , *Socijalna misao*, 3, p.79-91.

Nikolic-Ristanovic, V., Mrvic-Petrovic, N., Konstantinovic-Vilic, S., Knezic, B. and Stevanovic, I.. (1996) *Zene Krajine: Rat, egzodus i izbeglistvo (Women of Krajina: War, Exodus and Exile)* , Belgrade: IKSI.

Nikolic-Ristanovic, V. (1996) "War and Violence against Women" in J.Turpin and L. Lorentzen (eds.) *The Gendered New World Order: Militarism, Development and the Environment*, New York: Routledge, p. 195-211.

Nikolic-Ristanovic, V. (1996a) "Domestic Violence Against Women in the Conditions of War and Economical Crisis" in Sumner, C., Israel M., O'Connell, M. and Sarre, R. (eds) *International Victimology*, Canbera: Australian Institute of Criminology, p. 75-79.

Nikolic-Ristanovic, V (1996b) "War, Nationalism and Mothers", *Peace Review*, 3, p. 359-364

Nikolic-Ristanovic, V. (1998)."War and Crime in the former Yugoslavia" in V.Ruggiero. N.South and I.Taylor (eds) *The New European Criminology*, London: Routledge, p.462-480.

Nikolic-Ristanovic, V. (1998a)"Victims and Police in Belgrade", *International Review of Victimology*, 1, p. 49-63.

Nikolic-Ristanovic, V., Radisavljevic, S., Milivojevic, S. (1998)) "Self-Organizing of Women Here and in the World" (panel review), *Temida*, 3, p.49-58.

Nikolic-Ristanovic, V.(ed) (2000) *Women, Violence and War*, CEU Press, Budapest.

Nikolic-Ristanovic, V. and Milivojevic, S. (2000) "Viktimizacija zena nasiljem u porodici: uticaj socijalnih faktora vezanih za drustvene promene i zivotnu dob" (Victimization of Women by Domestic Violence: the Impact of Social Factors Connected to Social Change and Age), *Temida*, 1, p.20-28.

Nikolic-Ristanovic, V. (2001) "The Constriction of Identities in Media Images of Violence against Women" in G.Janhart, J.Gohrisch, D.Hahn, H.M.Nickel, I.Peinl, K.Schafgen (eds) *Gender in Transition in Eastern and Central Europe Proceedings*, Berlin:Trafo Verlag, p.284-295.

Nowakowska, U. (1999) "Violence Against Women: International Standards, Polish Reality", *Journal of Communist Studies and Transition Politics*, 1, p. 41-63.

Nurmi, R. (1999) "Mobile Russian Prostitution in Finland", paper presented at the 32nd Triennial Conference of the International Abolitionist Federation, "Breakdown of Borders", December 2-4, Copenhagen, Denmark.

Nutt, R.L. (1999) "Women's Gender-Role Socialization, Gender Role Conflict, and Abuse: A Review of Predisposing Factors" in M.Harway and M.O'Neil (eds) *What Causes Men's Violence Against Women?*, Thousand Oaks, London, New Delhi:Sage, p. 117-135.

Oleszczuk, T. and Buchowska, S. (1996) "The 'Pretty Woman Syndrome" in *One Year La Strada* (unpublished report), p.24-31.

O'Neil, M.J. and Harway, M. (1999) "Revised Multivariate Model Explaining Men's Risk Factors for Violence Against Women" in M.Harway and M.O'Neil (eds) *What Causes Men's Violence Against Women?*, Thousand Oaks, London, New Delhi:Sage, p.207-242.

O'Neil, M.J. and Nadeau, R.L. (1999) "Men's Gender-Role Conflict, Defense Mechanisms, and Self-Protective Defensive Strategies:Explaining Men's Violence Against Women From a Gender-Role Socialization Perspective" in M.Harway and M.O'Neil (eds) *What Causes Men's Violence Against Women?*, Thousand Oaks, London, New Delhi:Sage, p. 89-117.

Phinnemore, D. (1999) "The Challenge of EU Enlargement: EU and CEE perspectives" in K. Henderson *Back to Europe: Central and Eastern Europe and the European Union*, London:UCL Press.

Perow, C. (1979) "The Sixties Observed" in M.N.Zald and J.D.McCarthy *The Dynamics of Social Movements*, Cambridge: Winthrop Publishers, p.192-211.

Petrova, D. (1993) "The Winding Roud to Emancipation in Bulgaria", in N. Funk.and M. Mueller (eds) *Gender Politics and Post-Communism*, New Zork, Routledge, p.22-29.

Polovina, N. (1999) "Porodicni procesi u kontekstu ekonomske krize – od materijalnog do dusevnog siromasenja" (Family Processes in the Context of Economic Crises - From Material to Mental Impoverishment), *Socijalna misao*, 1-2, p. 57-67.

REFERENCES

Posarac, A. (1999) "Socijalne posledice krize: Siromastvo i nejednakost u Jugoslaviji" (Social Consequenses of the Crises: Poverty and Inequality in Yugoslavia),in *Ostvarivanje ekonomskih i socijalnih prava*, Belgrade:Beogradski centar za ljudska prava, p. 49-61.

Prokovik, V. (1998) "Siromastijata vo Republika Makedonija" (Poverty in Republic of Macedonia) in B. Nanveski and V. Stojanova (eds) *Socijalnata sigurnost na naselenieto vo Republika Makedonia vo uslovi na tranzicija*, Skopje: Friedrich Ebert Stiftung and Economski institut, p. 123-132.

Puzigaca, M (1999) "Strahovi i raspolozenja"(Fears and Moods) in S.Mihailovic (ed) *Javno mnjenje Srbije*, Beograd: Centar za proucavanje alternativa , UGS Nezavisnost, Udruzenje za unapredjivanje empirijskih istrazivanja, p. 107-125 .

Radoinova, D. *Domasnoto nasilie bub Varnenski okrug za period 1996-1998* (Domestic Violence in Varna District in the Period 1996-1998) (unpublished) .

Ranno signalizirane - polugodisen obzor: dekembri 1998- mai 1999 (Early Warning, December 1998 -May 1999), Sofia: UNDP.

Raichev, A., Kolev, K., Boundjoulov, A., Dimova, L. (2000) *Social Stratification in Bulgaria*, p. 70. Sofia. LIK.

Regional Report on Institutional Mechanisms for the Advancement of Women in the Countries of Central and Eastern Europe, The Report of NGOs (1999) Karat Coalition for Regional Action, Warsaw.

Reinharz,S. (1992) *Feminist Methods in the Social Research*, Oxford University Press, New York .

Rowbotham, S. (1992) *Women in Movement:Feminism and Social Action*, New York: Routledge.

Sabourin, T.Ch. (1996) "The Role of Communication in Verbal Abuse Between Spouses" in D.D. Cahn and S.A. Lloyd (1996) *Family Violence from a Communication Perspective*, Thousand Oaks: Sage, p.199-218.

Schur, E. M. (1987) *Labeling women deviant, Gender, Stigma and Social Control*, Random House.

Schechter, S. (1982) *Women and Male Violence – The Visions and Struggles of the Battered Women's Movement*, Boston: South End Press.

Sklair, L. (1991) *Sociology of the Global System*, Hertfordshire: Simon&Schuster

Sotirov, D. (1999) "Trafficking in Broken Dreams", in *South-East Europe Review*, 1, pp.69-76

Speder, Z. (1997) " Szegeny nok es ferfiak" (Poor Women and Poor Men) in K.Levai and G.Toth *Szerepvaltozasok* (Changing roles), Budapest :Tarki, p.121-139.

Srna, J. (1997) "Porodice u ratu i izbeglistvu"(Families in War and Exile), in Group of authors *Psihologija izbeglistva* (Psychology of Exile), Belgrade: Nauka, p. 29-35.

Stishova, E. (1996) "Full Frontal: Perestroika and Sexual Policy", in R.March.(ed) *Women in Russia and Ukraine*, Cambridge: Cambridge University Press, p. 189-195.

Stokes, G. (1997) *Three Eras of Political Change in Eastern Europe*, Oxford and New York: Oxford University Press.

Stordeur, R. and Stille, R. (1989) *Ending Men's Violence against their Partners: One Road to Peace*, Newbury Park, London and New Delhi:Sage.

Steinhilber, S. (2001) "Gender Relations and Labour Market Transformation: Status Quo and Policy Responses in Central and Eastern Europe" in G.Jahnert, J.Gohrisch, D.Hahn. H.Maria Nickel, I. Peinl, K.Schafgen *Gender in Transition in Eastern and Central Europe*, Berlin:Trafo Verlag, pp.201-214.

Szabo, M. (1994) "Greens, Cabbies, and Anti-Communists: Collective Action during Regime Transition in Hungary" in E.Larana, H. Johnston and J.R.Gusfield *Social Movements*, Philadelphia: Temple University Press, p.287-303.

Szalai, J.. and Orosz, E. (1992) Social Policy in Hungary in B.Deacon (ed) *The New Eastern Europe: Social policy, Past, Present and Future*, London:Sage, p.144-167.

Taylor, I., Jamieson, R. (1999) "Sex Trafficking and the Mainstream of Market Culture", *Crime,Law and Social Change*, 32, p 257-278.

Toth, O. (1993) "No Envy, No Pity", in N. Funk and M. Mueller,(ed) *Gender Politics and Post-Communism*, New York: Routledge, pp.213-223.

Toth, O. (1997) "Working Women, Changing Roles, Changing Attitudes", *The Hungary Quarterly*, vol 38, pp.69-77.

Toth, O. (1999) *Pocketbook of Hungarian Statistics 1999 - No 12 Violence in the Family*, Budapest:Tarki Central Statistical Office

REFERENCES

Trajkovski, D. (1998) "Semejstvoto vo sovremeniot sistem na socijalna zastita vo Republika Makedonija" (Family in Contemporary System of Social Welfare in Macedonia) in B.Nanevski and V. Stojanova (eds) *Socijalnata sigurnost na naselenieto vo Republika Makedonia vo uslovi na tranzicija*, Skopje: Friedrich Ebert Stiftung and Economski institut, p.69-76.

Turnock, D. and Carter, F. eds. (1999) *The States of Eastern Europe*, Vol.II South-Eastern Europe, Aldershot:Ashgate.

Turnock, D. (1999) "Hungary" in D.Turnock and F. Carter (eds) *The States of Eastern Europe*, Vol.I: North-Eastern Europe, Aldershot: Ashgate, pp.73-126.

Turpin, J and Kurtz, L.R., ed. (1997) *The Web of Violence, From Interpersonal to Global*, Urbana and Chicago, University of Illinois Press.

UNDP (1998) *Women in Poverty, An Assessment of the Bulgarian Anti-Poverty Policies and Strategies*, Sofia:International Labor Organization .

UNDP (1998a) *Poverty in Transition - Republic of Bulgaria*, Geneva: UNDP.

UNDP (1999) *The Status of Women in Macedonia.*

UNICEF (1997), *Women's status in FRY, the Survey's Coverage* (research report).

UNICEF (1999), *Women in Transition*, The MONEE Project CEE/CIS/Baltics, Regional Monitoring Reports, No.6., Florence:UNICEF International Child Development Center

Vaknin, S. (2000) "The Grow Out of Unemployment", http:/samvaknin.tripod.com

Valverde,M. (1985) *Sex, Power and Pleasure*, Toronto: Women's Press.

Vicheva, D., (1999) "Metamorphoses of the Crises in the Family", *Fair Play*, Digest of the Women's Alliance for Development, 2, pp.14-15.

Vidakovic, I. (1999) "Tribina: Strategije osnazivanja zena u posleratnom periodu" (Strategies of Empowering Women in Post-War Period), panel review, *Temida*, 2, p.55-58.

Vintileanu, I. and Babovic, B. (ed.) (2001) *Krijumcarenje ljudi:krijumcarenje zena i dece* (People Smuggling: Smuggling of Women and Children), Belgrade, CUPS.

Vlajkovic, J. (1997) "Psiholoski aspekti izbeglistva" (Psychological Aspects of Exile), in J. Vlajkovic *Psihologija izbeglistva* (Psychology of Exile), Beograd, Nauka, p. 21-36.

Vukovic, D. (1999) "Osiguranje za slucaj nezaposlenosti i ostvarivanje prava nezaposlenih lica"(Insurance in the Case of Unemployment and Realization of the Rights of Unemployed People), in *Ostvarivanje ekonomskih i socijalnih prava*, Belgrade: Beogradski centar za ljudska prava, p..352-370.

Waddington, D., Critcher, C. and Dicks, B. (1998) "All Jumbled up':Employed Women and Unemployed Husbands" in J. Popay, J.Hearn and J.Edwards (eds) *Men, Gender, Divisions and Welfare*, London and New York:Routledge, p.231-259.

WaD (1999) *Emerging Issues: Women in Bulgaria*, Sofia:WaD.

Walklate, S. (2001) *Gender, Crime and Criminal Justice*, Devon:Willan Publishing.

Wandycz, P. (1992) *The Price of Freedom*, Routledge: London

Watson, P. (1992) "General Relation, Education and Social Change in Poland", *Gender and Education*, 1-2, p. 127-147.

Watson, P. (1993) "Eastern Europe's Silent Revolution: Gender", *Sociology*, 3, pp 471-487.

Watson, P. (1996) "The Rise of Masculinism in Eastern Europe" in M. Threlfall *Mapping the Women's Movement*, London-New York:Verso, pp.216-231.

Watson, P. (2001) "Gender and Politics in Postcommunism" in G.Janhart, J.Gohrisch, D.Hahn, H.M.Nickel, I.Peinl, K.Schafgen (eds) *Gender in Transition in Eastern and Central Europe Proceedings*, Berlin:Trafo Verlag, p.37-49.

Wijers, M, Lap-Chew, L. (1997) *Trafficking in Women: Forced Labour and Slavery-like Practices in Marriage, Domestic Labour and Prostitution*, Utrecht: STV.

Williams, P. (1999) "Trafficking in Women and Children: A Market Perspective", *Transnational Organized Crime*, Special Issue "Illegal Immigration and Commercial Sex - the New Slave Trade" (ed. P.Williams), Vol. 3-4., p.145-170.

Wirth, J. *Women of the World Report - Central and Eastern Europe: Hungary* (forthcoming)

(Women - victims of aggression, Federal Government Report, 1999.

REFERENCES

Women in Black, (1994) "Radionica: sta je rat svakoj od nas ucinio na emotivnom, porodicnom, ekonomskom planu"(Workshop: What the War did to Everyone Among Us on Family, Emotional and Economic Level), in *Zene za mir*, Belgrade: Women in Blac, p. 98-117.

Women in Black (1994a),"Radionica: Embargo"(Workshop:Embargo), in *Zene za mir*, Belgrade: Women in Black, p. 118-136.

Yllo, K. (1993) "Through a Feminist Lens: Gender, Power and Violence" in R.J. Gelles. and D.R. Loseke (eds) *Current Controversies on Family Violence*, California:Sage, p.47-62.

Zajovic, S., (1995) "Zene i militarizam u Srbiji" (Women and Militarism in Serbia) in *Zene protiv rata*, 3-4, Belgrade: Women in Black, p.36-43.

Zlatanova, V. (2001) *Domasnoto nasilie* (Domestic Violence), Sofia: Unipres EOOD.

Zegarac, N., Brkic, M.,(1998) "Nasilje medju roditeljima skolske dece – rezultati istrazivanja"(Violence among Parents of School Children - Results of Research), *Temida*, 4, p.19-27.

INDEX

Social Indicators Research Series

1. V. Møller (ed.): *Quality of Life in South Africa.* 1997 ISBN 0-7923-4797-8
2. G. Baechler: *Violence Through Environmental Discrimination.* Causes, Rwanda Arena, and Conflict Model. 1999 ISBN 0-7923-5495-8
3. P. Bowles and L.T. Woods (eds.): *Japan after the Economic Miracle.* In Search of New Directories. 1999 ISBN 0-7923-6031-1
4. E. Diener and D.R. Rahtz (eds.): *Advances in Quality of Life Theory and Research.* Volume I. 1999 ISBN 0-7923-6060-5
5. Kwong-leung Tang (ed.): *Social Development in Asia.* 2000 ISBN 0-7923-6256-X
6. M.M. Beyerlein (ed.): *Work Teams: Past, Present and Future.* 2000 ISBN 0-7923-6699-9
7. A. Ben-Arieh, N.H. Kaufman, A.B. Andrews, R. Goerge, B.J. Lee, J.L. Aber (eds.): *Measuring and Monitoring Children's Well-Being.* 2001 ISBN 0-7923-6789-8
8. M.J. Sirgy: *Handbook of Quality-of-Life Research. An Ethical Marketing Perspective.* 2001 ISBN 1-4020-0172-X
9. G. Preyer and M. Bös (eds.): *Borderlines in a Globalized World.* New Perspectives in a Sociology of the World-System. 2002 ISBN 1-4020-0515-6
10. V. Nikolic-Ristanovic: *Social Change, Gender and Violence: Post-communist and war affected societies.* 2002 ISBN 1-4020-0726-4
11. M.R. Hagerty, J. Vogel and V. Møller: *Assessing Quality of Life and Living Conditions to Guide National Policy.* 2002 ISBN 1-4020-0727-2

KLUWER ACADEMIC PUBLISHERS – DORDRECHT / LONDON / BOSTON

MIX
Papier aus verantwortungsvollen Quellen
Paper from responsible sources
FSC® C105338

If you have any concerns about our products,
you can contact us on
ProductSafety@springernature.com

In case Publisher is established outside the EU,
the EU authorized representative is:
Springer Nature Customer Service Center GmbH
Europaplatz 3, 69115 Heidelberg, Germany

Printed by Libri Plureos GmbH
in Hamburg, Germany